Locating and Correcting
Reading Difficulties

Locating and Correcting Reading Difficulties

Fifth Edition

Eldon E. Ekwall

University of Texas at El Paso

Merrill Publishing Company
A Bell & Howell Information Company
Columbus   Toronto   London   Melbourne

Published by Merrill Publishing Company
A Bell & Howell Information Company
Columbus, Ohio 43216

This book was set in Century Schoolbook
Administrative Editor: Jeff Johnston
Production Coordinator: Julie Higgins
Art Coordinator: Ruth Ann Kimpel
Cover photo: David S. Strickler

Library of Congress Catalog Card Number 88–80958
International Standard Book Number: 0–675–20645–6

2 3 4 5 6 7 8 9 10—92 91 90 89

Printed in the United States of America

To:
Fred & Helen Martinez
and
Jim & Dusty Milson

Preface

The fifth edition of this book, like the previous editions, is designed to give busy teachers and students in reading education concrete methods of locating and correcting reading difficulties. It can be used in developmental, corrective, and remedial situations. Although the basic format of each chapter remains the same, the Reading Diagnosis Sheet at the beginning of the text has been substantially revised. The chapter sequence is new and now reflects the numbering of the items on the Reading Diagnosis Sheet. These changes, which were suggested by reviewers, will no doubt make the text easier to use.

This new edition contains additional concrete methods of teaching comprehension, especially through metacognitive techniques. There is also more material on vocabulary development. Several of the assessment instruments, such as the Quick Check for Basic Sight Words, The El Paso Phonics Survey, Materials for Testing Letter Knowledge, and the Materials for Testing Students' Knowledge of Contractions, have been revised. Three new appendices also have been added. Appendix J is a scope and sequence of reading skills that teachers should find useful in determining when certain skills should be mastered. Appendix Q is a chart for graphing students' progress in using repeated readings. The third new appendix (L), is a phonogram list and words for teaching vowel sounds and vowel rules. The author and his graduate students have found that many students make extremely rapid progress in phonics using the approach explained in appendix L.

The fifth edition has been designed so that teachers and students in reading education courses can use the materials in the appendices to build their own diagnostic kits. The appendices include materials for assessing students' knowledge of the alphabet, basic sight words, contractions, the use of context clues, phonics, and for testing their knowledge of vowel rules and syllable principles. Each of these appendices includes information on how to prepare the materials for classroom use. Specific directions and important points to remember are also included for administering each test or survey instrument. Other materials included in the appendices are a phonics primer and a quick test to determine if students should be given an entire basic sight word test. The appendix on sources of reading material (R) has also been updated and expanded.

While the fifth edition perhaps emphasizes a more global approach to the correction of reading difficulties, it also retains and adds still more materials and suggestions for correcting students who are in need of specific skills. The chapter on the use of computers has been thoroughly updated. Included are specific ways to use the computer in the teaching of reading and criteria for selecting and evaluating educational software and hardware. You will also find sources of software reviews, a list of companies that publish or distribute computer software for reading education, a list of magazines written for people who are interested in computer education, a list of the better known software directories, and an explanation of computer terminology.

You should first turn to the section entitled "How to Use this Book" where you will find an explanation of the format used. In each chapter there is a short section on how to recognize problems with reading skills, a brief discussion of pertinent information on problems, and specific recommendations on how to correct these difficulties. In some areas, you will also find games and activities to help strengthen or reinforce reading abilities. The text alternates use of masculine and feminine pronouns.

All of the ideas in this text have been tried and proven successful. You should remember, however, that what works well with one student may not be appropriate with another. Furthermore, ideas that are suitable for one grade level may not be suitable with another.

As with the first four editions, this text is not designed to present the theory and philosophy of reading. It is also not a substitute for a good reading methods course. It will, however, provide teachers and students in reading education with concrete procedures that can be successfully implemented in the classroom.

ACKNOWLEDGEMENTS

A number of excellent teachers, and other personnel concerned with the teaching of reading, have contributed numerous ideas and suggestions that I have found effective in teaching children to read. Although I cannot thank each of them individually, I would like to take this opportunity to express my sincerest appreciation for their contributions. I would also like to express my appreciation to a number of authors whose ideas have proven practical and to whom I am deeply indebted for the knowledge they have given me.

I would like to thank Nathan Davidson and Elise McGowan, my teaching assistants, and Alicia Meza, a faithful assistant, for their help while I was writing this text. I would also like to thank Johanna Cowart, Lynn Humphreys, Sheila Reyna, Shari Ritter, and Billie Wheeler for their contributions to Appendices J, L, and R, and Carol Ann Ekwall for her help with the fifth edition.

In addition, I would like to express my appreciation to Jeff Johnston, Jeff Putnam, and Julie Higgins of the Merrill staff. Jeff Johnston did his usual great job of managing the project and Jeff Putnam's editorial skills have made this a more readable text. The work of Dr. Jack Jones, Dr. Lana Low, Dr. Tim Morrison, and Sue Rogers who reviewed this edition of the text and made a number of constructive suggestions is also appreciated. I am also indebted to past reviewers whose suggestions have helped this become a more useful text.

E. E. E.

Contents

APPENDICES

How to Use This Book

Read the "Definition of Terms" to be sure you are familiar with all of them before you begin to read the text. Then read the "Reading Diagnosis Sheet," (p. 6), which lists 28 reading or reading-related abilities. After looking over the "Reading Diagnosis Sheet," read the entire book from beginning to end to ensure familiarity with the contents. Each of the first 24 chapters has a similar organization. First, an explanation is given for recognizing the difficulty with the ability listed. Then a discussion is presented to explain any pertinent problem. Specific recommendations for correcting any weaknesses in each of the abilities follow the discussion. Finally, in some chapters, there is a list of games and exercises to help correct these reading difficulties. In most cases you could not, or would not, be able to attempt everything listed as a recommendation; however, you can choose the techniques that seem most appropriate for your situation.

The reading diagnosis sheet is constructed to give you an opportunity to check each of the 28 abilities listed three times during the year. The time period between checks will depend upon the intensity of the help or the normal teaching program. It could be as often as once a month or once during each semester of the school year. You should attempt to locate student difficulties as early in the year as possible. The "Recognized By" section in each chapter will be helpful in determining whether or not certain skills are deficient. After determining which abilities are weak, tally the total number of students who are weak in each area and base your reading instruction on those areas in which the class as a whole is weakest. Then turn to the "Recommendations" and the "Games and Exercises" sections to use the suggestions given there.

The checklist does not categorize reading difficulties by the severity of the problem. You should be aware, however, that some of the items listed are of a more serious nature than others. Each discussion section explains how to determine whether the difficulty needs treatment, or whether it is only a symptom of a more serious problem. For example, word-by-word reading, improper phrasing, and repetitions usually are symptoms of more serious problems, such as difficulty in comprehension and/or word analysis or word recognition. In this situation, treatment for these larger problems probably would cause the symptoms of word-by-word reading, improper phrasing, and repetition to disappear automatically. You should read each discussion section carefully to ensure adequate diagnosis and determine the proper improvement procedure.

After noting on the reading diagnosis sheet the skills in which your students are weak, you may then turn to the table of contents which will help you to quickly locate corrective procedures for each of the problems listed on the reading diagnosis sheet. For example, students who have difficulty with basic sight words can be helped by using the corrective procedures beginning on p. 43 (as shown in the table of contents), those who have an inability to skim can be helped by using the procedures beginning on p. 155, and so on.

Following the "Reading Diagnosis Sheet" there is a section entitled "Making Your Own Diagnostic Kit from the Appendices." Become familiar with this section, so you may begin to make your own diagnostic kit as you read the various sections for which testing or assessment materials are included in the appendices. After becoming familiar with the text, you may wish to reproduce copies of the reading diagnosis sheet in order to have a record for each member of the class, or with each student with whom you are working that has difficulties in reading.

It will be easier to locate certain difficulties if you use the code for marking in oral diagnosis, which is listed in appendix A. This code will enable you to find exactly what type of mistakes students make in their reading. With a little practice, you will become adept at marking certain mistakes that students make in their oral reading. You will, of course, need a copy of what the student is reading (preferably double-spaced) to mark as the student reads. You will also find this "marked" or "coded" copy useful in rechecking a student's reading to note the amount of progress in overcoming earlier difficulties.

Sometimes a particular suggestion will be appropriate with a younger child but will be inappropriate for an older student. I have not listed various suggestions as appropriate for certain grades or age levels. You will need to exercise your own judgment based upon the severity of the problem and the age and attitude of the child. I have, however, made note that some problems are beyond the beginning-reading stage.

Definition of Terms

Affix A term meaning *to fasten,* usually applied to suffixes and prefixes collectively.

Basal Reader A reading textbook designed for a specific grade level. These usually contain material designed to enhance specific skills, such as word attack, vocabulary, and comprehension skills.

Basic Sight Word These are words that are used many times over in the reading material written for children and adults. One of the most common basic sight word lists is the *Dolch Basic Sight Vocabulary**, which contains no nouns but is a 220-word list of "service words." In appendix D you will find the *Ekwall Basic Sight Word List,* along with instructions for assessing students' knowledge of these words.

Blend Combinations of two or three letters blended together into sounds while retaining the sounds of the individual letters: e.g., *cr* in *crayon,* and *pl* in *plate.*

Choral Reading Reading done orally by two or more students from the same passage at the same time.

Diagnosis A careful investigation of a problem carried out to determine the amount and sequence of remediation needed by a student with reading difficulties.

Digraph A combination of two letters recording (representing) a single sound. There are consonant digraphs and vowel digraphs. An example of a consonant digraph would be *ph* in the word *digraph.* In this case, the *ph* stands for the /f/ sound. An example of a vowel digraph would be the *ea* in the word *each.* In saying the sound represented by the letters of a digraph (phoneme), one does not change the position of the mouth from the beginning to the end of the sound.

---

*Edward W. Dolch, *Methods in Reading* (Champaign, Illinois: Garrard Publishing, 1955), pp. 373–74.

Diphthong   A combination of two vowel letters that are both heard in making a compound sound: e.g., *ow* in *cow,* and *oy* in *boy.* In pronouncing a diphthong sound, the position of the mouth is moved from the beginning to the end of the diphthong.

Grapheme   A grapheme is the written representation of a phoneme: e.g., the word *dog* has three distinct sounds that are represented with the graphemes *d, o,* and *g.* The word *straight* has five phonemes that are represented by the graphemes *s, t, r, aigh,* and *t* (See *phoneme*).

Kinesthetic Method   The use of the senses of touch, hearing, seeing, and muscle movement to teach letters or words. The approach usually involves tracing over words with the index and middle fingers while sounding the part being traced.

Levels of Reading

> **Independent or free reading level**   The student can function adequately without the teacher's help at this level. Comprehension should average 90 percent or better, and word recognition should average 99 percent or better.

> **Instructional reading level**   The student can function adequately with teacher guidance and yet be challenged to stimulate his reading growth. Comprehension should average 75 percent or better, and word recognition should average 90 percent or better.

> **Frustration reading level**   The student cannot function adequately. In reading at this level the student often shows signs of tension and discomfort. Vocalization is often present. Comprehension averages 50 percent or less, and word recognition averages 90 percent or less.

Phoneme   The smallest unit of speech sound in a language, e.g., in the word *dog* there are three phonemes /d/, /o/, and /g/. (When a letter is found between two slash marks as the *d, o,* and *g* above, it means the sounds for which the letter stands.)

Phonics   The study of sound-symbol (phoneme-grapheme) relationships as they apply to the teaching of reading—usually used in beginning reading.

Reading Programs

> **Developmental**   The normal classroom instructional program followed by the teacher to meet the needs of pupils who are progressing at a normal rate in terms of their capacity.

> **Corrective**   A program of instruction usually conducted by a classroom teacher, within the class setting, to correct mild reading difficulties.

> **Remedial**   A program of instruction, usually carried on outside the regular classroom, to teach specific developmental reading skills to students with severe reading difficulties.

Sight Word   Any word that a reader has seen many times in the past and is able to recognize instantly without using word attack skills. This term should not be confused with *basic sight word.*

Structural Analysis   Now often referred to as *morphology,* which is concerned with the study of meaning-bearing units such as root words, prefixes, suffixes, possessives, plurals, accent rules, and in some cases, syllable principles and vowel rules. Some authors disagree as to whether syllable principles and vowel rules should be considered under the heading of *phonics* or *structural analysis.*

Word-Analysis Skills   The skills a reader must use to determine how to pronounce a word when it is not recognized instantly. (The word-analysis skills are usually considered to be *phonics, structural analysis, context clues, configuration clues* and *dictionary skills.*)

Word-Attack Skills   A term that means the same as word analysis skills.

Word-Recognition Skills   The ability of a reader to recognize words, usually referring only to recognition without the aid of word analysis.

Reading Diagnosis Sheet

#	1st Check	2nd Check	3rd Check	Item	Category
1				Word-by-word reading	Oral Reading
2				Incorrect phrasing	
3				Poor pronunciation	
4				Omissions	
5				Repetitions	
6				Inversions or reversals	
7				Insertions	
8				Substitutions	
9				Basic sight words not known	
10				Sight vocabulary not up to grade level	
11				Guesses at words	
12				Consonant sounds not known	
13				Vowel sounds not known	
14				Vowel pairs and/or consonant clusters not known (digraphs, diphthongs, blends)	
15				Lacks desirable structural analysis (Morphology)	
16				Unable to use context clues	
17				Contractions not known	
18				Comprehension inadequate	Oral Silent
19				Vocabulary inadequate	
20				Unaided recall scanty	Study Skills
21				Response poorly organized	
22				Unable to locate information	
23				Inability to skim	
24				Inability to adjust rate to difficulty of material	
25				Low rate of speed	
26				High rate at expense of accuracy	
27				Voicing-lip movement	Other Abilities
28				Lacks knowledge of the alphabet	
29				Written recall limited by spelling ability	
30				Undeveloped dictionary skills	

TEACHER
SCHOOL
NAME
GRADE

The items listed above represent the most common difficulties encountered by pupils in the reading program. Following each numbered item are spaces for notation of that specific difficulty. This may be done at intervals of several months. One might use a check to indicate difficulty recognized or the following letters to represent an even more accurate appraisal:

Making Your Own Diagnostic Kit From the Appendices

You will note that in the present edition of this book, materials are included in appendices B through I for developing your own diagnostic kit for use in locating students who have difficulties in reading. Each appendix is arranged as follows:

Preparing for the Test. In this section you will find instructions for removing and preparing the material in this book for use in testing. In most cases, the directions include removing an answer sheet, which is to be duplicated. Directions are also included for removing and laminating a stimulus sheet. It is suggested that material in each of these appendices be filed, so that they may easily be retrieved. I file each test or assessment device in a large manila envelope and then label each envelope as one would do with a file folder. These are then kept in a portable file box, so it may easily be transported from place-to-place as may be needed in various testing situations.

Specific Directions for Giving Each Test or Assessment Device. In this section, you will find specific directions to use in administering each test or assessment device.

Important Points to Remember. In administering any test or assessment device, there are certain techniques that you will find helpful and others that should be avoided. This section, found in each appendix, includes this information.

Following is a list of various appendices and testing or assessment devices that you should have in your kit when it is completed:

Appendix B A test of letter knowledge

Appendix C A quick check to determine whether students should be given an entire basic sight word test.

Appendix D The *Ekwall Basic Sight Word Test*

Appendix E A test for students' knowledge of contractions

Appendix F A test for students' ability to use context clues

Appendix G   *Quick Survey Word List* and the *El Paso Phonics Survey. The Quick Survey Word List* is used to determine whether or not students who are expected to read at approximately the fourth-grade level, or above, would need to be given a phonics test and other corresponding tests such as the one in appendix I. Students who do well on the *Quick Survey Word List* would not need further phonics testing. Therefore, the use of this survey can sometimes save considerable time in the diagnostic process.

Appendix H   Materials for testing students' knowledge of vowel rules and syllable principles

1

Word-by-Word Reading

RECOGNIZED BY

Pupil pauses after each word and does not allow the words to flow as they would in a conversation.

DISCUSSION

Word-by-word reading may be caused by a failure to instantly recognize a number of sight words, failure to comprehend (to some extent), or an over-dependence on phonics, or it may be a bad habit. Young students who are beginning to read are often word-by-word readers. However, as their sight vocabulary continues to grow, they should lose this habit.

You should determine whether word-by-word reading is caused by habit, lack of word recognition, or lack of comprehension. This determination may be made as follows. Give the student something to read at a much lower reading level. If she continues to read poorly, the problem may then be assumed to be a bad habit. If she immediately improves, it can generally be considered either a problem with comprehension or with word recognition. You must then decide between these two problems. Ask the student questions about the more difficult material she was reading word-by-word. If the student can answer approximately 75 percent of the questions correctly, then her problem probably lies in the area of word recognition. If she cannot answer approximately 75 percent of the questions correctly, she may be having trouble with comprehension. You may also take a few of the more difficult words from the reading passage and put them on flash cards to see if the student has instant recognition of these words in isolation. If the student has trouble with word recognition, the suggestions listed in items (A) through (D) will be helpful. If the difficulty lies in the development of poor reading habits, the recommendations under items (E) through (L) will be more helpful. However, if the student is having difficulty with comprehension, you should follow the suggestions listed under "Comprehension Inadequate," chapter 18.

Remember that students can only read with fluency when they are thoroughly familiar with the vocabulary in the material that they are required to read. Therefore, if a student is having difficulty with the vocabulary in the material, you should not try the types of suggestions listed in items (E) through (L). You would be treating the symptoms rather than the actual cause of the difficulty.

RECOMMENDATIONS

A. Use reading material on a lower level of difficulty.

B. Use materials with which the pupil is so familiar that the vocabulary presents no problem.

C. Have the children write their own stories and read them aloud. Tape-record their reading of these stories and contrast it with their reading of less familiar stories. Discuss the differences and their need for smooth, fluent reading.

D. If word-by-word reading is caused by an insufficient sight vocabulary, you should follow the suggestions listed under "Incorrect Phrasing," chapter 2, item (A), and those listed under "Sight Vocabulary Not Up to Grade Level," chapter 11.

E. Have the pupil read in conjunction with a tape recording of the passage. It is often difficult for an adult to read with expression at a rate that will be comfortable for a child to follow. Some teachers prefer to use another good student at the same grade level to do the reading on the tape recorder.

F. Provide experience in choral reading. This activity may be with as few as two pupils or as many as the entire class.

G. Use mechanical devices that require readers to attain certain speeds. If these mechanical devices are not available, the instructor may have the pupils pace their reading with their hands, forcing their eyes to keep up with the pace set by their hands. (Caution! Do not allow the eye to pace the hand.) This may be done either orally or silently. Remember there is little emphasis on reading speed in the primary grades, and very little emphasis is given to teaching speed reading in the middle grades. Therefore, the mechanical devices are only to maintain a comfortable pace and not to increase speed per se.

H. Give a series of timed silent reading exercises. The addition of the time factor will usually make the student aware of this habit. The same cautions pertaining to grade level should be observed here as for item (G). In doing the timed reading exercises you may wish to use the "Repeated Readings Chart" shown in appendix Q. This chart is designed to allow the teacher to compare students' speed and number of errors on 10 trials using the same passage.

I.   Allow pupils to choose stories that they feel are exciting, and then let them read their selections aloud.

J.   Have the children read and dramatize conversation.

K.   Have the children read poetry. They should read it over until it becomes easy for them.

L.   Discuss reading as talk written down. Record several children's talk and then record the reading of dialogue. Let the children listen and compare the differences between talk and dialogue.

M.   Use commercial materials such as the *Plays for Echo Reading* published by Harcourt Brace Jovanovich, which are designed to develop expressive fluent oral reading.

2

Incorrect Phrasing

RECOGNIZED BY

Pupil fails to read in natural phrasing or linguistic units. He may fail to take a breath at the proper place and will often ignore punctuation, especially commas.

DISCUSSION

The causes of incorrect phrasing may be insufficient word recognition, insufficient comprehension, or the development of poor reading habits. You should first determine the cause. Give the student an unorganized list of all the words from a passage that he will read later. The passage should be at a reading level in which the student is experiencing difficulty. If he does not know approximately 95 percent of the words in the list, you can assume that the lack of word recognition is contributing to the problem of incorrect phrasing. Have the student read the story from which the words came and then answer at least six questions from that story. If the student continues to phrase incorrectly and fails to answer at least 75 percent of the questions, and yet knows 95 percent or more of the words, probably comprehension difficulties are a major contributor to the problem.

Reading material is not too difficult for a student if he has instant recognition of 96 percent or more of the words and can answer at least 75 percent of a series of questions over the passage. If the material is not too difficult in terms of vocabulary and comprehension, and a student continues to phrase incorrectly, you may assume that either he has poor reading habits or he does not understand the meaning of various punctuation marks. Remember that it is difficult for older students, even though they are good readers, to read stories on a primer or first-grade level and then answer the type of comprehension questions commonly given to children who are actually working at this level.

You should keep this in mind if it is necessary to use material of a very low reading level.

If insufficient word recognition skills are a contributing factor in incorrect phrasing, then the suggestions in items (A) through (F) should be beneficial. If incorrect phrasing is caused by poor oral reading habits or a failure to understand the meaning of certain punctuation marks, the suggestions listed under items (H) through (Q) are appropriate. If, however, the cause of incorrect phrasing is a lack of comprehension, consult item (G) in the recommendations and refer to the appropriate chapter. If incorrect phrasing is caused by lack of word recognition or a lack of comprehension, you would be treating only the symptom and not the cause by using the recommendations listed in items (H) through (Q).

RECOMMENDATIONS

A. If insufficient word recognition is a major contributor to the problem of incorrect phrasing, it is, of course, necessary to increase the student's sight vocabulary. A word becomes a sight word after it has been read many times. Some writers and researchers have estimated that it takes from twenty to seventy exposures to a word before it actually becomes a *sight word*. A student who has not built up a sight vocabulary equivalent to his grade level must read and read and read in order to expose himself to as many new words as many times as possible. (See appendix R for sources of high-interest low-level vocabulary books.)

B. If the cause of incorrect phrasing is a limited sight vocabulary, then the suggestions recommended in chapter 11, "Sight Vocabulary Not Up to Grade Level," will be helpful.

C. Use the *Sight Phrase Cards* published by Garrard Press. (See appendix R.)

D. Compile lists of common prepositional phrases and have the students practice reading these phrases. (See appendix M.)

E. Listen to tape recordings of properly phrased reading while the student follows the same written material.

F. Use material that presents no vocabulary problem, allowing the pupils to concentrate on phrasing without experiencing difficulty in word attack.

G. If incorrect phrasing is caused by a lack of comprehension, then the recommendations in chapter 18, "Comprehension Inadequate," or chapter 19, "Vocabulary Inadequate," will be helpful.

H. Demonstrate proper phrasing by reading to the class.

I. Review the meanings of various punctuation marks and discuss how these help the student to phrase properly. It often helps to draw an analogy between traffic signs and punctuation marks: i.e., commas are likened to yield the right-of-way signs and periods are likened to stop signs.

J. Reproduce certain reading passages divided into phrases as in the following sentence:

Fred and Mary   were on their way   to the movies.

In doing this, you may find that there is more carry-over if a space is left between the phrases rather than using a dash(—) or a slash(/) to separate the phrases.

K. Use mechanical devices (see appendix R) that will force the reader to read more quickly. Be sure that whole phrases appear at the same time on the screen. You can easily make special filmstrips for this purpose. These can be used in a regular filmstrip projector, they may be programmed on a computer, or they can be used in an automatic slide projector with one phrase of a story appearing on each slide. Remember the precaution stated previously in "Word-by-Word Reading"—mechanical devices used with young children should be set at a comfortable pace. They should not be used for reading speed per se.

L. Have the children read and dramatize conversation.

M. Provide choral reading with several readers who phrase properly.

N. Write sentences using crayons. Make each phrase a different color. After reading sentences in color have the students read them in black and white print. In the following example the different styles of type represent different colors.

Fred and Mary   **were on their way**   to the movies.

O. Ditto or mimeograph songs. Have the students read these without the music.

P. Have students read orally phrases that extend only to the end of the line. After practicing with these phrases, students read phrases that carry over onto the next line; however, there should be more than the normal amount of space between each phrase. Gradually go from this style to normal writing.

Q. Use commercial materials such as the *Plays for Echo Reading* published by Harcourt Brace Jovanovich, which are designed to promote fluent oral reading.

GAMES AND EXERCISES

Bouncing for Words

Purpose: To provide practice on basic sight words, other sight words, or sight phrases

Materials: Group-size (6" X 3") cards for the basic sight words, sight words in general, or sight phrases to be learned
A chair for each child
A basketball or volleyball

Procedure:

Each child is given one phrase card. He stands behind a chair and places his card face up on the seat of the chair. The leader, one of the children in the group, bounces the ball to the first child. As the child catches the ball, he says the phrase. If the student says it correctly, he then picks up the card. If the student misses the phrase the card remains on the chair. Play continues until all the children have a turn at their phrases. At the end of the game, the children exchange cards and play continues. Any child who could not say the phrase when he caught the ball is told the phrase and keeps the phrase card until all the cards are exchanged at the end of the next game.

Use sight word cards instead of phrase cards, or use two teams. Instead of beginning with the children in a circle, have opposite teams face each other with eight or ten feet between each team. The leader then rotates the bounces between teams. The team with the least number of cards on its chairs after a certain number of sets or games is the winner.

Search

Purpose: To provide practice on the basic sight words or on phrasing

Materials: Three or more identical packs of word cards or three or more identical packs of sight phrase cards

Procedure:

Three or more children sit around a table, each with a pack of phrase or word cards that are identical to those of the rest of the players. One child looks at his pack and calls a phrase. The remaining players then see who can find the same phrase. The child who finds the phrase first places the card face up in the middle of the table and scores a point for himself. Play continues until a certain number of points are scored by an individual.

Pony Express

Purpose: To provide practice on phrasing

Materials: Pocket chart
Sight phrase cards

Procedure:

Fill a pocket chart with sight cards. Each word may represent a letter in the pony express saddlebag. The children come one at a time to claim their letters and read them to the rest of the class. After all cards have been removed from the chart the children exchange cards (letters) and begin again by mailing their letters (placing them back in the pocket chart).

A Phrasing Scope

Purpose: To provide practice in proper phrasing

Materials: Pieces of paper about 5" wide
A piece of cardboard a little larger than the strips of paper
Two dowel pins about ½" in diameter and 7" long

Procedure:

Paste the pieces of paper into a long strip. Type a story, either original or from a book, on the strip. Type only one phrase on a line and double space the lines. Next, fold the piece of cardboard and seal the sides, leaving the top and bottom open. Cut a window near the top of the cardboard. Slide the strip of paper through the cardboard and attach a round stick (½" dowel) at each end of the strip of paper. The pupil rolls the paper from the bottom to the top and reads the story as each phrase passes through the window's opening. See example following:

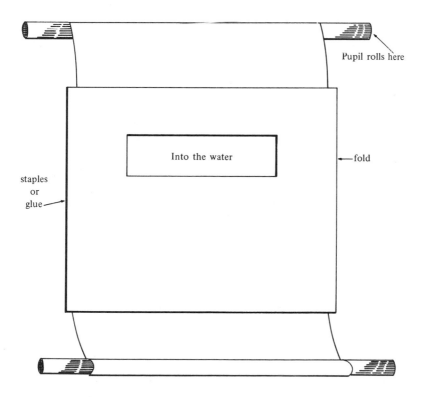

Sets

Purpose:　　To learn new phrases and to provide practice on reading those already known

Materials:　Two decks of identical phrase cards; number of cards used depends on the number of players, use four phrase cards for each player

Procedure:

Deal one deck of phrase cards, so each player has four different phrases. Place all duplicate phrases from the second deck faceup in several rows on the table. Begin by pointing to a phrase and saying it. The student who has the matching phrase picks it up and says it as he places it in his hand to make a matching "set." Play continues until one player has a complete set of four matches. The student must then read all of the phrases in his hand as they are placed on the desk or table. If the student cannot read them, play continues until another student has a complete matching set and can read them without help. The winner is, of course, the first student who obtains a complete matching set and is able to read all phrases from each set.

Drawing for Phrases

Purpose:　　To provide practice on reading basic sight words and phrases

Materials:　Three small boxes
　　　　　　1 inch squares of tagboard

Procedure:

In this game it is beneficial to have a disabled reader work with a good reader. Write a number of different prepositions on one-inch squares of tagboard and place them in Box One. Use words such as *with, in, under,* and *over* that would fit with almost any noun. In Box Two place one-inch tagboard squares with the words *the* and *a.* In Box Three place a few one-inch tagboard squares with nouns on them such as *house* and *chair.* Ask students to draw one square from each box to form a phrase. After all squares have been drawn and the phrases read, the squares may then be rearranged to form more phrases. You may wish to have the students write down the phrases to see who can get the most phrases. The written list is also useful for reviewing the phrases at a later date.

3

Poor Pronunciation

RECOGNIZED BY

Pupil fails to pronounce a word as it should be pronounced.

DISCUSSION

Mispronunciation of words is one of the most serious reading problems of disabled readers. The problem may be caused by one or a combination of the following factors: (1) the student may be weak in knowledge of phonics; (2) the student may possess, but not use, a knowledge of phonics; (3) the student may have some hearing defect; (4) the student may not understand diacritical markings; (5) the student may be a careless reader; and (6) the student may have some speech defect or accent. In any case, a careful diagnosis is called for before a program of correction is started. The following paragraphs suggest ways of diagnosing the various reasons for poor pronunciation.

Child has weakness in phonics knowledge The *El Paso Phonics Survey* found in appendix G can be used to quickly spot those areas of weakness in the student's knowledge of phonics. Teachers should be extra careful in selecting a phonics test to use. Extensive research at the Reading Center at the University of Texas at El Paso has shown that few, if any, group phonics tests examine what a student actually does in applying phonic word-attack skills. Therefore, such tests do not aid diagnostic teaching. This inadequacy is also true of some individual phonics tests. However, the *El Paso Phonics Survey* does require the student to respond in a situation similar to actual application of skills.

Child has phonics knowledge but does not use it properly The test mentioned above actually tests the student's ability to use phonics as well as phonics knowledge itself. The teacher may want to supplement test results by observing the ways in which the student attacks or fails to attack new words.

Hearing defect An auditory-discrimination test is easy to administer and will determine if a student has difficulty discriminating between somewhat similar sounds. The inability to discriminate between certain sounds can lead to the mispronunciation of words. This knowledge, supplemented with informal hearing tests, such as determining if the student hears a normal voice at the distance most children hear it, will help you decide if a hearing defect is contributing to the reading difficulty. Pupils indicating difficulty in any of these areas should be further examined by a specialist.

No knowledge of diacritical markings   Informal exercises constructed by the teacher, based upon the dictionary, may help. In an individual case this might include asking a student to read certain words from a dictionary in which the diacritical markings are shown. Once again, this type of task closely parallels that of reading.

Careless reading   You should stop the reader at a mispronounced word and ask for the correct pronunciation. If the student usually says it correctly, the problem may be one of carelessness. This would still not exclude the possibility that training in various forms of word analysis might be beneficial.

Speech defect or accent   Ask the student to repeat sentences that are given orally. Use words that were mispronounced in previous reading. Words read incorrectly, but spoken correctly, are not speech problems.

Some students never seem to develop the ability to apply various rules that are required for the successful use of certain phonics skills. For this type of student, the suggestions recommended under item (B) may prove more satisfactory in helping word attack problems.

RECOMMENDATIONS

For a child who has a weakness in phonics knowledge:

A. Teach the phonics skills in which a weakness is indicated by the *El Paso Phonics Survey* (see appendix G). For sample exercises see "Games and Exercises," chapter 13.

B. Use the phonogram list in appendix L as suggested under "Using the Phonogram List to Teach Phonics."

C. Have students make their own lists of common letter combinations that are generally phonetically regular such as *-tion, -ance,* and *-edge* as they are encountered and learned.

D. Make lists of prefixes and suffixes; however, do not expect the children to learn the meaning of many of these. Focus only on the children being able to pronounce these affixes. (See list of suffixes and prefixes in appendix N.)

E. Have the children make word cards or lists and build their own file of words that they habitually mispronounce. Allow for periodic, independent study of these words. An old shoe box makes an excellent file box for indexing word cards.

For a child who has phonics knowledge but does not use it properly:

F. For the child who has a knowledge of phonics but does not use it properly, repeated readings often bring about favorable results in a fairly short time. Try this method first. Use the repeated readings chart as explained in appendix Q.

G. A student who does not use phonics knowledge properly can also benefit from the following exercise using the phonogram list in appendix L:

1. Have the student first pronounce *sent;* then give her a number of other words and nonsense words to pronounce that end in *ent,* such as *dent, pent,* and *bent.* This exercise will give the student practice in using various consonant sounds in conjunction with various word endings.

2. Do the same as (1), using consonant blends with various combinations; for example, pronounce *slash,* then give a number of other words and nonsense words ending in *ash,* such as cr*ash,* fl*ash,* and sc*ash.*

As the student reads, ask her to try to pronounce difficult words aloud. You should determine which sounds she knows but is not using. Use these sounds in constructing exercises similar to the two shown above or others appropriate for improving the particular phrase of phonic elements not being used correctly.

H. When the pupil mispronounces a word in oral reading, call attention to the correct pronunciation with as little fuss as possible. Ignoring the mistake tends to reinforce the wrong pronunciation with the pupil as well as with any other members of the class who are listening. Help the pupil to analyze the correct pronunciation.

For a child who has a mild hearing defect:

I. To teach certain sounds with which pupils are having difficulty, do the following:

1. Set up pairs with only one different sound: e.g., *hit—heat.*
2. Make sure the students can hear the sound differences.
3. Make sure the students can say the words.
4. Use each word in a sentence and then have the students say the single sound following that sentence.

J. Have students hold their throats with their hands to feel the difference in vibration from one word to another or from one letter to another.

K. Play games that deal with sounds. For example, the first student says, "I am a *ch.*" The rest of the students then guess whether she is a chicken, chipmunk, etc. This gives all students many exposures to word beginnings.

For a child who has no knowledge of diacritical markings:

L. Teach the child how to use the diacritical marks found in the dictionary. Try to find words and letter combinations similar to those missed by the child. For example, the child may use the short /o/ sound in the word *torn*. To correct this you might construct an exercise such as the following:

Directions: Fill in the blanks with the correct word and then use your dictionary to mark the correct vowel sound of the word you placed in the blank.

1. The old coat was *(wôrn)*. (join   worn   to)
2. The old *(hôrn)* sounded as if it were new. (horn   man   sled)
3. They looked at the old man in *(scôrn)*. (hurry   worry   scorn)
4. Please do not *(wôrry)* about the money. (open   worry   destroy)

For a child who is a careless reader:

M. Use the repeated readings chart as described in appendix Q.

For a child with a speech defect or accent:

N. Refer to audiologist for suggestions.

4

Omissions

RECOGNIZED BY

Pupil omits words, phrases, or both. Sometimes only letters are omitted.

DISCUSSION

Omissions in reading are usually caused by insufficient word recognition or word-analysis skills, in which case they are deliberate. On the other hand, the student may have developed a habit of omitting certain words, in which case, they would be nondeliberate. Omissions are the second most common type of miscue. Before beginning a program of help, you should try to determine the cause. To determine if the omission of words is deliberate, ask the student to pronounce any words omitted after he has read a passage. If the student knows the word or words, assume that the omission was nondeliberate and that the problem is either one of carelessness or the development of a bad habit. If the student does not know the word, and the omission was deliberate, then the problem is likely to be lack of word recognition or word-analysis skills. You could have the student read the material at the level in which he is making omissions and note the percentage of words omitted. Then give the student an easier passage. You should note whether or not omissions still occur. If the omissions continue with approximately the same percent of occurrence, assume that they are a result of a bad habit. If, however, the percent of omissions markedly decreases, assume that the student has insufficient word recognition or word-analysis skills.

The student may lack word-attack skills in the areas of phonics, structural analysis, or context clues, or the student may to some extent lack comprehension. If the problem stems from one of these difficulties, the suggestions in items (A) through (E) will probably be of little or no value since the omissions are actually only symptoms of a larger problem with word-analysis difficulties. It is then necessary to determine in which of the word-analysis areas the student is deficient. The procedures and suggestions recommended for each case are given in the following chapters and pages:

Phonics—Chapters 13, 14, and 15
Structural Analysis—Chapter 16
Context Clues—Chapter 17
Comprehension—Chapter 18

If the student is able to analyze new words but does not have instant recognition of words that, for his grade level, should have become sight words, he probably lacks word-recognition skills. It would then be necessary to help the student build a sight vocabulary. To improve this area, as well as to help the child to recognize this problem, see "Sight Vocabulary Not Up to Grade Level," chapter 11.

If the student's problem is determined to be one of poor habit or of carelessness, the suggestions listed under items (A) through (F) should be helpful. You should also keep in mind that unless the student's errors are rather frequent and affect comprehension to some extent, they may not be worth worrying about.

RECOMMENDATIONS

A. Call the reader's attention to omissions when they occur. Making an immediate correction is the first step toward breaking the habit.

B. Have the student do repeated readings as described in appendix Q. After calling the student's attention to the problem as mentioned in "A" above, you may find that this method works extremely well.

C. If whole words or phrases are consistently skipped, the pupil may be required to point to each word as he reads it. The author has found that it is helpful to ask the reader to pick up his finger and then bring it down on each word as it is read. This keeps the reader from pointing to words that are ahead of the actual word being read. This technique should also be stopped as soon as possible.

D. Have several children choral read or let one child read with a tape recording of a reading passage.

E. Ask detailed questions that require thorough reading. Ask about only a sentence or paragraph at a time. Students often will omit adjectives. In this case it is often helpful to give the student a list of questions such as, Was the bear big or little? and What color were the flowers? The student will be forced to focus on adjectives that could otherwise easily be omitted.

F. Giving help with word middles or endings often will help the problem of omitting these parts of words. The student's attention might be called to certain middles and endings, and you may make lists of common letter combinations.

G. To focus attention to words omitted by the reader, tape-record a passage and then give the student a copy of the material as it is played back to him. Have the student follow along and point to each word as it is read. Have him circle all words omitted. After the reading, discuss possible reasons for his omitting the words and the importance of not doing so.

H. As the student reads, ask him to outline the first letter of each word read as follows:

Sam plays baseball in the park.

This will be helpful for students who make many omissions. You will, of course, want to discontinue this as soon as the student stops making omissions.

Another variation of the procedure above is to have the student underline the first letters of words as follows:

Mary went with her mother to the store.

Following this you may wish to have the student draw lines over or below words in phrases or natural linguistic units as he reads. An example of this is:

Fred has a large brown cat.

5

Repetitions

RECOGNIZED BY

Pupil rereads words or phrases.

DISCUSSION

The causes of repetitions in students' reading are similar to the causes of omissions in reading—that is, poor word-recognition skills, poor word-analysis skills, or the development of a bad habit. A problem with word recognition skills is the most common of the causes. It should be pointed out, however, that sometimes a student repeats certain words in order to correct a reading error. If this happens only on certain words that are known to be new to the student, it should, in most cases, be ignored. If the words not recognized by the pupil are ones that normally should be sight words for that pupil, it can be assumed that she is deficient in word recognition skills. In this case, the recommendations under "Sight Vocabulary Not Up to Grade Level," chapter 11 should be beneficial.

The problem of word-analysis difficulties may be in any of the following areas: (1) phonics, (2) structural analysis, (3) use of context clues, or (4) use of the dictionary (less frequently). If the problem is in one of these areas, the recommendations suggested in items (A) through (E) would probably be of little or no value since the repetitions are only a symptom of the larger problems of word-recognition or word-analysis difficulties. You would need to determine in which area of word analysis the pupil was deficient. These procedures and the suggestions recommended in each case are given in the chapters and pages as follows:

Phonics—Chapters 13, 14, and 15
Structural Analysis—Chapter 16
Context Clues—Chapter 17
Dictionary Skills—Chapter 28

You can determine, to some extent, whether poor word-recognition or word-analysis skills is the cause of repetitions by having the pupil read material at the level in which she is making repetitions. Note the percent of words or phrases repeated. Then give the pupil a much easier passage and note whether or not there is a definite decrease in the percent of repetitions. If there is, the problem is probably insufficient word-recognition or word-analysis skills. If, on the other hand, a student continues to make as many repetitions as she did on the more difficult passage, then the problem is probably a bad habit.

If you determine that the problem results from bad habits, then the recommendations listed under items (A) through (G) should prove beneficial. Also, following the suggestions listed under items (H) and (I) may give the pupil the confidence she needs to break the habit.

RECOMMENDATIONS

A. Call the repetitions to the student's attention. This is the initial step in breaking the bad habit.

B. Use the repeated readings chart shown in appendix Q.

C. Have the student read with a tape recording of the material in the reading passage.

D. Have the students choral read.

E. Use mechanical devices that are designed to project a certain number of words per minute and that prevent the reader from regressing. (See appendix R.) When working with children in the primary grades, you should not worry about speed itself. You must make sure the instrument does not move at a rate too fast for the normal reading rate of the reader.

F. Have the student set a certain pace with her hand and keep up with this pace as she reads. Do not let the eyes pace the hand.

G. To focus attention to words repeated by the reader, tape-record a passage read and then give the student a copy of the material as it is played back to her. Have the student follow along pointing to each word and underlining any words as they are repeated. After completing the passage, discuss any reasons that the student believes are causing her to repeat words or phrases.

H. Provide easier or more familiar material in which the vocabulary presents no problem.

I. Let the students read the material silently before they attempt to read orally.

6

Inversions or Reversals

RECOGNIZED BY

Pupil reads words from right to left instead of the normal left-to-right sequence, e.g., *was* for *saw,* or *pot* for *top.*

Pupil reads letters in reverse, e.g., *d* for *b,* or *p* for *g.*

Pupil makes partial reversals in words (the letters within words), e.g., *ant* for *nat.*

Pupil reverses words within sentences, e.g., the *rat* chased the *cat,* instead of the *cat* chased the *rat.*

DISCUSSION

Reversals or inversions may be caused by a number of factors. The student may have failed to develop a left-to-right eye movement or a left-to-right reading pattern. (This problem, if and when it exists, is difficult to determine.) The student may have not developed a strong enough visual image for the word and may miscall the word because he is not giving enough detail to the context. The student may suffer from some neurological impairment, or he may fail to realize that the order or position in which letters appear does make a difference. Another possible factor is immaturity. (It is much more common for a student of five, six, or even seven years old to make inversions or reversals than a child who is eight years old.)

Observation and questioning will, in some cases, help locate the cause of the reversals. However, unless the problem is a difficult one caused by a neuro-logical disfunction, you need not be concerned with which of the above causes is the major contributor. The recommendations are the same in any case. Many children who make reversals tend to outgrow the problem after a few months of school. However, if the problem persists after several weeks of instruction, especially if the student is over the age of eight, you may wish to refer the pupil to a psychologist or neurologist. However, be prepared to receive recommendations that you continue doing the things listed above!

For many years reading teachers have believed that students who made many reversals or inversions tended to have more severe difficulties than students who made other types of errors. More recent research has tended to refute this belief. We now believe that, if checked carefully, you are likely to find that children who make numerous reversals will also make just as high a percentage of other types of errors.

RECOMMENDATIONS

Probably the most important thing you can do to help the student correct the problem is to call his attention to the context in which the word is used. If the student is made aware of the context, then he will have a tendency to correct the problem on his own. To do this, give the student a number of sentences in which the word or words being reversed could only logically be used in one context. It may be helpful to have the student work at the sentence level, rather than at the paragraph or passage level, so he can focus more on the context. The following is an example:

Fred *was* going with Tom to the movies.
Lori *saw* a big dog on the way home.

A. After discussing the problem with the student, give him sentences in which words that he tends to reverse are covered by a small piece of paper. Allow him to read to the end of the sentence, using the context, to determine the word he feels should be in the sentence. Then allow him to uncover the word and check the accuracy of his use of context.

B. Emphasize left-to-right in all reading activities. The following methods may be helpful:

1. Cover words or sentences with your hand or a card and read the word or sentence as you uncover it. Then, have the student do the same. The student may find it helpful to make a window marker as shown. The child uses it as he would a regular marker but lets the line of print show through the slot.

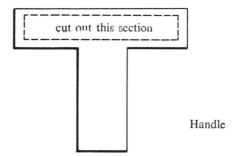

2. Have the student underline the word or sentence, sounding the word as it is underlined or reading the sentence as it is underlined.
3. Teach the child to pace his reading with his hand, practicing a left-to-right movement.
4. Draw arrows pointing from left to right under troublesome words.

C. Let the child use a typewriter to practice words with which he has difficulty. This will enable him to see the word formed from left to right.

D. Pair the letters that are causing difficulty (such as *p* and *q*). Have the pupil trace the letters with his index and middle fingers, sounding each letter as it is traced.

E. If whole words are reversed, you can have the pupil trace the word and then attempt to write it from memory.

F. Use a magnetic board with three-dimensional letters. Have the pupil manipulate letters to form words commonly reversed.

G. Write in pairs the words sometimes reversed (was-*saw*, net-*ten*, war-*raw*, trap-*part*). Use one word in a sentence and ask pupils to point to or write the word used.

H. Use a colored letter at the beginning of words commonly confused. Discontinue this practice as soon as the word no longer presents any difficulty for the child.

I. Blindfold the pupil and form letters or words with which he is having difficulty using three-dimensional letters. Have the pupil trace the letter and say it as you trace it on his back, making sure that your finger follows the same part of the letter on the student's back that his does in tracing the three-dimensional letter.

J. To help make the student aware of the importance of sequence of words commonly reversed, place one word commonly reversed over another. Then have the pupil draw lines from the first letter of the top word to the first letter of the bottom word. Have the student say each letter as he begins to draw the line from it and each letter as the line reaches it:

K. Write two words commonly reversed side by side. Ask the student to number the letters in the first word by placing a number under each letter. Then ask him to assign the same numbers to the letters in the second word:

```
s a w   w a s      o n   n o
1 2 3   3 2 1      1 2   2 1
```

7

Insertions

RECOGNIZED BY

Pupil adds words that are not present in the sentences. For example, in the sentence, "The dog chased the little boy," the pupil may add *big* to make the sentence read, "The *big* dog chased the little boy."

DISCUSSION

Insertions are the third most common type of miscue made by students in oral reading. They are often not as serious as other types of errors. A possible cause of insertions is that the student's oral language development may surpass her reading level or that she may anticipate what is coming next and read that instead of what is actually written. Insertions that make sense within the context of the sentence indicate the student's awareness or comprehension of the material being read. In this case, you may assume the insertions are caused from either carelessness or oral language development beyond the reading level of the student. When insertions do not make sense within the context of the sentence, you may assume that comprehension problems are involved. The recommendations listed in items (A) through (G) are appropriate when the problem is carelessness or when the oral language development of the student surpasses her reading ability. If students make this type of error, you should first determine whether they appear often, or are serious enough, to be concerned. If they appear rather seldom, it may be best to ignore them. If the cause of the insertions is a lack of comprehension, then the recommendations in "Comprehension Inadequate," chapter 18, are recommended.

RECOMMENDATIONS

A. Call the student's attention to the insertion. Sometimes she is not aware of the habit. Allowing the student to continue only provides reinforcement for the mistakes.

B. Use the repeated readings chart as explained in appendix Q.

C. Ask questions that require an exact answer. If the student usually follows a certain pattern in making insertions (such as adding adjectives), you may wish to provide questions for the student to review before reading the story. These questions can focus on the descriptions of the objects in the story described by the adjectives that are often inserted. This will focus the student's reading on the material as it is being read. Use questions such as Does it say how big the frog was? and Was it a sunny warm day, a sunny cold day, or just a sunny day?

D. Have students choral read.

E. Have the student read along with a passage that has been tape-recorded.

F. If the student makes many insertions, have her point to each word as it is read. Have the student lift her finger up and bring it down on each word as it is read. Do not allow the student to continue this technique after the habit has disappeared.

G. Play a tape recording in which the student made insertions. Ask the student to follow the written passage. Have the student write on the written passage the insertions that were made on the oral reading of the material. Use the student-corrected passages as a basis for discussing the problem.

8

Substitutions

RECOGNIZED BY

Pupil substitutes one word for another.

DISCUSSION

Substitutions are the most common type of miscue or oral reading error. The child who substitutes one word for another is probably either a careless reader or a reader who has not developed adequate word-recognition skills. The substitutions made by many readers are nearly correct within the context of the material being read: e.g., "The man drove the *automobile*" might be read "The man drove the *car*." If these minor mistakes do not appear too often, it may be best to ignore the problem. If, however, they consistently occur, some steps should be taken. Substitutions that are not in the proper context of the sentence usually are caused by word-recognition difficulty. When help is given with word-recognition skills, the problem of substitutions usually disappears. You should determine whether substitutions are caused by carelessness or insufficient word-recognition skills and plan help accordingly. You should note whether certain substitutions appear only in the child's reading or whether they occur in his speech as well.

If the substitutions made by the pupil are not in the proper context of the sentence, they are probably caused by the lack of word-recognition skills. In that case, the recommendations under items (A) through (E) should be helpful. If, however, substitutions are caused by carelessness, the recommendations under items (F) through (M) should be helpful.

RECOMMENDATIONS

A. If there are many words that are not known, then the suggestions listed under chapter 11 (Sight Vocabulary Not Up to Grade Level) should be used. When the student's sight vocabulary is brought up to grade level, then the problem of making substitutions will probably disappear.

B. Work on beginning syllables and/or sounds that cause difficulty. (See appendix K.)

C. Use the difficult words in multiple-choice sentences, such as the following examples:

1. John's father gave him a (watch, witch, water) for his birthday.
2. He (though, thought, through) he would be the tallest boy in the class.
3. He asked his father (what, where, when) they would leave.
4. She said, "The books belong to (them, that, this)."

D. Use the words in sentences where the student must complete the word in order to make the sentence sensible. Following are examples.

1. Can you tell me wh____ they will be home?
2. Does th____ book belong to Lori?
3. The stunt driver drove his car t____ the wall of fire.
4. Jamie said, "That funny l____ dog belongs to me."

E. Sometimes students feel they must make a continual response while they are reading. When such students do not know a strange word, they are likely to substitute whatever word comes into their minds rather than take the time to use analysis skills. Assure these students that they will be given ample amount of time to attack a word before you or a classmate tells them the word.

F. Call attention to the mistake and correct it when it occurs.

G. Use the repeated readings chart as explained in appendix Q.

H. Have the student trace over the first letter or underline the first letter of each word in the sentence as shown below:

Debbie went with Tom to the movies.

Debbie went with Tom to the movies.

Do not ask the student to continue this practice for a long period of time. Use it only to break the habit and then stop using it.

I. Have the pupils choral read.

J. Have the pupils read along with a passage that has been tape-recorded.

K. Ask questions about the subject matter that will reflect the pupil's mistakes. Have him read to make corrections.

L. Have the pupils follow a printed copy of what they have read as it is played on a tape recorder. As they listen, have them circle words for which substitutions were made. Use this student-corrected material when discussing the problem.

M. Some students, especially when they are under pressure during a test or in a situation somewhat different from their normal environment, will feel pressure to read rather rapidly. If you sense that a student is reading more rapidly than he should or normally does, stop him and explain that it is not necessary to read faster than usual.

9

Guesses at Words

RECOGNIZED BY

Pupil guesses at new words instead of analyzing the correct pronunciation.

DISCUSSION

Guessing at words may be the result of one or several factors. The pupil may not possess a knowledge of phonics or structural analysis. She may not know how to systematically sound out a word, or she may not be using context clues. Before attempting to help the pupil, you should determine which of the factors are responsible for the pupil's guessing at words. A very effective way of determining why a pupil guesses at words is to *ask her.* You should ask whether she knows the sound of the first letter, the blend, the vowel combinations, the first syllable, and so forth. Also, you should check to see whether the student knows how to blend sounds together rapidly. Finally, ask questions to determine whether she is aware of the context in which the word is used. If it is determined that the pupil has no knowledge of phonics or structural analysis, the suggestion listed under item (A) should be followed. If she has knowledge of phonics, but doesn't use it, then the suggestions listed under items (B) through (D) will be helpful. Pupils who do not make use of the context should be given help as recommended in items (E) through (I).

RECOMMENDATIONS

A. Administer the *El Paso Phonics Survey* (appendix G) or a similar test that tests in a situation that approximates what the student would have to do if actually reading in your classroom. Give help where needed according to the results of the test. Recommendations for correcting difficulties in the areas of phonics and structural analysis are found in the following chapters:

Phonics—Chapters 13, 14, and 15
Structural Analysis—Chapter 16

B. While the child is reading orally, the teacher should call attention to the words at which she guesses. At the same time, help should be given in the systematic analysis of the word. This will start the reader into the habit of analyzing her own difficult words. Help the student to sound the first sound, the second, and on through to the end of the word. Then give help in blending these sounds together.

In doing this with older students, you may find it helpful to practice on phonetically regular "nonsense" words. To make phonetically regular nonsense words, use phonetically regular "real" words and replace the consonants; e.g., in a two-syllable word such as "tulip," make the nonsense word "lupit."

C. Use the repeated readings chart as explained in appendix Q.

D. Have the student trace over or underline the first and last letters and middle vowel(s) of words at which she pauses:

It was a very h̶ụ̶mid day.

It was a very hum̲i̲d day.

E. As the pupil reads, circle or underline the words that she guesses. Replace these words with blank lines and have the student reread the material. Ask her to fill in the correct words from context.

F. Try to develop the habit of having the pupil reread several words preceding the difficult word and sound out at least the first one or two sounds of the difficult word. Then read several words following the difficult word. This strategy will develop the habit of using context as well as the beginning sounds. The pupil will learn to sound more of the word than the first syllable as the need arises. For example: "The large black dog was ch ____ on the bone." If the pupil has read *on the bone* and hears the sound of *ch,* she will in most cases say *chewing.*

G. Give the pupil sentences in which there is one difficult word which she has guessed in her oral reading. Have her work independently, using the method described in item (E), to determine correctness of the difficult words.

H. Teach the pupil that there are a number of types of context clues. The student does not have to categorize them; however, working with several different kinds of context clues will enable her to become more adept in their use. For example:

1. Definition context clues:
   The word *mongrel* sometimes refers to a *dog* of mixed breeds.

2. Synonym context clues:
   The team was *gleeful* and the coach was also *jubilant* because they had won the game.
3. Contrasting words:
   He was *antisocial,* but she was *friendly.*
4. Common sayings or expressions:
   It was *dark* as *pitch.*

I. Use commercially prepared materials designed to improve use of context clues. (See appendix R.)

10

Basic Sight Words Not Known

RECOGNIZED BY

Pupil is unable to read some or all of the basic sight words—those words of high utility that make up from 50 to 65 percent of the words in most reading material. The percent would, of course, be higher when written at a lower reading level.

DISCUSSION

There are several lists of the common or basic sight words. One is provided in appendix D. These are the words that make up half or more of the reading matter in elementary reading material. Since these words appear frequently, it is important that a child recognize them instantly. If children do not have these words in their sight vocabulary, or cannot recognize them instantly, they cannot become fluent readers. Children often confuse certain basic sight words, especially those with similar beginnings, e.g., *whe*n, *whe*re, and *wha*t; or *thi*s, *tha*t, and *tho*se.

The test of the basic sight words often is given by showing the pupil four words and asking him to circle or underline the words you pronounce. The ability to distinguish a word from a choice of four words is not, however, the same as the ability to pronounce the word in print. You frequently will find that older students can score 100 percent on a basic sight word test if given in this manner, but that the same students may not be able to pronounce many of the same words when they are asked to read them.

When testing for students' knowledge of basic sight words, the words should be presented for approximately one second each. If you give more time than this, then, to some extent, the test becomes a measure of word-analysis skills rather than a test of sight words. You can have the student read words from a list; however, you cannot control the time each word is exposed to the student. Another way to test basic sight words is to use flash cards and allow the student about one second for each word. This has drawbacks because it is difficult for the teacher to manipulate the flash cards and mark right and wrong answers at the same time. Another problem occurs when a student thinks he knows a word and asks the teacher to wait momentarily, usually by saying "wait, wait." When the teacher does not give this extra time, the student tends to get angry or frustrated and direct that anger or frustration at the teacher.

A better way to determine which words are or are not known by a student is to use a computer to give a brief (tachistoscopic) presentation of each word. The student sits in front of the computer screen and pronounces each word as it appears. The teacher is seated close enough to the student to hear each response. This will give the teacher time to mark right and wrong answers and write the phonetic pronunciation for incorrect answers. The teacher can then analyze beginning consonant, consonant cluster, ending consonant, and medial vowel(s) sounds to determine whether certain students possess certain weaknesses. (See appendix R under *Laser Designs* for source for ordering the basic sight words test on a computer disk.)

If you have the student read basic sight words from a list, remember to count any word wrong at which the student pauses for more than about one second. Having students read the basic sight words from a list is a quick way to check those students you think, but are not quite sure, know most words.

If you decide to use flash cards to test students' knowledge of basic sight words, you may wish to place the words the student gets right on one pile and those he gets wrong on another. However, keep in mind that some students get rather frustrated in seeing the pile of wrong cards grow. If time allows you may wish to stop and teach each word missed to those students who do not miss a high percentage of the total.

You can find the point at which particular words should be known by a student in appendix D. The first digit of the designation refers to grade level, and the second digit after the decimal refers to the month. These digits designate the point at which the student should master each word. Keep in mind, however, that each student's background of experience and the basal series from which he has been taught may cause considerable variance.

A quick way to determine if students know most of the basic sight words is found in appendix C.

RECOMMENDATIONS

If a student knows most of the basic sight words, then the suggestions listed in items (A) through (J) and the games and exercises will be helpful in teaching the words. However, if the student does not know a considerable number of basic sight words, there is probably no faster or more efficient way of teaching these words than through the use of the language-experience approach and the neurological-impress method. (These methods are explained in chapter 29.) In using these methods, you will not be focusing on any particular basic sight word. However, since the words appear so often, they will soon become known because they are used over and over either in the stories that the student writes using the language-experience approach or in the stories he reads using the neurological-impress method.

A. Have the pupil write troublesome words on cards (8½″ × 3″). Trace the word using the index and middle fingers. Sound the word as it is traced. After the pupil knows the word, it should no longer be sounded. (Some words do not sound as they are spelled. In this case the sounding part should be omitted.) Use cards to form sentences. Also give sentences with the sight words omitted. Have the pupil fill in blanks with the appropriate word from his pile of cards.

   If you wish to emphasize a kinesthetic approach in having the student write words using the middle and index finger, the following idea from Edward J. Dwyer and Rona F. Flippo has been suggested.* Take a piece of acetate such as that used on overhead projectors. Run this through a sewing machine with an unthreaded needle to make rows of holes approximately ¼ inch apart. This will make the bottom surface rough when it is complete. Attach the acetate with the rough side up to a piece of cardboard using bookbinding tape on one side so it can be raised or opened as one would do with the front page of a book. When a new word is to be learned, print it on a flash card and place it under the acetate cover so that it is between the acetate and cardboard. Then have the student trace over the word. The series of raised holes made by the sewing machine needle in the acetate will give it a three dimensional effect.

B. Use the sight words that cause difficulty in sentences. Underline the words that cause difficulty as in the following examples:

   1. I <u>thought</u> it was you.
   2. I could not go even <u>though</u> I have time.
   3. He ran right <u>through</u> the stop sign.

C. Pictures can be used to illustrate some words, such as *play, wash, work, small,* and *sing.* Use a picture with a sentence that describes it and the sight word underlined, or have the children make picture dictionaries:

---

* From Dwyer, Edward J. & Flippo, Rona F. Multisensory approaches to teaching spelling. *Journal of Reading,* November 1983, 27, 171–72.

The thimble is small.

The dog likes to play.

D. Have the pupil write troublesome words on a card (8½″ × 3″) and then pantomime the action described by the word; e.g., *pull, sleep, ride, jump.*

E. Place one word that is different in a line of words. Ask the pupil to circle the one that says "what", e.g., *when, when, what, when, when.*

F. Use words commonly confused in multiple-choice situations. Have the pupils underline the correct word:

1. He wanted to (walk, <u>wash</u>) his clothes.
2. He didn't know (when, <u>what</u>) to do.
3. He put it over (<u>there</u>, their).
4. I (well, <u>will</u>) go with you.

G. Have the pupil read the entire sentence, look at the beginning and end of the word, and then try to pronounce it on the basis of its context and configuration.

H. For slow learners who have difficulty with certain words, try cutting letters from sandpaper or velvet so that the child can "feel" the word as he pronounces it. Follow the same procedure described in item (A). For certain students it is helpful to put a thin layer of salt or fine sand in a shoe box lid and let them practice writing the word in the salt or sand.

I. Place a piece of paper over a piece of screen wire such as the wire used on screen doors of a house. Before doing this, it is a good idea to cover the edges of the screen wire with bookbinding tape, so the rough edges do not cut anyone. Writing on the paper on the screen wire with a crayon will leave a series of raised dots. Have the student trace basic sight words in this manner, then have him trace over the words, saying them as they are traced.

J. Each day pass out a few basic sight words on cards to students. Each student in turn goes to the board and writes his word. The class should try to say it aloud. After it is pronounced correctly, have them write it in a notebook. On some days have students select words from their notebooks and write them on the chalkboard. Then ask various members of the class to say these words.

GAMES AND EXERCISES

(Also see "Games and Exercises" for improving sight vocabulary, chapter 11. Many of the games and exercises listed there are appropriate for improving knowledge of basic sight words.)

Dominoes

Purpose: To provide practice in word discrimination

Materials: Flash cards, divided in half by a line, in which a different word is on each side of the line. (See examples.) Make sure that the words are repeated several times on different cards.

the	what		and	the

a	and		go	a

Procedure:

After mixing the cards, the game proceeds the same as dominoes. The child pronounces the word as he matches it.

Word Order

Purpose: To provide practice on basic sight words, other sight words, or to provide practice in recognition of phonic elements.

Materials: Dittoed sheets of words arranged in the same manner as the following example.

A. why ____   B. c ____
   what ____   d ____
   when ____   g ____
   where ____   b ____
   which ____   f ____

C. cat ____   D. sound ____
   mule ____   frog ____
   cage ____   wolf ____
   pill ____   rabbit ____
   duck ____   pass ____

Procedure:

Play a recording or read words or sounds to the children who have the dittoed sheets. Each set of words should, however, concentrate on practice in only one area. The directions for the preceding sets would be similar to the following example.

Set A: Number the words in the order in which they are read.

Set B: Number the letters that correspond with the same beginning sound that you hear in the following words (in the order they are given): *book, food, good, can, dog.*

Set C: Put numeral *1* in front of the word with a long /a/ sound.
Put *2* in front of the word with a short /u/ sound.
Put *3* in front of the word with a short /a/ sound.
Put *4* in front of the word with a long /u/ sound.
Put *5* in front of the word with a short /i/ sound.

Set D: Number the words, in the order they are given, that have ending letter sounds. Give the following sounds: /f/, /t/, /g/, /d/, /s/.

Passport

Purpose: To provide practice on the basic sight words or other sight words

Materials: Use either group-size (6″ × 3″) or individual-size cards (3″ × 1½″). One set is given to the group of children and one is kept by the captain, who is usually a child who knows the words quite well.

Procedure:

Each child is given one or several words (passports). In order to get aboard the boat, he must show his passports to the captain. When the captain calls the port (the word or words) from his deck of cards, the person who has a card matching the captain's must show it to him to get off the boat.

Variation in Procedure:

The same game can be played with the sound of the consonants and vowels. In this case, the captain has word cards, and the child who has a letter matching the sound of the first letter in the word called by the captain shows his passport (letter) and is allowed to leave the boat.

Word in the Box

Purpose: To provide review and reinforcement on words that present problems to pupils

Materials: A large box
Word cards with words on them that have given the children trouble in their reading

Procedure:

The children sit in a circle around the box. You either read or play a tape recording of a story. Before hearing the story, each child is given a card on which there is a word from the story. When that word is read in the story, the child says "___ goes in the box" and throws the word in the box. The child then is given another word, so he may continue in the game.

Word Football

Purpose: To provide practice on the recognition of basic sight words or other sight words.

Materials: A large sheet of drawing paper
A small replica of a football
Word cards.

Procedure:

Draw a football field on a large piece of paper. The game begins at the fifty-yard line where the football is placed. The word cards are then placed faceup on the table, and two children, or two teams, take turns reading them. If a child reads a word correctly, he moves the ball ten yards toward the opponent's goal. If he reads the word incorrectly, it is considered a fumble, and the ball goes ten yards toward his own goal. Each time the ball crosses into the end zone, six points are scored. The scoring side then gets to read one more word to try for the extra point.

Word Checkers

Purpose: To provide practice in word recognition or phonic sounds

Materials: Checkerboard
Small squares of paper with sight words or phonic sounds on them

Procedure:

You or the child covers the black squares with the words. The game is played the same as regular checkers, but the player must say the word that appears on the square before a checker is placed on that space.

Variation in Procedure:

Phonic sounds may be used instead of words.

Pack of Trouble

Purpose: To discover which children do not know certain words and to provide special help in such cases

Materials: Word cards using the vocabulary currently being studied
             Blank cards on which you can print words.

Procedure:

You flash word cards to individual students and ask them to pronounce the words as quickly as possible. Whenever a child misses a word, he is given that word and makes a copy of it to keep. The student then can give the original back to you. Each child develops his own pack of trouble, which he can use for study with another individual or with a small group. As soon as the student masters a word, he may give it back to you. The idea is, of course, to keep your pack of trouble as small as possible.

Climbing the Word Ladder

Purpose: To provide practice on basic sight words, on sight words in general, or on sight phrases

Materials: A number of card packs of ten words. On the cards can be basic sight words, other sight words, or sight phrases.
             A small ladder that will hold ten cards. The rungs of the ladder may be made from wood 3/4" round and the vertical poles from wood of 1" × 2". See illustration following.

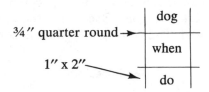

Procedure:

Each child receives a pack of cards and tries to try to climb the ladder with them. Cards are laid on each rung of the ladder. The child then tries to climb it by saying the words. After the child has mastered his own words, he exchanges packs and begins again with new words.

Hands Up (Words)

Purpose: To provide practice on recognition of basic sight words or other sight words.

Materials: Group-size cards (6″ × 3″)

Procedure:

Quickly flash a word card around the group allowing each child to see it. The child whose turn it is to pronounce the word then has a chance to do so. If the student pronounces the word correctly, he is given the word card. If the student does not pronounce the word correctly, then he is required to raise his hand. When the next card is flashed, the second child has a chance to say it. If, however, the child who has his hand up can pronounce the word before the second child, he gets the card and may put his hand down. The second child then receives a chance at another word. If he misses that word, then that child must hold up his hand, and so on. The object is to get the most cards. There may also be a number of children with their hands up at any one time. If this is the case, the one who pronounces the word first gets the card.

Surprise Words

Purpose: To reinforce knowledge of the basic sight words or sight words

Materials: Word cards to fit pocket chart
            A pocket chart

Procedure:

Fill the pocket chart with words that are currently being studied. Turn the cards so only the backs are showing. The children take turns coming up to the chart and taking a surprise word. If they can pronounce the word, they get to keep it; if they cannot, they must leave it in the chart. The child with the most words at the end of a certain time period wins the game.

Gamble for Words

Purpose: To provide practice on either basic sight words or other sight words

Materials: Pocket chart
            Cards with either the basic sight words or any sight word on them
            A die

Procedure:

Place the words to be worked on in a pocket chart or on the shelves of a pegboard unit. One child then rolls a die. He may pick up the same number of cards from the chart as the number indicated on the die. He must, however, be able to say each word as he picks it up. The turn then passes to another child. The object is to see who can get the most words. This game may be played using either a student vs. student approach or a team vs. team approach. You may set a time limit for the game or limit the game to a certain number of refills of the pocket chart.

Word Match

Purpose: To provide practice on word recognition

Materials: A pack of word cards in which every card has a word on it that is duplicated; that is, there should be two cards for each word to be used. The number of cards will depend on the number of players involved.

Procedure:

The players are each dealt four cards, which are placed faceup in front of each player. Five cards are then placed faceup in the middle of the table. The remainder of the pack is placed facedown in the middle of the table. If the first player has a card that matches any of the five faceup cards in the middle of the table, he picks it up, pronounces the word, and keeps the pair, placing them facedown in front of him. The student may continue playing until he can make no more pairs. The student then draws to fill his hand to four cards and replaces the five faceup cards on the table. If, in this process, cards that match are drawn and placed on the table, they are left for the individual who has the next turn. Play continues to the first player on the left. If a player can match a card in the middle of the table but cannot pronounce the word, he must place his card on the middle and leave it. If the following player can pronounce the word, he receives the pair. The winner is the person with the most cards when all of the cards are paired.

Rolling for Words

Purpose: To teach and provide practice on basic sight words

Materials: Three colors of construction paper
             A die
             Three small boxes

Procedure:

Cut the colored construction paper into one-inch squares. Print a basic sight word on each square. Put the squares into separate boxes according to the color of the paper. You may wish to put primer words on one color, first-grade words on another color, and so on. The players throw the die to see who starts the game. The student with the highest number starts by selecting as many words from any one box as the number on the die. If he fails to say any one of the words, he loses all the words from that turn; and after being told the missing word by the teacher, the student returns the words to the appropriate box. Play continues to the first player's left. The winner is the one with the most words when all three boxes are empty, and the game ends.

Finding Rhyming Words

Purpose: To teach and reinforce basic sight words

Materials: Flash cards of basic sight words from which rhyming words can be made
            A pocket chart

Procedure:

Place the flash cards in the pocket chart. You then say, "I want a word that rhymes with *fat*." Students take turns looking for a word to rhyme with the one given by you. If the student cannot find the word, he is given a word to hold by you or by another student who knows it. The winners are those students who are holding no words at the end of the game.

Finding Phrases

Purpose: To reinforce knowledge of the basic sight words

Materials: Pocket chart
            Basic sight word cards $3'' \times 8\frac{1}{2}''$

Procedure:

Place the words in the pocket chart to make four or five phrases (for example, *is in* and *wants to go*). Then say a sentence such as, "The boy wants to go." Students take turns going to the pocket chart and placing their hands on the phrase from the sentence and reading it. If a student fails to read it correctly, he must take the cards from that phrase to be studied. The object is to have no cards at the end of the game.

The Password

Purpose: To provide practice on especially difficult basic sight words

Materials: Straight or safety pins
             3″ × 8½″ cards

Procedure:

Take a group of students who are having trouble with the same basic sight words. Write one of the basic sight words on each card, and go over the words thoroughly with the children. Then pin one card on each student. Throughout the day, whenever one student must deal with another or whenever you wish to get a response from that student, call the basic sight word written on the student's card rather than his name before that student is to respond. This can be done daily with different groups of words and students.

Concentration

Purpose: To develop the ability to recognize basic sight words

Materials: Basic sight word flash cards in which each card has a duplicate

Procedure:

Find 10 to 12 cards and their duplicate cards (total of 20 to 24). Shuffle the cards and lay them facedown on the table. The first student turns up a card and says the word. He then turns up another card trying to find the duplicate of the first one turned up. If the second card is not a duplicate of the first or if the student does not know the word, he turns them facedown, and the next student takes his turn. If a student is able to turn up one card, say the word, and then turn up the duplicate of that card, he gets to keep the pair. As play continues, students will, of course, find it easier to find matching pairs. The person with the most pairs at the end of the game wins.

11

Sight Vocabulary Not Up to Grade Level

RECOGNIZED BY

Pupil fails to instantly recognize words thought to be common for or below grade level. (Failure is not limited to words commonly called *basic* sight words.)

DISCUSSION

In advancing from grade to grade, the pupil should increase her sight vocabulary at each grade level. A pupil's sight vocabulary is not up to grade level unless she can correctly pronounce 95 percent of the words in a book or textbook at her grade level. The pupil who, for some reason, has not developed an adequate number of sight words at each grade level is greatly handicapped since she must analyze many more words than a normal reader. This child is more likely to encounter reading material on her frustration level.

You should not determine whether a library book is at a certain grade level from the publisher's recommendation unless that recommendation has been made on the basis of one of the better readability formulas. You can, however, expect a reading textbook to be written at approximately the level for which it was intended to be used. Even when using a textbook at a certain level to determine if a student is deficient in her sight vocabulary, you should take passages from several parts of the book to ensure an accurate diagnosis.

RECOMMENDATIONS

The first, and most important, recommendation to help a student increase the size of her sight vocabulary is to have the student read widely on many subjects. If the student has adequate word-attack skills and is calling the words correctly, then she will automatically learn many new sight words by seeing them a number of times. However, if the student does not have adequate word attack skills for her grade level, then the use of the language-experience approach and the neurological-impress method (See chapter 29) will probably do more to increase the student's overall sight vocabulary than any other corrective procedures you can use.

A. Have the pupil read as widely as possible on her free or low instructional level. In doing so, she will learn new words from their context. (See appendix R for high-interest low-vocabulary books.)

B. Have the pupil start a card file of new words. Write the word and the definition on the front of the card. On the back, write the word in its proper context in a sentence (never write just the word and the dictionary definition alone).

C. Many basal readers have lists of new words introduced in the book. Sometimes these are at the end of each chapter. Determine the grade level appropriate to begin with (where the child knows approximately 95 percent of the words in these lists) and read stories from basal readers to her. Discuss the meanings of new words as you come to them. Following this, have the child read the stories. Give her help when it is needed.

D. Build on the pupil's background of experience as much as possible. Use films, filmstrips, records, tape recordings, or anything that will build her listening-speaking vocabulary. This will make it easier for the student to acquire new words through context clues.

E. Use picture word cards on which the unknown word appears under a picture illustrating that word. When making these, it is also helpful to use the word in a sentence as well as by itself. Have the pupils work in pairs or small groups to learn these new words from the word cards. Have the children work cooperatively to build a file of pictures representing scenes, action events, and so forth in stories. Before the children begin to read the new stories, discuss these picture files with them. Pictures may also be put in scrapbooks, and pages may be divided into sections (represented by letters) on numbered pages. You can then make a tape recording to go along with the scrapbook. The script for the tape recording might read as follows:

> On page three of the scrapbook in picture (A), you see a picture of a waterfall. In the story you are going to read today, a man goes over a waterfall in a boat. The boat probably looks like the one in picture (B). The men have been camping in the woods and probably look like the men in picture (C).

Put the children at listening stations and have them prepare for reading a story by listening to these tapes and looking at the scrapbooks.

F. Have the pupils pantomime certain words such as *write, hear,* and *walk.* Make sure the pupils see the word immediately before, during, and after the pantomime.

G. Teach the pupils one method they can follow consistently in attacking a new word. The following procedure may be used:

1. Look at the word.
2. See if any part of it looks like a word you already know.
3. How does it begin? How does it end?
4. Read the other words in the line and see what you think it should be.
5. Listen for the word in the rest of the lesson or when others speak.

GAMES AND EXERCISES

Sight Words in Context

Purpose: To provide practice on sight words and context clues

Materials: Pocket chart
Group-size word cards
Tape recorder

Procedure:

Place eight to ten words in the bottom pockets of the pocket chart. These should be new words on which you wish to provide practice. Play a tape recording of a short story that uses the words in the bottom rows of the pocket chart. Say the word and at the same time ring a bell or sound a buzzer. At the signal, the student picks the correct card from the eight to ten choices in the bottom rows and places it in the top row of the pocket chart. Be sure to pause briefly after the word to give the student a chance to look for it. You will need to allow for longer pauses at the beginning of the story when there are more words at the bottom of the pocket chart. The cards should be placed in order from left to right beginning with Row One. When the top row is full, the cards begin the left-to-right sequence in Row Two and so on until all cards have been transferred from the bottom to the top of the chart. After all the words are transferred from the bottom to the top of the chart, you can check the words with the student in the following manner: "In Row One, the first word is ____, the next word is ____," etc. This makes the exercise self-correctional when it is programmed on the tape along with the rest of the exercise.

Variation in Procedure:

Instead of saying the word as a bell or buzzer rings, ring the buzzer and let the student find the word from context.

Zingo

Purpose: To provide practice in the recognition of the basic sight words or other sight words

Materials: A number of word cards (7" × 7") with 25 squares, each of which has a different sight word on it
A list of each of the sight words
A number of kernels of corn, buttons, or beans

Procedure:

This game is played like bingo. Read a word from the word list and ask the children to hunt for that word on their word (Zingo) cards. When they find the word pronounced, they place a kernel of corn or some other marker on it. The first child to get five spaces filled in any direction is the winner. After a child has won, she should pronounce the words covered by the marker. This will insure that the children not only recognize words by sight but that they also can say them.

Construct your word list so that you can allow various individuals to win if you so desire: e.g., Zingo Card 3 may win by saying words 2, 8, 10, 12, and 15. Although this is a prearranged game, it will enable you to allow the pupils who need motivation to win.

Racetrack

Purpose: To provide practice in recognition of basic sight words or other sight words

Materials: A large sheet of drawing paper
Two duplicate sets of individual-size word cards (3" × 1½")
Two toy automobiles

Procedure:

Draw an oval track on the drawing paper to resemble a racetrack. Be sure to put in a start and finish line. Divide the track into sections in which there are printed drill words. Each of the two players has a toy automobile and is placed on the starting line of the track. Each player has a set of small word cards that are a duplicate of those of the opposing player and are the same as the words on the racetrack. Each player places his pile of cards faceup. One player then reads the word on her top card. If the word is the same as the one in the first space of the racetrack, she moves her auto to that space. If it is not the same, she may not move. Her card is placed on the bottom of the deck, and the other player takes a turn. The winner is the first player to go around the racetrack to the finish line. Be sure cards are shuffled well before each game.

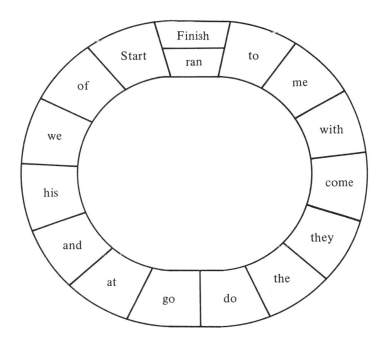

Treasure Hunt

Purpose: To provide practice on the basic sight words or other sight words

Materials: Sight word cards with a word on one side and a direction on the back such as Go to a word that starts with *c*, or Go to a word that starts with *w*.

Procedure:

A number of word cards are placed on the top of the children's desks with sight words showing. To begin the hunt, give two or three people different cards with the directions faceup. The children immediately start to hunt for words with the beginning letters as indicated. When they find a word that starts with one of the letters, they say it. They may then turn the card over and get directions for the next step in the treasure hunt. The last card should have a picture of a treasure chest on the back of it instead of directions to look further. You will need to arrange the card sets, so each child goes through the same number of steps.

Donkey

Purpose: To provide practice on basic sight words or other sight words

Materials: Make a deck of cards using one new word causing difficulty on each. You may use any number of players. In the deck you should include three to five cards with the word *donkey* written on them.

Procedure:

Deal all cards to the players facedown. The players then take turns turning up a card, pronouncing it, and placing it in a pool in the middle of the table. When the *donkey* card appears, the player drawing it says *"donkey"* and throws it in the center of the table. All the players try to grab the *donkey* card. The one who gets it may keep it and all cards that have been thrown into the pool. The winner of the game is the player who ends up with all of the cards or the most cards when all *donkey* cards have been drawn.

The Head Chair

Purpose: To provide practice on the recognition of the basic sight words or other sight words.

Materials: Group-size word cards (6″ × 3″)

Procedure:

Arrange students' chairs in a circle and mark one as the head chair. Begin play by flashing a card to the person in the head chair. If the child says the word correctly, she stays in her chair. If the student misses the word, she goes to the end chair; and all the children from this child to the end move over one chair. Continue around the circle from the head chair to the end chair. The object is to try to end up in the head chair.

Variation in Procedure:

If you are working with a relatively small group, have all of the chairs facing you. This will enable all of the children to see all of the words.

Cops and Robbers

Purpose: To provide practice on the recognition of basic sight words or other sight words.

Materials: Tagboard
Word cards

Procedure:

On a piece of tagboard construct an irregular course of dots and then connect the dots with lines. At points along the course place hideouts, dried up water-holes, deserts, etc. The game is played with two children—one a bank robber, one a police officer. The bank robber will place her marker on the course as far from the officer's marker as possible. The game begins with each player turning over a word card from a pack placed facedown on the table. The student reads the word on the card and then moves the number of dots denoted by a number appearing in one of the corners of the word card. The robber tries to avoid the officer. The game ends when the robber is captured. A more difficult game can be made by increasing the number of moves allowed according to the difficulty of the word given.

Team Sight Word Race

Purpose: To provide drill on basic sight words or other sight words

Materials: A group-size (6″ × 3″) set of basic sight word cards or sight words on which you want to provide practice

Procedure:

The children are divided into two teams. Each team member takes a turn attempting to pronounce a word turned up from a pile of sight words. If one team member misses, the opposite team then receives a chance to pronounce that word in addition to the team member's regular turn. Score is kept on the number of words each team pronounces correctly. Do not have the members sit down when they miss a word, but have each team member go to the back of the line after each try whether successful or not. This enables all members of each team to gain equal practice and does not eliminate those people who need practice most.

Variation in Procedure:

Instead of using single or isolated words, use phrase cards or sentence cards in which the word being emphasized is underlined. Allow the children to make the cards with a final check by you. You can use a number of smaller teams and have several races going at one time.

Stand Up

Purpose: To provide practice on the recognition of the basic sight words or other sight words

Materials: Group-size word cards (6″ × 3″)

Procedure:

The children are seated in a group around you. One child stands behind the chair of another child who is sitting with her chair facing you. You then flash a card. If the child who was standing pronounces the word before the child in the chair, then the child who was sitting must stand up behind someone else.

Word Hunt

Purpose: To provide practice on the basic sight words or other sight words

Materials: Blindfolds
             Group-size word cards (6″ × 3″)

Procedure:

Have several children cover their eyes. The rest of the group hide the cards where they can be found easily. When all the cards are hidden, the children who are "it" are given a signal to immediately take off their blindfolds and begin hunting for the cards. A child may pick up a card if she knows the word on it. No cards may be taken unless the word is known. The child who finds the most words is the winner.

Seven Up

Purpose: To provide practice on word recognition and word meaning

Materials: Group-size word cards (6" × 3"). Be sure there are seven times as many cards as children playing.

Procedure:

The children sit in a circle with flash cards in a pile facedown in the center of the group. Each child takes a turn by turning over a card and reading it. If the student reads it correctly, she keeps it. When a student has seven correct cards, she stands up. The game continues until all the children are standing. The children then sit down and see how fast they can make a sentence with some or all of their seven cards. Be sure both nouns and verbs are included in the stack. As soon as a child has made a sentence, she stands. This play continues until all the children who can make sentences of their words have done so.

Noun Label

Purpose: To teach nouns to non-English speaking children and to improve the vocabulary of those students who are deficient in their vocabulary development. It may, of course, be used in the early stages of reading in the regular developmental program.

Materials: Group-size word cards (6" × 3") with the names of common nouns written on them
8½" × 11" tagboard sheets with a picture of one of the common nouns on the top half of the sheet.

Procedure:

The pictures on the tagboard sheets are placed on the tray of the chalkboard. The children are then given words that correspond to the pictures. They come up to the chalkboard and place their words under the appropriate pictures. See the following example.

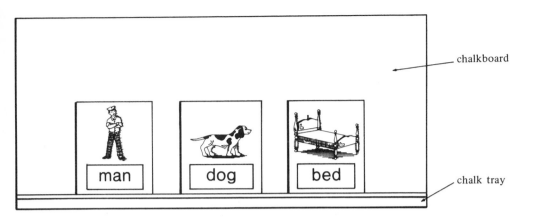

Erase Relay

Purpose: To provide practice in recognizing newly learned words

Materials: A list of words on which you wish to provide practice

Procedure:

Write on the chalkboard two columns of words that are approximately equal in difficulty. Write as many words on the board as there are children in the relay. The children then choose sides or are numbered 1, 2, 1, 2, and so on and stand in two lines at right angles to the chalkboard. At the signal, the first child in each line points at the first word in her respective column of words and pronounces that word. If the student pronounces it correctly, she is allowed to erase the word. The game is won by the side that erases all the words first.

Variation in Procedure:

Do the same exercise using such sounds as long vowels, short vowels, consonants, consonant blends, prefixes, suffixes, and word parts.

Words and Pictures

Purpose: To learn and review the common nouns

Materials: Envelopes
Make word cards that are divided as shown in the following example. On one side the word should appear, and on the other side there should be a picture representing that word. After the cards are completed, they should be cut into two pieces. Each should be cut with a different pattern along the cut edge; however, both sides should be approximately the same size. Put about 10 of these word cards and pictures (20 pieces) inside each envelope and pass them out to the children.

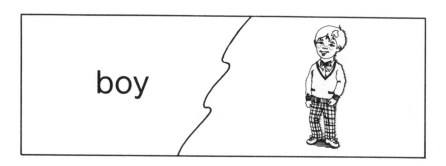

Procedure:

The children should be told to first line up the words in a column. After this is done, they will pronounce the first word and check to see if it is right by putting the picture representing that word beside it. The cut edges will, of course, match if the child knows the word. If the student does not know the word, she may continue to match the word and pictures until the edges do fit, thus, the game will be self-correcting. Pass the envelopes around, and let each child do each set.

What Is It?—What Does It Mean?

Purpose: To provide practice on the recognition and definitions of sight words encountered in daily reading lessons

Materials: Use lists of words that are new to the children in various reading groups. The words should be divided to indicate that Word Two came from the lesson being studied by Group Two, etc.

Procedure:

This game should be used after the children have had words introduced to them in their reading groups. Divide the children into teams, so children from different reading groups will be working together. If possible, use these same teams in school work other than reading. This way children are not singled out by their reading groups but are working together in group activities. At the time of the game, section off the two teams and start by writing a word on the board for the first child in team (A). If she is in Reading Group Three, the word would be from the story on which Group Three is working. In other words, each member on the team is given a word that is from her reading group's story. The child is to pronounce the word and then use it in a sentence. If the student just pronounces it, then she gets one point. If the student does not know how to pronounce it but can explain what it means or what it is, she gets three points. If the student can do both, she gets five points. If the student cannot do either, then she receives no points. A word is then put on the board for a child on team (B), and so forth. A score is kept on the board, so everyone can see it. The team with the most points at the end of a designated amount of time is the winner.

Golfing

Purpose: To provide practice on the basic sight words or other sight words

Materials: Nine packs of word cards. Each pack should have 10 sight words in it.
A player and a scorekeeper

Procedure:

The player takes the first pack, shuffles the cards, and places them facedown in front of her. She takes a card from the top of the pack, turns it faceup, and reads it. If she misses a word, the scorekeeper makes one mark on the scoring sheet. The number incorrect for the first pack is the player's score for the first hole. The student continues in this manner through the nine packs, trying to receive as small a score as possible.

What Word Am I?

Purpose: To provide practice with sight words

Materials: Two duplicate sets of cards with sight words printed on them

Procedure:

Divide the class into two groups. Each child has a word card pinned on her back. The duplicates of the cards are spread out on a table. The object of the game is to see which group can guess all their words first. The children take turns going to the table, picking up a word card, and asking, "Am I ____?" saying the word that is on the card. If the student chooses the card that matches the word on her back and pronounces it correctly, she keeps the card. If the student selects a card that doesn't match, she puts the card down on the table and takes her seat. The game continues until one group guesses all its words.

Jumping the Fence

Purpose: To provide practice on the basic sight words or other sight words

Materials: Flash cards with sight words on them
White tape

Procedure:

Place the flash cards in a row leading to the fence (white tape on the floor). A child who reads a word correctly jumps over the card and advances toward the fence. She may jump the fence when she reaches it. If she misses a word, she sits down and another child has a turn.

Baseball

Purpose: To provide practice with the basic sight words, other sight words, or phonic sounds

Materials: Flash cards with basic sight words, other sight words, or phonic sounds on them

Procedure:

The four corners of the classroom may serve as bases and home plate. Two teams of players participate. One child goes to home plate. The pitcher then holds up a flash card. The child pronounces the word, defines it if possible, and uses it in a sentence. If the student is correct, she advances to first base. This continues until the bases are loaded. Runs are scored as the children cross home plate. An out occurs when a child misses a word. There are three outs per team. The team with the highest score wins the game.

Variation in Procedure:

The flash cards may be vowel or consonant sounds, and the child must give a word that has the same beginning or ending sound on the card.

Flinch*

Purpose: This game is adaptable and may be varied to reinforce many reading skills, but it is especially valuable in developing vocabulary in the content areas. This game works well with two to four players and may be played with as many as six.

Materials: The deck is composed of 52 cards numbered from 0–12. In each deck there will be four cards numbered *0,* four numbered *1,* four numbered *2,* and so on. On another part of the card there will be a word. Use terms or words peculiar to the unit and any other words in the basal text that are new or difficult.

Procedure:

The dealer shuffles and deals out all of the cards one at a time. Each player stacks the cards facedown on the table in front of her. The first player to the left of the dealer draws the top card from her pile, and pronounces the word. If the player pronounces the word incorrectly, her opponents tell her the word, which is then placed on the bottom of the original stack to be redrawn at a later time. If the player pronounces the word correctly, she tries to find a place to play the card. Zero cards (treated as wild cards) play on any opponent's discard pile. Number (1) cards are played to start card piles in the middle of

---

*Invented by Mrs. Alice Hays of Imperial, Nebraska.

a table. Any other number card plays only if it is an adjacent number to one showing on an opponent's discard pile or to the top card of a pile in the center: e.g., a (7) card would play on either a (6) or (8) card. If a player pronounces the word correctly but cannot play the card either on an opponent's discard pile or on a center pile, she places it face up beside her original stack. This is her discard pile. A player continues to draw from her original pile, to pronounce the word, and to play the card. Her turn ends when she must play on her discard pile. Play rotates to the left. Should a player fail to see a play, any opponent may call it, and then each player, in turn, gives the person over-looking her play an extra card, which is placed on the bottom of her original stack. The game ends when one player disposes of all of the cards in her original stack.

The Witch

Purpose: To provide practice with sight words. This game works well with four players if 20 cards are used.

Materials: Use a deck containing about 20 cards with one additional card that has a witch on it. Print one word on half of the cards. Duplicate the first set of words on the other half of the cards.

Procedure:

One person deals out all the cards; players pick them up and look at them. Beginning with the person at the dealer's left, the players take turns drawing cards—each player draws from the person on her right. As pairs are formed, the words are pronounced, and the pair is placed on the table. Play continues until all cards are matched. The player left with the witch is the loser and receives a *w*. The next time she loses, she is a *wi,* and so on. The object is to try to avoid losing enough times to spell *witch*.

Word-Object Hunt

Purpose: To teach or reinforce words used as nouns

Materials: A number of flash cards with the names of various objects written on them

Procedure:

Each student is given about 12 cards that she spreads out before her. You then say, "I went to the grocery store to buy b____." Any student may raise her hand if she has an object that starts with *b* and would normally be bought at a grocery store. You then verify the answer, and all students get a chance to look at the word. The game may be varied by not giving the beginning letter and by using the names of objects bought in various stores.

Silly Sentences

Purpose: To teach or reinforce sight words

Materials: Plain cardboard flash cards or flash cards with flannel backing and a flannel board

Procedure:

Lay out sentences in mixed-up order either on a table or on a flannel board. Have students take turns coming up and unscrambling the sentences and reading them after they are placed in a sensible order. Make sure all students get a chance to read each logically ordered sentence.

Tape-Recorded Object Search

Purpose: To teach or reinforce sight words

Materials: Tape recorder
Cassettes
Envelopes
Sight word cards

Procedure:

Tape-record a message that says, "Lay all of your cards out in front of you in two rows. There are eight cards. Place four cards in the top row and four cards in the bottom row. Turn the tape recorder off until you have done this." (Allow a four-second pause.) "Listen carefully. We need a scale to weigh the package. Pick up the word *scale*." (Allow about five seconds per word.) "The word *scale* has a number four on the back of it. Check to see if you got it right." When playing this game, make sure each card is numbered 1–8, so they can easily be checked. Place a tape cassette and eight cards in each envelope. Number the envelopes and give students sheets with corresponding numbers on them, so they can check off each envelope after it has been completed.

Matching Nouns and Verbs

Purpose: To teach or reinforce sight words

Materials: Envelopes
Sight word cards

Procedure:

In each envelope place about ten nouns and ten verbs, such as the following examples:

birds fly
brooms sweep
people talk

Instruct students to match the noun with the proper verb. Number the correct pairs with matching numbers, so the students can check the pairs on their own. Number the envelopes and give students sheets with corresponding numbers, so they can check off each envelope after it has been completed.

Matching Noun Pictures with Words

Purpose: To teach various noun sight words

Materials: Pictures cut from catalogs and other sources
Small cards
Envelopes

Procedure:

Place about 15 or 20 pictures in each envelope and the name of the object in the picture on a small card. On the back of the card and matching picture write a number so that each match. Also number each envelope. Pass out envelopes to students and instruct them to match the pictures with their written names. When they are done, they can look at the numbers on the back of each card and pictures to make sure they have matched them correctly. Give students a sheet of paper with as many numbers on it as you have envelopes. When they complete each envelope, they should check it off their numbered sheet. This will ensure that each student does each envelope.

12

Contractions Not Known

RECOGNIZED BY

Pupil is unable to pronounce contractions when he encounters them in print. For writing purposes, it is also important to be able to tell what two words each contraction stands for and to be able to make contractions from various words. A test for students' knowledge of contractions may be found in appendix E.

DISCUSSION

It will sometimes become apparent that a major part of what sounds like poor oral reading is really a student's lack of knowledge of contraction.

When testing for student's knowledge of contractions, the teacher should show the student the contraction and ask him to pronounce it. If he can pronounce the word, it will usually suffice for reading purposes. (For example, for reading purposes the student must pronounce *can't,* but she does not necessarily need to know it means *cannot.*) You may wish to have the student tell what two words the contraction stands for, so you know if he will be able to use it in his written work. Following is a list of contractions and the point at which students should know them, according to the scope and sequence shown in appendix J.

RECOMMENDATIONS

A. For any contraction not known, write the two words it stands for and then the contraction on the chalkboard. Have students make up sentences using both the contracted and noncontracted form. See the example.

let us   let's

1. Let us go with Mother and Father.
2. Let's go with Mother and Father.

Grade Level	*Words*		
1.9	aren't	can't	don't
	weren't	couldn't	didn't
	wasn't	hadn't	won't
	haven't	isn't	wouldn't
2.5	anybody'd	he'll	it's
	here's	I'll	let's
	she'll	that's	where's
	they'll	I'm	who'll
	there's	we'll	there'll
	what's	you'll	
2.9	doesn't	hasn't	you'd
	he'd	you're	he's
	I'd	we've	I've
	they've	she'd	who'd
	she's	they'd	we'd
	they're	we're	you've

NOTE: 2.9 means the word should be known at the ninth month of the second grade, 3.5 means it should be known by the fifth month of the third grade, and so on. This information is based on an analysis of when these contractions were commonly taught in six sets of well-known basal readers.

B. Give students a matching exercise by placing a few contractions on slips of paper in an envelope. Number each contraction. In the same envelope place slips that name the two words each contraction stands for and write the matching number of the contraction on the back. Students should then try to match the contractions with the correct words by placing them side by side as illustrated in the example.

1. let's	let us
2. don't	do not

After the student has completed the exercise, he can turn the cards in the right-hand column over to see if the numbers on the back match the numbers on the slips in the left-hand column.

C. Give students paragraphs to read in which several words could be contracted. Underline these words. Instruct students to change words to a contraction as they read. See the example following.

Frank said to Jim, "We have only two days before you are going to leave." "Yes," said Jim, "I am waiting to go, and I have already packed my suitcase."

After doing this type of exercise, discuss why contractions are used and which form, long or short, sounds more natural in common speech.

D. Conduct contraction races between two students. Tell the students two words and see who can call out the contraction first. Also give contractions and have students call out the words that are contracted.

E. Give students newspaper articles and have them underline all contractions and words that could have been contracted.

F. As children talk, call attention to the contractions they use by writing them down. Discuss why they used the contracted form.

13

Consonant Sounds Not Known

RECOGNIZED BY

Pupil is unable to give the correct sounds and variant sounds of the consonants. (See appendix G.)

DISCUSSION

Before beginning a program of help in phonics, you will find it helpful to administer a phonics test such as the *El Paso Phonics Survey* found in appendix G. If a student is deficient in nearly all areas, e.g., initial consonants, consonant clusters, etc., you may wish to start from the beginning with the teaching of phonics. In this case you will find that, for most students, work with the phonogram list as described in appendix L will enable the student to quickly learn a great many initial consonants, consonant blends, and consonant digraphs in a relatively short time.

RECOMMENDATIONS

A. If the student does not know a great many of the initial consonants, consonant clusters, vowels, vowel teams, and special letter combinations, use the phonogram list as described in appendix L.

B. Construct flash cards on which the consonant is shown along with a picture illustrating a word that uses that consonant, e.g., *b* in *b*all, and *c* in *c*at. On the opposite side of the flash card print the letter only. This can be used as the pupil progresses in ability. See example following.

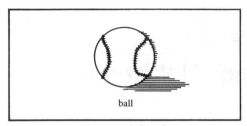

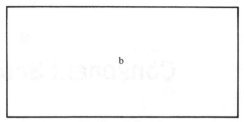

Front of Card   Back of Card

C. Put the consonant letters on cards (3″ × 3″). Divide these cards into groups of 10 each. Lay out separate groups of letters, so the pupil can see all 10 at once. As you call the sounds of letters, or as they are played from a tape recording, have the pupil pick up the correct card to match the sound of the letter. As there are fewer words to observe— that is, after some have already been picked up—you will need to speed up the rate at which you pronounce the remaining words. The following timing seems to work well: pronounce the first word, wait 7 seconds; pronounce the second word and wait 7 seconds again; then 6, 6, 5, 5, 4, 4, and 3 seconds. Many students are unable to manipulate the cards in less time than this.

D. Tape-record words and have the children write the letter that stands for the beginning, ending, or both beginning and ending sounds of these words. See the following example:

Directions: As you hear a word called on the tape, write the letter that begins the word. (Tape script says, "Number one is *come,* number two is *dog,*" and so on.)

1. c
2. d
3.
4.
5.

E. Use the same system as in item (D). Instead of having the pupils write letters they hear, have them pick up the card that matches the beginning or ending letter they hear in the words.

F. Put various consonant letters on the board and have the children make lists of the words that begin with these letters.

G. Record the consonant letters with their sounds and let the students hear these as many times as it is necessary to learn them. They should, however, have a chart they can follow to see the letters as they hear the sound.

H. Use commercial charts that are available for teaching consonants. Records that give the proper pronunciation of the consonant sounds are also available. (See appendix R.)

I. Use commercially prepared games designed to teach consonants and consonant usage. (See appendix R.)

GAMES AND EXERCISES

Phonic Rummy

Purpose: To provide practice in various phonic elements. This game works well with two to four players when using 36 cards, or up to six players when using 48 or 52 cards.

Materials: A deck of cards with phonic elements that you wish to teach. On each card will appear one phonic element and four words that use that particular phonic element. One of the four words will be underlined. The deck may consist of 36, 40, 44, 48, or 52 cards. For each phonic element there will be four cards, each of which has a different word underlined. A deck of 36 cards would involve 9 phonic elements; 40 cards would involve 10 phonic elements. See the following example of the cards:

i	*ay*	*gr*
did	stay	green
pit	<u>may</u>	<u>grass</u>
if	play	grow
<u>fish</u>	clay	grab

Procedure:

The dealer shuffles the cards and deals eight cards facedown to each player. The rest of the cards are placed facedown in the center of the table. The first player to the left of the dealer calls for a word using a certain phonic element on which he wishes to build. (See the examples.) For example, the student might say, "I want Sam to give me *fish* from the *i* group" and would pronounce the short /i/ sound. If Sam had that card, he would give it to the caller. The player (caller) then continues to call for certain cards from specific people. If the person called upon does not have the card, the player takes a card from the center pile; and the next player to the left takes his turn. When a player completes a "book" (i.e., he has all four cards from a certain phonic element), he lays it down. Players can only lay down "books" when it is their turn to draw. The object is to get the most books before someone empties her hand.

Think

Purpose: To provide practice with initial vowels, consonants, and initial consonant blends. This game works well with four players.

Materials: Enough small cards so that each letter of the alphabet and each initial blend can be printed on a separate card. There may be more than one card for each vowel.

Procedure:

Place the cards facedown on the table. The players take turns selecting a card and naming a word that begins with the same letter or blend. If someone cannot name a word within five seconds, she puts the card back. The winner is the person who has the greatest number of cards after the entire pile has been drawn.

Checkers

Purpose: To provide practice on various vowel or consonant sounds, and to improve auditory discrimination.

Materials: Cards with phonic elements such as consonant sounds, vowel digraphs, and diphthongs on them
Large squares of paper in two contrasting colors

Procedure:

Draw a checkerboard on the floor or place sheets of construction paper on the floor in a checkerboard pattern. Divide the children into two groups and place each group back to back on the two middle rows. Each group must not have more children in it than there are squares across one row of the checkerboard. Each child stands on a square and holds one card with a sound on it. You call the words (these may be prerecorded on the tape recorder) that have the sounds that correspond with the sounds on the cards the children hold. When a child hears a word that has her sound in it, she may move one square toward the outer part of the checkerboard. The object of the game is for one side to reach the king row first. If a child misses a sound, or moves when she should not, then her side has to move a player back one space. There may be times when several children will move at once depending, of course, on the words chosen by you.

Variation in Procedure:

Play the same game, but ask comprehension questions over a reading assignment that all the children have read.

Word Trail

Purpose: To provide practice on consonants, consonant blends, vowels, digraphs and diphthongs

Materials: A piece of tagboard
A list of phonic elements to be taught
A die

Procedure:

Draw a margin (approximately two inches) around the sheet of tagboard. Divide the margin into spaces large enough for inserting the phonic elements for practice. On the corners and in several spaces between corners insert penalties and rewards such as, Take another turn or Move back three spaces. The players then take turns shaking the die and moving their players (perhaps pieces of corn) along the spaces, saying each phonic element as they move. If they cannot say a certain phonic element, they must stop on the space behind it and wait for another turn. The first player around the "word trail" is the winner.

Any Card

Purpose: To provide practice with consonants, consonant digraphs, consonant blends, and rhyming sounds. This game can be played with two to four players.

Materials: A deck of 36 to 52 cards with words such as the following:

pan	fun	sock	mill	call	harm
man	bun	knock	still	fall	charm
can	run	shock	kill	ball	farm

Also include four cards with *any card* written on them.

Procedure:

A player deals out five cards. The player to the left of the dealer plays any one of his cards and names it. The next player plays a card that either rhymes or begins with the same letter as the first card. For example, if *sun* has been played, *bun* (rhyming with *sun*) or *sock* (with the same first letter) could be played. If a child cannot play, she draws from the pile in the center until she can play or has drawn three times. If the student has the card with *any card* written on it, she may play this card and name any appropriate word. The first player who runs out of cards wins the game.

I'm Thinking of a Word

Purpose: To provide practice in auditory discrimination and the recognition of beginning, ending, or both beginning and ending sounds

Materials: Pocket chart
Cards with words that begin with various consonants
Cards with words that end with various consonants

Procedure:

Fill the pocket chart with about 10 cards, each of which has a different beginning sound. The first student says, "I'm thinking of a word that begins like
/d/." (The student gives the *d* sound.) The student draws a card, trying to get
the word beginning with that sound. She gets to keep the card as long as she
matches a sound and word. She may thus take all of the cards from the pocket
chart. If the student gives a sound and draws a word that does not begin with
that sound, play then passes to the next student. If the student gets all of the
cards, another student then follows the same procedure. The same procedure
can be used with ending sounds.

Variation in Procedure:

There are many possible variations of this game. You may have children come
to the front and say, "I'm thinking . . . ," and call on someone to guess the word.
Another game might have a child put letters in the pocket chart and say, "My
word is *dog*." The other children then have to find a *d* or *g* depending on whether
you are working with beginning or ending sounds. The children also may play
the same game and be required to find both the beginning and ending sounds.

Catch the Stick

Purpose: To improve auditory discrimination and to improve the children's
ability to make the connection between sounds and letters

Materials: A number of group-size cards (6″ × 3″) with the beginning consonant sounds on them
A yardstick

Procedure:

Seat the children in as small a circle as possible for the number of children
you wish to have play the game. Ten to twelve children are optimum. The
children are all given a different beginning consonant sound on a group-size
card. One child stands in the center of the circle and holds a yardstick in an
upright position with one end on the floor and the top end held in place by the
tip of her finger. The child in the center then pronounces a word that begins
with a consonant. At the same time the student pronounces the word, she takes
the tip of her finger off the top of the yardstick. The child who has the beginning
letter of the word named by the child in the center of the circle must catch
the yardstick before it falls on the floor. If the child who had the consonant
letter catches the stick, she returns to her seat and the person in the center
must say another word. However, if she does not catch the stick, then she must
change places with the child in the center and give her card to the child she
is replacing.

Blending Wheel

Purpose: To provide practice on blending beginning consonants, consonant blends, and/or beginning consonant digraphs

Materials: Two cardboard circles, one of which is approximately two inches smaller in diameter (convenient sizes are 8″ and 10″)

Procedure:

Fasten the two circles together with a paper fastener as shown in the following illustration. The outside circle should have word roots or major parts of a word on it, and the inside circle should have a specific consonant, consonant blend, or consonant digraph on which you wish to provide practice. Have the child rotate one of the circles and practice blending the root or word part with the consonant, consonant blend, or consonant digraph.

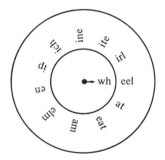

Word Puzzles

Purpose: To provide practice in recognizing blend sounds and to provide practice in blending

Materials: Envelopes
            Word cards

Procedure:

Cut a few word cards of equal size. Print a word containing a blend that has been taught, e.g., *gl*ad, *st*and, on each card. Cut each word in two between the blend and the remainder of the word. Place about eight to ten of these in each envelope and pass out the envelopes to the children. The children then assemble the blends and word parts to make words. After being checked by you, the envelopes are exchanged so that each child eventually assembles the words in each envelope.

Phonics Posters

Purpose: To develop an awareness of related sounds

Materials: Tagboard
            Old magazines or old textbooks

Procedure:

At the top of a piece of tagboard place a letter or combination of letters. Have the children find pictures of objects in magazines or old readers that start with the sound or sounds displayed in the heading. These object pictures should be cut out and mounted on the tagboard to provide practice for the individuals who need special help.

Poet Play

Purpose: To help children develop an awareness of sound similarities through the use of rhyming words

Materials: Pocket chart
            Word cards
            Envelopes

Procedure:

Give the children envelopes containing a number of word cards. Place a master word in the pocket chart and have the children locate in their envelopes a word that rhymes with the one posted. Number the envelopes and allow the children to exchange them after each round, so they will become familiar with a great many words and their sound similarities.

Stand-Up

Purpose: To provide practice in discriminating between like and unlike sounds

Procedure:

When there is extra time before lunch or dismissal, you might use this game. It is both interesting and beneficial. You call, "All those whose names start like *meat* may stand up and get their coats." Repeat as many times as needed to dismiss the children. As a variation, use letters that are in the middle or end of children's names. The children also might use this same method to choose groups or sides in other games.

Rhyme Time

Purpose: To discover which children are having auditory discrimination problems and to provide practice through the use of related phonic sounds

Materials: Tagboard
               Word cards

Procedure:

Write sentences on the tagboard. On small word cards print a variety of words that will rhyme with selected words given in the sentences. Have the children locate and match their cards with the rhyming words in the sentences. Place each set of cards in an envelope and number the envelopes, so the children can keep a record of the sets on which they have worked. See the example following:

1.   The <u>dog</u> bit the mailperson. (log, hog, etc.)

2.   The candy tasted <u>sweet</u>. (treat, beat)

3.   <u>Look</u> out the window. (took, book)

4.   The wall had a large <u>crack</u>. (back, sack)

5.   He cut down the apple <u>tree</u>. (see, flee)

Making and Exchanging Picture Dictionaries

Purpose: To learn initial consonant sounds

Materials: Old notebooks or paper to be bound together
               Crayons and/or paints
               Magazines and other materials containing pictures

Procedure:

Have students cut out or draw pictures representing various initial consonant sounds. Under the picture write the letter or letters of the initial sounds and the word that stands for the picture. Also under each picture use the word in a sentence. After the students have finished their books, have them exchange dictionaries, so each student learns to read every other student's dictionary.

Hard and Soft *C* and *G*

Purpose: To teach the rules for hard and soft *c* and *g*

Materials: Rule chart with pockets and flash cards with various *c* or *g* words
               on them

Procedure:

Construct a large chart about 8½″ × 11″ like the chart that follows. The bottom half should contain two large pockets marked as shown. The top half should contain the rule for soft and hard *c* and *g*. Students are then given a number of flash cards with soft and hard *g* words on them. They put each card into the appropriate pocket according to the rule stated on the chart. Students may check their own work if the words *hard* or *soft* are written on the back of each flash card. (Do the same for *c*.)

G followed by *e, i,* or *y* usually has a soft sound.

If *g* is followed by any other letter, it usually has a hard sound.

Hard *g*	Soft *g*
(game)	(gentle)

14

Vowel Sounds Not Known

RECOGNIZED BY

Pupil is unable to give the correct sounds and variant sounds of the vowels, as well as vowel teams and special letter combinations, such as *al, ur,* etc. To check the vowel sounds, use the *El Paso Phonics Survey* found in appendix G. A test for checking students' knowledge of vowel rules and syllabication principles is found in appendix H. (Keep in mind that you cannot accurately assess students' knowledge of vowel rules until they have mastered the vowel sounds.)

DISCUSSION

In the past there have been many rules that supposedly should be learned by students who are learning phonics as an aid to word-attack skills. However, research studies over the past 20 years have shown that some of the rules formerly taught have little utility in reading programs. Rules that appear to be worthwhile teaching are as follows:

1. If there is only one vowel letter and it appears at the end of a word, the letter usually has a long sound. Note that this is only true for one-syllable words.
2. A single vowel in a syllable usually has a short sound if it is not the last letter in a syllable or is not followed by *r.*
3. A vowel followed by *r* usually has a sound that is neither long nor short.
4. When *y* is preceded by a consonant in a one-syllable word, the *y* usually has the sound of long *i*; but in words of two or more syllables the final *y* usually has the sound of long *e.* Some people hear it as short *i.*
5. In words ending in vowel-consonant *e,* the *e* is silent, and the vowel may be either long or short. Try the long sound first.

6. When *ai, ay, ea, ee,* and *oa* are found together, the first vowel is usually long and the second is silent.

7. The vowel pair *ow* may have either the long *o* sound as in low or the *ou* sound as in owl.

8. When *au, aw, ou, oi,* and *oy* are found together, they usually blend or form a diphthong.

9. The *oo* sound is either long as in moon or short as in book.

10. If *a* is the only vowel in a syllable and it is followed by *l* or *w,* then the *a* will usually be neither long nor short, but will have the *awe* sound heard in ball and awl.

These rules certainly do not cover all the rules or exceptions; however, learning too many rules often proves almost as fruitless as knowing none. Furthermore, a student who has passed the primary grades (first, second, and third) will often find it difficult to learn by the use of rules. You should not attempt to give a great deal of remediation until you are fairly sure what areas of phonics are causing difficulty for the pupil. The *El Paso Phonics Survey* will help to determine where the student is weak. This test will not only help determine whether the student knows the sounds and rules, but will also show whether he is able to apply them in the analysis of a word.

RECOMMENDATIONS

A. It is helpful to teach the long and short vowel sounds in words which have the vowel-consonant-final *e* configuration for long vowel sounds and words which have the CVC configuration for the short vowel sounds. Remember, however, that as the student progresses into multisyllable words, the vowel-consonant-final *e* rule does not apply to as high a percentage of words. Later, students should probably be taught that when they encounter the vowel-consonant-final *e,* they should try the long vowel first and then the short sound for the first vowel.

The procedure for teaching the long and short vowel sounds, as well as words for that purpose, is given in appendix L. However it will be briefly reviewed here:

1. If you wish to teach the long and short vowel sounds for *a,* choose the following words:

    mat   hat   rat   fat

    Discuss the sound represented by short *a.* Then present the words listed above. If the student cannot pronounce them, help him to do so. Then present the following words:

    mate   hate   rate   fate

Then discuss the fact that when the *e* is added, the first vowel takes on its long sound and when it is removed it takes on its short sound. Review the long sound as you did the short vowel sound. Then present other words such as those shown below from appendix L. Cover up the final e in each word and ask the student to pronounce the word. Then remove the final "e" and ask the student to give the word without the final "e."

pale   gale

Use the words in appendix L to teach each of the long and short vowel sounds in the same manner. The advantage of this method of teaching the vowel sounds is that students learn these two fundamental rules at the same time.

B. Construct flash cards in which the vowel is shown along with both the word and a picture illustrating a word that uses that vowel, e.g., short *a* in h*a*t, long *a* in r*a*ke. On the opposite side print only the vowel letter marked long or short to be used as the pupil progresses in ability. When using this method with an entire class, you can substitute 2″ × 2″ slides or transparencies for the overhead projector for flash cards. An example follows:

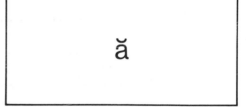

Front of Card   Back of Card

C. Have the children circle or underline the words that have vowels with the same sound as the first word in the line. See the following examples.

1. Long—lone, dog, of, to
2. Rat—car, bear, happy, same
3. Line—with, win, wild, is
4. Treat—tread, same, easy, well

D. Record the vowel letters with their sounds and variant sounds and play them to the students as many times as it is necessary to learn them. They should, however, have a chart they can follow to see the letter as they hear the sound.

E. Put the vowel letters on cards (3″ × 3″). Use the breve (˘) or the macron (−) to indicate the short and long sounds. Divide these cards into groups of 10 each. Lay out separate groups of letters, so the pupil can see 10 at once. As you call the sounds of the vowel letters, or as they are played from a tape recording, have the pupil pick up the correct card to match the sound of the letter. (See directions under item (B) for "Consonant Sounds Not Known," chapter 13.)

F. Use the same system as in item (E). Instead of having the children match letters they hear, have them write the letter matching the letter sound (phoneme) they hear in words.

G. Use commercial charts that are available for teaching vowels. Records to accompany the sounds are also available. (See appendix R.)

H. Use commercially prepared games designed for teaching the vowels and vowel usage. (See appendix R.)

GAMES AND EXERCISES

Game Board for Sorting Vowel Sounds

Purpose: To learn to hear various vowel sounds

Materials: Pictures or words with various vowel sounds in them
Construct a board as follows:

	A	E	I	O	U
Long					
Short					
R = Controlled					

Procedure:

Have students sort pictures or words into the correct intersecting squares (pictures must be used with beginning readers) according to the sound in the name of the object in the picture. For example, *hen* would go under the square under the *e* column and the row across from *short*. The pictures from some commercially sold games such as *Vowel Lotto* work well with this game board.

Vowel Tic-tac-toe

Purpose: To learn vowel sounds

Materials: Flash cards with the following written on them:

Short *a*	Long *a*	R-controlled *a*
Short *e*	Long *e*	R-controlled *e*
Short *i*	Long *i*	R-controlled *i*
Short *o*	Long *o*	R-controlled *o*
Short *u*	Long *u*	R-controlled *u*

Procedure:

Have the two students who are playing tic-tac-toe draw a vowel card. Then, instead of marking each square with *X* or *O*, the student writes words that have the sound on his card. If, for example, one student gets short *o* and the other gets long *a*, then each person must write a word with that sound when it is his turn to play instead of making the traditional *X* or *O*. An example of a partially finished game is shown:

```
          |     |
   cake    |     |
          |     |
 _____|_____|_____
          | hot |
          |     |
 _____|_____|_____
          |     |
   make    | pot |
          |     |
```

Variation in Procedure:

This is also a good learning device if the two participants have to draw a new card before each move. When playing the game this way, use two different colors of chalk or pencil to help remember which words belong to each player.

Sorting Pictures According to Matching Vowel Sounds

Purpose: To teach short and long vowel sounds

Materials: Construct a large chart using all 10 of the short and long vowel sounds on pictures placed on pockets as shown. On the top half of the chart, glue a large envelope in place. Find many pictures representing various short and long vowel sounds and place them in the large envelope.

Procedure:

Construct the chart similar to the example.

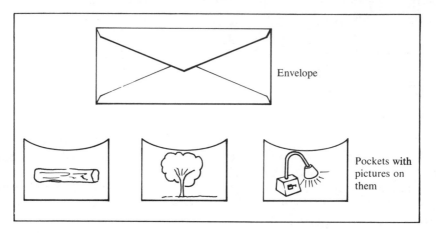

NOTE: This illustration shows only three pictures, a log, tree, and light. There should, of course, be 10 pictures, each representing a short or long vowel sound.

Have students take pictures from the large envelope and say the word related to the picture. Remind them to listen for the vowel sound they hear in that word. Then have them find the corresponding vowel sound from the picture on the pockets below and place the picture from the large envelope in the proper pocket. This activity can be made self-checking by numbering the backs of the pictures from the large envelope to correspond with the small pocket it should go in; i.e., after students have placed all of the pictures from the large envelope in the small pockets, they can merely turn the pictures over to see if they match the numbers on the small pockets.

Sorting Vowel Sounds

Purpose: To learn to hear various vowel sounds

Materials: Ten shoe boxes for each group
             About 100 word cards, each using the sound of only one vowel

Procedure:

You or a team captain draws a card. Students read it and listen for a specific vowel sound. They then analyze the word and place it into the correctly marked short or long *a, e, i, o,* or *u* shoe box.

Vowel Relay

Purpose: To give practice in blending and learning sight words

Purpose: To give practice in blending and learning sight words

Materials: Flash cards with various sounds (graphemes) such as the following:

Long *a*	Short *a*	R-controlled *a*	L-controlled *a*
Long *e*	Short *e*	R-controlled *e*	W-controlled *a*
Long *i*	Short *i*	R-controlled *i*	W-controlled *o*
Long *o*	Short *o*	R-controlled *o*	W-controlled *e*
Long *u*	Short *u*	R-controlled *u*	

Procedure:

Divide the students into two groups and the chalkboard into two parts. Each group lines up in front of its half of the chalkboard. The pile of cards is divided in half and placed in the chalk tray below each of the two divisions of the chalkboard. When you say "Go," the two front players each move up and turn over a card. Each player must write a word using his designated vowel sound in a period of ten seconds. However, a new player cannot move up until you again say "Go" in ten seconds. If the student cannot think of a word, he draws a line. The next player moves up and turns over another card when you say "Go." The team that has all of its cards turned over with the most correct words is the winner.

NOTE: Much of the material listed under "Games and Exercises" in chapter 13 can be adapted for teaching the vowel sounds.

15

Blends, Digraphs, or Diphthongs
Not Known

RECOGNIZED BY

Pupil is unable to give the correct sounds of the blends, digraphs, or diphthongs.

DISCUSSION

As with the consonant and vowel sounds, it is essential that the pupil know the blends, digraphs, and diphthong sounds in order to analyze certain words. The *El Paso Phonics Survey* in appendix G will help you determine which areas are causing the most difficulty for the pupil. It also will help you to determine if the pupil possesses a knowledge of the blends, digraphs, or diphthong sounds but does not use her knowledge. The test should be administered before beginning a program of help in this area.

RECOMMENDATIONS

A. As with the initial consonant sounds, if a student does not know a number of consonant blends, use the phonogram list as explained in appendix L. You are likely to find that the student learns most of these in a relatively short time. You can then retest the student and teach those that are still not known.

B. For teaching vowel digraphs and diphthongs, use the phonogram list to find words with the digraphs or diphthongs not known. Use the tape recorder to provide drill on those combinations, as explained in appendix L. For example, give students who do not know the *ai* sounds words such as *aid, braid, laid, maid,* and *paid,* and *ail, hail, nail, pail, quail,* etc.

C. Construct flash cards in which the blend, digraph, or diphthong is shown along with a picture that illustrates a word using that letter combination. See appendix K for suggested words. On the opposite side of the card, print only the blend, digraph, or diphthong to be used as the pupil progresses in ability. When using this method with an entire class, you can substitute 2″ × 2″ slides or transparencies for the overhead projector for the flash cards. [See illustration of card under item (A), "Vowel Sounds Not Known," chapter 14.]

D. Record the letter combinations with their sounds and let the students hear these as many times as it is necessary to learn them. They should, however, have a chart they can follow to see the letter combinations as they hear the sounds. Ask each pupil to point to the letters as she hears them on the tape.

E. Put diphthongs, digraphs, and blends on cards (3″ × 3″). Divide these cards into groups of 10 each. Lay out separate groups of diphthongs, digraphs, and blends and allow the pupil to see all 10 at once. As you call the sounds of these various letter combinations or as they are played from a tape recording, have the pupil pick up the correct card to match the sound of the letter combinations. [See directions under item (B), "Consonant Sounds Not Known," chapter 13.]

F. Use the same system mentioned in item (E), only tape-record words and have the pupil pick up the letter combinations she hears in these words.

G. Use commercial charts that are available for teaching various letter combinations. Recordings to accompany these sounds are also available. (See appendix R.)

H. Use commercially prepared games that the children can play individually or in groups. (See appendix R.)

Games and Exercises

See "Games and Exercises," chapter 13, and "Games and Exercises," chapter 14. Much of the material listed in these two sections can be adapted to the teaching of blends, digraphs, and diphthongs.

16

Lacks Desirable Structural Analysis (Morphology)

RECOGNIZED BY

Pupil is unable to gain clues to the pronunciation of a word or its meaning by finding familiar elements of that word within the word. (See definition of structural analysis in the definition of terms.)

DISCUSSION

Structural analysis begins when the child is able to recognize the root word in words with *s, ed,* or similar endings, e.g., *run* in *runs* and *look* in *looked.* From this beginning the student should learn to recognize the parts that make up compound words, such as *tooth* and *ache* in *toothache,* and *green* and *house* in *greenhouse.* She should also begin to recognize common roots, suffixes, and prefixes. Most authorities in the field of reading believe it is not good, however, to look for little words within bigger words since the smaller words may not have their usual pronunciation. The child should learn the principles of syllabication; they will enable her to divide words into pronounceable units. A syllabication test is found in appendix H, and a test for contractions is found in appendix E.

One of the best ways to determine if a student is having difficulty with structural analysis is to ask her to read orally. While the student reads orally, you can note the types of errors she makes and can also ask questions to ascertain if she knows certain root words, ending sounds, beginning sounds, word families, parts of compound words, contractions, and affixes. Teachers who are familiar with the components of structural analysis will usually find a definite pattern of mistakes within a certain area or overlapping into several areas.

RECOMMENDATIONS

A. Use the phonogram list as described in appendix L.

B. Make lists of the common word endings and have the children underline these endings and pronounce their sounds.

C. Use multiple-choice questions that require the pupil to put the proper endings on words. See examples following.

1. The boy was (looked, looks, looking) in the window.
2. That is (John, John's, Johns) ball and bat.
3. The boys came (early, earlier, earliest) than the girls.

D. Make lists or flash cards of the common roots, prefixes, and suffixes. Use these in forming new words. You may have a drill on these sounds, but do not require memorization of the meanings of affixes. (See appendix N for list of suffixes and prefixes.)

E. Make lists or flash cards of common letter combinations such as *tion* and *ult*. A drill on these may be helpful; however, try to avoid listing letter combinations that have sounds that may vary according to the word in which they are used. Lists may be made on transparencies for the overhead projector or on large pieces of cardboard.

F. Make lists of and discuss compound words as the pupil encounters them in her reading lessons.

G. Make lists of all the words that can be made from certain roots. For example:

1. work—works, working, worked
2. carry—carrying, carrier, carried, carries
3. faith—faithful, faithless
4. lodge—lodger, lodging, lodged, lodgment

H. Write a number of words on the board with prefixes that mean the same thing, e.g., *imperfect, united, irreplaceable*. Have the pupils add to the list. Underline roots or prefixes and discuss them.

I. Make a list of words to which the pupil adds prefixes or suffixes to give a certain meaning to the word. Following is an example.

Directions: Add a suffix to make these words mean *one who does* or *that which does:*

work	extract
elevate	pretend
play	repel
contract	admires

J. Construct drills in which the pupil may learn words by filling in blanks according to the proper context. Two examples follow.

1. Hydroelectric refers to the production of electricity by the use of ____. (water)
2. Something that existed before is ____. (preexistent)

K. Teach the pupil the syllabication principles and work through a number of words to enable her to become proficient at dividing words into syllables. The main syllabication principles follow.

1. When two consonants stand between two vowels, the word is usually divided between the consonants, e.g., *dag-ger* and *cir-cus.*
2. When one consonant stands between two vowels, the consonant is more likely to go with the second syllable unless the vowel on the right is a final *e,* in which case there is no syllable division; e.g., *mo-tor, pa-per,* and *re-ceive.*
3. When a word ends in a consonant and *le,* the consonant usually begins the last syllable, e.g., *ca-ble.*
4. Compound words are usually divided between the word parts and between syllables within these parts, e.g., *tooth-ache, mas-ter-mind.*
5. In most cases, do not divide the letters in consonant digraphs or consonant blends. (See appendix K for lists of consonant digraphs and consonant blends.)
6. Prefixes and suffixes are usually separate syllables. Examples: *dis-own, north-ward.* Use appendix N as a study aid to help pupils recognize prefixes and suffixes.

GAMES AND EXERCISES

Prefix and Suffix Baseball

Purpose: To provide practice in recognizing prefixes, suffixes and their meanings

Materials: Make cards with a prefix such as *un* ____ or a suffix such as ____ *ly* on them. Be sure to include the line to indicate whether it is a prefix or a suffix.

Procedure:

This game is not to be used until considerable work has been done with prefixes and suffixes. English-speaking children have less trouble with the game since they already have a large vocabulary and only need to realize that these words contain prefixes and suffixes.

Each of the two teams chooses a pitcher who will "pitch" a word to the "batter." The batter will think of a word to go with the prefix or suffix and then pronounce it. If the student does this much but cannot use it in a sentence, she has made a "single." If the student can think of a word, pronounce it, and use it in a sentence, she hits a "double." After the children become more adept at the game, you may wish to confine the hits to singles to slow down the game.

Caution! Remember only a few suffix and prefix meanings are consistent enough to warrant memorizing their meanings.

Dig Up the Root

Purpose: To develop recognition of word roots and attached affixes

Materials: Pocket chart
             Word cards

Procedure:

Divide the pocket chart into two columns. On the left-hand side, list a number of root words. In an adjacent column, randomly list words composed of the root words plus an affix. Have the children match the root word in the first column with the root and its affix in the second column.

1. finish   undecided
2. reach   finishing
3. determine   replace
4. decided   nationality
5. place   reached
6. nation   predetermine

Prefix and Suffix Chart

Purpose: To teach the meanings and uses of suffixes and prefixes

Materials: Chart similar to the following example

Procedure:

Construct a chart like the following and have the students fill in the blank spaces. Place an X in the spaces that are not applicable.

Prefix	Prefix Meaning	Root	Whole Word	Suffix	Suffix Meaning
un	—	do	undo	x	x
x	x	soft	softly	—	in a way
x	x	play	playful	ful	—
—	from	port	—	x	x
pre	—	—	—	x	x
x	x	care	—	—	without
re	—	gain	—	x	x

Spinning for Suffixes (For small groups of 2–5 people)

Purpose: To give practice in recognizing and attaching suffixes. Also this game will help the pupil to learn the meanings of certain suffixes.

Materials: A heavy piece of cardboard or a piece of plywood cut in a circle about two to three feet in diameter. Around the edge of the board, write a few suffixes, so they occupy the same positions as the numbers on the face of a clock. See example.

Extra overlays of paper to attach to the face of the circle. These overlays will enable you to readily change the suffixes with which you are working.

A pointer in the center of the circle that can be spun.

A number of word cards that can be used with each overlay. For example, for the suffixes *ed, ing,* and *tion* on the overlay, you might use the word *direct* on a word card.

A shoebox.

Procedure:

Pass out an equal number of word cards to each member of the group. You or a student then spins the pointer, which stops on a certain suffix. You call on each member of the group, and ask them to take their top card and try to attach the suffix at which the pointer stopped. The children may be asked to spell and pronounce the word, and then define what it means. When a child has done this correctly, she puts her card in a box. The child who has all her cards in the box first is the winner.

Variation in Procedure:

Make overlays that contain prefixes to fit on the face of the circle and play the game in the same manner as was done with the suffixes.

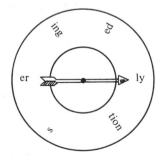

Send Over

Purpose: To provide practice in structural analysis by adding various endings to verbs

Materials: Large cards with a verb printed on each of them

Procedure:

Two teams are formed by any method the students may wish. Each team is given half the cards. When the first team holds up one of its cards and says "send (name of person) over," that person must then say four forms of the verb correctly. If the student is correct, she chooses one member of the other team to be on her side. If the student is incorrect, she must go over to the opposing team. The game ends when the teams run out of verbs or when all players are on one team.

Go Fish

Purpose: To provide practice in structural analysis

Materials: A deck of cards, approximately the same size as regular playing cards. Each card should have a particular form of a verb printed on it; e.g., *jump, jumps, jumped, jumping*. There should be four cards in each book and as many books as desired. A book consists of the four forms of a verb.

Procedure:

Each player is dealt four cards. The remainder of the pack is placed facedown in the center of the table. Each player in turn asks another player for a specific card to complete her book. If the student receives the card, she may ask again, and may continue to ask as long as she receives the card she wanted. If the person does not have the desired card, she tells the player to "go fish," and the player must draw from the pile in the center. If the player draws the card she asked for, she may ask another player for a card. When a book is completed, it is placed facedown in front of the player. If the player does not draw what she has asked for, then it is the next player's turn. The winner is the player with the most books when all books have been assembled.

Variation of Procedure:

A variation of this game is to have pairs of cards, for example *sands-sand, shoe-shoes,* and to have players "fish" for pairs instead of books.

Endings

Purpose: To provide practice in structural analysis

Materials: A number of cards with suffixes or word endings printed on them

Procedure:

Divide the class into two equal teams. On the chalkboard, list a number of familiar root words such as *run, sleep, help, rain, ask,* and *splash.* In a circle on the floor place cards of suffixes such as *s, ed, d, ing,* and *y.* In the center of the circle a blindfolded team member is turned around. The student points to a card and the blindfold is removed. She goes to the chalkboard, chooses a word, and adds the ending to it (writing the new words on the board). She then pronounces the word. If the word is written correctly, she scores a point. If the word is pronounced correctly, she scores another point. If the word is written incorrectly, the rival team scores a point. The first team to receive 25 points wins.

17

Inadequate Ability to Use Context Clues

RECOGNIZED BY

Pupil is unable to derive meaning or pronunciation of a word from the way it is used in a sentence.

DISCUSSION

The use of context clues can be one of the student's greatest helps in determining the meaning of unfamiliar words. It is often one of the easiest reading skills to teach; yet many students are unaware that the use of context clues can be an effective method of deriving the meaning or the pronunciation of words.

A test for determining if a student is able to use context clues effectively is found in appendix F. When using the test for use of context clues, it is important that the student read at his independent level or at an easy instructional level. Do not expect students who are reading at a difficult instructional level or at their frustration level to be able to use context clues effectively. (An explanation of each of these three levels is found in the section entitled "Definition of Terms.")

You can determine if a student is having difficulties using context clues by listening to him read orally. While the student reads, note whether words missed are ones that normally can be recognized from context. Also question the student about the meaning of certain words where that meaning is evident from the context. In silent reading, ask the student to underline the words that he does not know either how to pronounce or how to define. The same procedure can be used in either case.

RECOMMENDATIONS

A. Show the student that it is possible to derive the meaning of words from their context. Show specific examples.

   1. The careless boy did his work in a *haphazard* manner.
   2. He felt that although his work was *imperfect,* it was still good.
   3. When he tried to *insert* the letter in the mailbox, the mailbox was too full.
   4. They called in a *mediator* to help settle the problems between labor and management.

B. Begin by constructing sentences or short paragraphs in which words that students should be able to determine by their context are omitted. In place of each key word, insert an initial consonant and then *x*s for the rest of the letters in the words. See the example below:

   When Jack <u>ix</u> in a hurry, he always <u>rxxx</u> home from school.

   When students have become proficient at this, advance to the next step, which is to replace key words with *x*s for each letter.

   When Jack <u>xx</u> in a hurry he always <u>xxxx</u> home from school.

   After students are able to get most of the words that were omitted by replacing the letters with *x*s, then leave blank lines to replace the entire words that have been omitted.

   When Jack _____ in a hurry he always _____ home from school.

C. Use multiple choice questions in which the student fills in blanks: e.g., "Jack _____a black pony (rock, rode, rod)." Using words that look alike also will give the student practice in phonic and structural analysis.

D. Make tape recordings in which key words are omitted. Give the pupil a copy of the script and have him fill in the blank spaces as the tape is played.

E. Have the student practice reading up to a word, sounding at least the first sound, and then reading several words following the unknown word: "A cow and her c_____ drank from the water hole (calf)." In this case the pupil should be able to say *calf* if it is in his listening-speaking vocabulary. The student should also realize that a calf is the offspring of a cow.

F. Make sentences that can be completed by circling or underlining a picture, such as in the example.

   Directions: Circle the picture that correctly completes the sentence.

   The hen sat on her

G. Give a series of sentences in which only part of a word missing from context is spelled. See the examples.

1. The __ __ __ f __ ce of the water was smooth.
2. All of the Boy __ __ __ __ ts werc cold when they arrived home.
3. The explorers climbed the __ __ __ nt __ __ n.
4. Is your son in the air __ __ __ __ __ __, __ __ vy, or m __ ri __ __ s?

H. Use pictures to illustrate certain words omitted from a tape-recorded story. Lay the pictures (approximately 10) in front of the pupil. As the recording is played, have the pupil pick up the picture that is appropriate to illustrate the missing words. Sound a bell for the missing word.

I. Make a series of sentences using words that are spelled alike but may have different pronunciations or meanings: *read, lead.* Have the pupil read sentences using these in proper context.

> She *read* the book.
> She will *read* the story.
> It was made out of *lead.*
> She had the *lead* in the play.

J. Use commercially prepared materials designed especially for improving the student's ability to use context clues. (See appendix R.)

18

Comprehension Inadequate

RECOGNIZED BY

Pupil cannot answer questions about subject matter he has read or cannot tell what he has read.

DISCUSSION

Several factors about the reader affect his comprehension of the reading material. Other factors that affect a student's comprehension are related to the material he reads. Some factors that affect comprehension in terms of the reader are as follows:

1. *The knowledge the reader brings to the subject.* This means that what a student knows about a particular subject is directly related to how much he will understand about that subject when he reads. In the field of reading education, there is now considerable controversy about whether comprehension is a "top down" or a "bottom up" process. Some reading specialists believe that comprehension is affected more by the knowledge the student brings to the subject and believe that the "top down" model may be most important. On the other hand, others believe that comprehension is affected more by the material the student is reading and would argue that the "bottom up" model is more important. There is a need to study the contribution of both theories; however, common sense tells us that comprehension is a mixture of the two. Unless one is researching the importance of one theory or the other, an argument about this aspect of comprehension seems rather fruitless.

2. *The reader's interest in the subject.* A student will understand more of what he reads if he is particularly interested in the subject.

3. *The reader's purpose for reading.* A student who has a purpose for reading is more likely to understand more of what he reads than a student reading the same material who has no special interest in the subject. For example, if a student wishes to learn how to operate a computer to play a particular game, then he will be more likely to understand more of what is read than a student, of equal ability, who has no desire to operate the computer or to play a particular game on that computer.

4. *The reader's ability to decode words rapidly.* If the student must stop to puzzle over new words, he cannot be expected to comprehend well. The whole process of reading, when many of the words are not in the student's vocabulary, becomes "mind-boggling." The student must give so much attention to the decoding of new words that attending to comprehension to any degree is difficult.

Some factors that affect comprehension in terms of the material being read are as follows:

1. *Number of hard words.* Hard words are usually considered to be those that are not on a particular word list according to a readability formula. This means that the more words on a higher grade level, the more difficult the material is likely to be to comprehend.

2. *Length of the sentences.* Research has consistently shown that longer and more complex sentences within a passage are more difficult to comprehend than are shorter, simpler sentences.

3. *Syntax.* Syntax is the way words are put together. Adults have a tendency to make their writing more complex by using such words as whereas, however, and the like. This tends to make the material being read more difficult to comprehend. Given a set of words (for example, 500 of the most commonly used words) to use to write a story, an adult and a second-grade student would probably write a story about the same subject, yet the adult would string the words together in such a way (syntax) that the story would be more difficult for another second-grade student to comprehend than the story by the second grader.

Attempting to teach comprehension once a student has learned the basic word-attack skills will often be the most difficult problem in the teaching of reading. Perhaps the methods of teaching reading have contributed to the problem. Comprehension is often *tested* but seldom *taught.* In fact, the only instruction some students receive in comprehension skills is in the form of questions over a paragraph or story. This questioning may help the student to develop a strategy for comprehending on his own, but it does not "teach" the student how to comprehend.

An important point that the classroom teacher should keep in mind when using the basal reader is that *the stories in that reader are only a tool in teaching reading comprehension and word-attack skills.* One often sees detailed descriptions of story maps or of how one can apply schema theory to help students understand the stories in the basal reader. However, this kind of information is only worthwhile to the student if it carries over to other reading the student will have to do for the rest of his life. The stories in the basal reader are often interesting and impart considerable information to the student, but the ultimate goal of developing the student's ability to comprehend everything he reads, at or near his grade level, is lost if all he ends up comprehending are the stories in the basal reader.

Perhaps the study of metacognition has added more knowledge about what educators must do in order to help a student learn to comprehend than any other technique with which the author is familiar. Since cognition is the process of thinking, metacognition is the process of understanding *how* a person thinks or the process of monitoring one's thinking. An example of cognition in the area of reading comprehension would be a student thinking about what he is reading. An example of the use of metacognition would be the student examining how much he is understanding about the subject matter while he is reading. Practical methods of using metacognition to improve reading comprehension will be discussed in the first section under Recommendations.

Studies on the nature of comprehension have shown that although reading specialists often refer to comprehension subskills, they cannot really prove these subskills exist. Reading specialists definitely know that comprehension involves both a word or vocabulary factor and a group of skills that might be referred to as "other comprehension skills." Even though they cannot prove that these other comprehension skills exist, it is perhaps useful to list some for teaching purposes. These skills include the ability to do the following:

1. Recognize main ideas
2. Recognize important details
3. Develop visual images
4. Predict outcomes
5. Follow directions
6. Recognize an author's organization
7. Do critical reading

There are several commonly used methods of checking students' ability to comprehend. One of the most widely used methods is the standardized test. Some standardized tests in the field of reading are divided into two main sections—reading vocabulary and reading comprehension. Perhaps this is a misnomer since a good reading vocabulary is really essential for reading comprehension; thus, reading vocabulary is actually one of the subskills of reading comprehension. Since vocabulary is such an important subskill of comprehension, procedures for dealing with vocabulary are found in the next chapter. When using standardized tests to assess reading ability, a teacher should note if a score made by an individual is higher than what the student could have achieved by simply guessing. Some standardized tests have no provision for enabling teachers to measure the reading ability in students of extremely limited reading ability, i.e., a student may be able to achieve a score that is one to three levels above that at which he is actually reading. You should also remember that standardized reading tests are designed, for the most part, to measure the reading ability of a group rather than that of an individual.

Another method of assessing reading comprehension ability is to have students read passages from their basal reader or from other material that is at their grade level. After reading, the students should be asked questions that test their ability to remember facts, make inferences, get main ideas and understand the vocabulary. The major drawback with this approach is that it is difficult for the teacher to construct meaningful questions. The author has found that some questions that may appear relatively easy are seldom understood when they are used with a number of different students. At the same time and for no apparent reason, some questions are almost always answered correctly. When using this method to check comprehension, you should consider the student to be comprehending on a level equivalent to that at which the material is written if the student can answer at least 75 percent of the questions correctly.

A third approach to measuring comprehension is the use of commercial reading inventories. Although some studies have shown that the questions on some of these are sometimes irrelevant or could be answered without reading the passages over which they were constructed, in most cases, the teacher can be assured that the questions are superior to those that he might construct on the spur of the moment.

Another approach that is very useful in determining how well a student comprehends, as well as how his reading ability matches the level of the material he is reading, is the cloze procedure. A detailed description of how to use the cloze procedure is given in appendix I.

RECOMMENDATIONS

A. One research study indicated that the principle differences between younger students who comprehended well and those that did not were that the good comprehenders were able to develop mental images as they read, and they reread when they did not comprehend. Based on this information, the teacher should strive to help students develop mental images. Teach the student to be aware of mental images he is forming as he reads. Have the student read a sentence or two and then ask if he was able to actually see the scene or the action described in what he read. If the student cannot do this, then read the same sentence and tell the student what you saw in your "mind's eye" as you read. Ask the student to read the same material and attempt to get approximately the same mental image. In beginning to develop this skill, be sure to use reading passages that contain information with which the student is already somewhat familiar. Keep in mind that the mental image that a student is able to get will depend on his background of experience.

B. Another skill students should develop, based on the research mentioned above, is that of rereading something that does not seem to make sense when they read it the first time. In the beginning stages, ask students to read one sentence at a time and then ask themselves, "Do I know what the author is saying?" If the answer to this is "yes," instruct the student to keep on reading. On the other hand, if the answer is "no," instruct the student to reread that sentence. Continue to practice this skill until the student has developed the ability to monitor his thought processes while reading.

C. One of the most effective methods to teach students to monitor their thought processes is to develop a code to mark their reactions to each paragraph. The code system will vary somewhat according to the grade level of the students involved. To develop the system, give a group of students a paragraph that is rather difficult for even the better readers. Before having them read the paragraph, tell them that you are about to have them read something that you believe will be rather difficult for them. Ask them to be aware of what happens to them as they read. Point out that most students have some sort of strategy for deriving meaning when a passage is somewhat difficult, so they should think about these strategies as they read. Following their reading use the overhead projector or the chalkboard to record their responses. Assign each logical response a code. Responses typical of middle or upper elementary-grade students would be as follows:

> RRS—I had to reread a sentence because I lost what the author was saying.
> RRP—I had to reread the whole paragraph and then I understood.
> CGVI—I couldn't get a visual image.
> GVI—I got a visual image of what the author was talking about.
> DKWM—I didn't know a word meaning.
> UCGWM—I didn't know the meaning of a word, but I figured it out from the way it was used in the sentence. (Used context to get word meaning)
> DU—I didn't understand what was there.
> UJF—I understood just fine.

Others you might expect to get less often might be as follows:

W—I am wondering why I have to read this?

UEC—The student used "expanded context." The students will, of course, not be likely to refer to this as using expanded context but rather something on the order of "I saw the word in the paragraph above (or in the title, etc.) and went back to read it there to see if I would figure out what it means."

CITQ—Can I think of a question over this material? Once students have begun to use metacognitive techniques, they are likely to begin to give answers similar to this one.

BNR—I was bothered by noise in the room or from an airplane flying overhead.

VI—Very interesting

Once a set of responses somewhat similar to those above is elicited, place them on something more permanent, such as a piece of chart paper or a bulletin board, so that they are in full view of all students at all times when using this technique. Use a paper cutter to cut a number of strips of paper about 1" wide and 11" long from sheets of 8½" × 11" paper. Ask students to align the bottom of the strip of paper with the bottom of the page of the material they are to read. Then ask students to use these codes to mark each paragraph you have assigned. The material might be their basal reader, their science or social studies text or any other material that you feel is appropriate for their grade level.

In doing this activity, be flexible in determining the code students are to use. For example, in the original development of the code, students may not list all of the things they believed happened to them as they read. In this case allow for more to be added or for some, seldom used, to be removed.

This procedure will enable the good comprehenders to teach the poor comprehenders their procedures for coping with difficult material.

D. Young students should be counseled on the importance of getting meaning from reading. Young readers, low achievers, and disabled readers all seem to share the characteristic of believing that fluent oral reading and decoding are their ultimate goals. Do not take it for granted that some students know that comprehension of the material read is the most important purpose for reading. For younger students, it will also be helpful to discuss the vocabulary of reading: what is a "sound," "paragraph," or "sentence"? Studies have shown that many students, as late as first grade, do not know the difference between a letter, a word, and a sentence.

E. Stress the necessity for the student to be able to recognize words for which he does not know the meaning while he reads. Instruct the student to attempt to determine the meaning of unknown words from their context. If the student is unable to derive the meaning of the word from context, then stress the necessity of using the dictionary. Most people become somewhat "expert" at omitting or ignoring words for which they do not know the meaning. Simply being aware of this habit will be most helpful in breaking the habit. Think back to a time when you looked up a word in the dictionary. Then you may have noticed that same word several times in the very near future. Chances are that you had encountered the same word many times in the past but had simply *ignored* it. Once you knew the meaning of the word, you became much more aware of how often it appeared in materials that you were reading.

F. Stress the need for students to change their reading speeds depending upon the kind of materials they read. Many students read everything at the same rate. You could show students that a story problem in a math book would not be read at the same rate as a newspaper story about a familiar subject.

G. Teach students to predict what may lie ahead as they read. In instructing students to do this, you may wish to have them read up to a certain point in a story or passage. Then discuss what they think the author will write next, based on what they have already read.

H. Instruct students to anticipate what questions the author or teacher might ask over a story or passage after it has been read. In order to do this, have students read a paragraph and then discuss what they think the author or you might ask them over the material. Practice this until students are proficient in this skill. Show students the difference between main ideas or overall comprehension of a passage and the comprehension or learning of only minor facts or details.

I. Teach students to constantly ask *who, what, when, where,* and *why* as they read.

J. Use some type of marker for words that you think students will find difficult to understand. For example, you might put an asterisk before words that you feel will be difficult for students or an "x" before words that you believe they will not know. This will help them to be more aware of new words.

K. Talk to children about how stories progress from page to page to show a sequence of events and make students aware of the headings in social studies and science books. Discuss the reason authors use headings and how they may be used to improve the students' understanding of the material they read.

L. Place all of the sentences of a paragraph on the board or on an overhead projector and discuss their importance to the overall understanding of the paragraph. You may wish to have students place the sentences in order according to their importance in the paragraph, e.g., putting the most important sentence first, the next most important sentence second and so on.

M. Teach students to learn to distinguish when text does or does not make sense to them. You may wish to provide practice in this skill by re-writing a passage and adding sentences within the text that contribute nothing to its meaning. Then have students read the material and attempt to locate those sentences that do not contribute to the overall comprehension of the material. This will help students monitor their comprehension in the future.

N. Tell students to think about the material they read, so when they complete the assignment, they will be able to explain the material to other students. This too will help students monitor their comprehension as they read.

O. Ask students to pretend they are the teacher while they read. Have them attempt to think of as many questions as they can over each paragraph.

P. Students' ability to monitor their comprehension as they read may be enhanced by using story frames such as those suggested by Gerald F. Fowler.* Fowler suggests that story frames be introduced shortly after students have read a selection. Five types of story frames are presented here. Note that all five types may not be appropriate for all types of stories; however, you will find that several can often be used in many stories. It is suggested that you first introduce students to one of the simpler types of story frames, such as the one on Figure 1, after students have completed reading a story. Answers to the questions posed by the story frames may then be solicited from the entire class. After students become more adept at using each type of story frame, they may then be given to students prior to reading a story as an advance organizer to help them monitor their comprehension as they read.

You may have to modify these story frames to fit the story you are working on. For example, you may start with "This story begins when" and then add "and then." Following this you may add words that appropriately follow the sequence of events for the story such as, "next," "following that," and "the problem is solved when."

Procedures for Improving Overall Comprehension

A. Set a purpose for reading before students begin to read. Have them skim the material and make predictions about the nature of the material and what they may expect to get from it. These predictions may be made from captions under pictures, the actual pictures, and from any headings that may appear in the story or article.

**Figure 1
Story summary with one
character included**

Our story is about _____
_____. _____ is an
important character in our story. ___
tried to _____
The story ends when _____
_____
_____.

**Figure 2
Important idea or plot**

In this story the problems starts
when _____. After that,
_____
_____.
Next, _____
_____. Then, _____
_____. The problem is
finally solved when _____
_____. The story ends_____
_____
_____.

**Figure 3
Setting**

This story takes place _____
_____. I know this because the
author uses the words "_____

_____." Other clues that
show when the story takes place are
_____
_____.

**Figure 4
Character analysis**

_____ is an important character
in our story. ___ is important because
_____. Once, he/she
_____. Another time,
_____. I think that
_____ is _____
(character's name)   (character trait)
because _____.

**Figure 5
Character comparison**

_____ and _____ are two
characters in our story. _____
                    (character's name)
is _____ while
           (trait)
_____ is _____
(other character)   (trait)
For instance, ___ tries to ___.
___ learns a lesson when ___
_____
_____.

B. Teach students to find material that is not too difficult for them by counting about 100 words of the material they are about to read. Tell them when they read these 100 words, they should not find more than one or two words they do not know. This refers to material the students would be reading without having any type of review of the words and content before they begin reading. Research in this area shows that students cannot be expected to comprehend well unless they have rapid word recognition of the material.

C. Having students combine sentences can also be an effective aid to the improvement of overall comprehension. Use the basal reader to find various sentences that can be combined. In using this method, you may

*Reprinted with permission of Gerald L. Fowler and the International Reading Association from "Developing Comprehension Skills in Primary Students Through the Use of Story Frames," by Gerald L. Fowler, in *Reading Teacher,* November 1982.

wish to call children's attention to the use of words such as *and, but, therefore, however, neither, either, which, that,* etc. You may also wish to develop, with students' help, a permanent list of these words. They can then be placed on chart paper or a bulletin board and kept in a place where all students can readily refer to them.

In doing this exercise, you may also wish to indicate which sentences should be combined by placing a number after each sentence and then giving students a sheet indicating which sentences should be combined. For example, the sheet may appear as the following:

¶ 1: 1 & 2
¶ 3: 1, 2, & 3, etc.

You may also wish to have them use words from certain sentences to form their sentence (sometimes called embedding). In this case, you may wish to indicate which words are to be embedded using a coding system such as this:

¶ 1: 1, 2 (cute), 3 (angry)
¶ 1: 4, 5, & 6

Example of original paragraph

Fred had a pet coyote. It was very cute. It sometimes got very angry. When Fred went to school it sometimes followed him. When the coyote followed Fred he sometimes had to take it back home. Then Fred was late for school.

Example of combined paragraph

Fred had a pet coyote that was very cute, but sometimes it got very angry. Sometimes Fred's coyote would follow him to school and then he would have to take it back home, which made Fred late for school.

D. One method of making students familiar with the new words and content of the material they are about to read is to make an audiovisual presentation of the vocabulary and concepts. For example, if the students are about to begin a unit on weather in their science book, the teacher might find or have the students find various pictures that represent concepts and the vocabulary that students are likely to encounter. In a unit on weather, new words might be *barometer, hygrometer,* and *thermometer.* After finding pictures of these instruments, the students can paste them on sheets of paper and place them in a review notebook. The words listed above might be found in three different sections of a page. Each section would be labeled "A," "B," and "C," and in each section one of the words listed above would appear along with a picture of that instrument. See picture following.

The teacher or advanced students would then write and record a narrative to go along with the material in the notebook. Before students begin reading, they would go to a listening station with the notebook

SECTION A	SECTION B	SECTION C
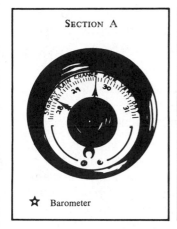		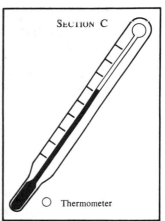
☆ Barometer	☐ Hygrometer	○ Thermometer

and audio tape to prepare them for the concepts and vocabulary of that unit in the textbook. The script for a unit on weather might be as follows: "Look on page one in section A where you will find a picture of a barometer. The word *barometer* is written by the star. Note the spelling of this word b-a-r-o-m-e-t-e-r. A barometer is used to predict what the weather will be like in the future. When a barometer shows a high reading, the weather is likely to be fair. And when the barometer shows a low reading, we might expect wind and maybe rain or snow. Now look in section B where. . . ."

E. Students who word-by-word read or who do not use proper phrasing when they read are not likely to comprehend as well as students who do use proper phrasing. One way to improve a student's ability to phrase is to give him material and indicate where he might phrase properly, as in the following sentence:

> Tom's dog/was very little/but he could/run as fast/as most dogs/much larger/ than he.

F. Another method of getting students to phrase properly is to have them read dialogue or use materials such as *Plays for Echo Reading* published by Harcourt Brace Jovanovich. (See appendix R.)

G. Constantly make the point to students that reading can be a source of information to help them with hobbies and any other subjects they would like to know more about. Refer them to various source books, encyclopedias, etc.

Ability to Recognize Main Ideas

A. You should work with pupils to help them find the main idea and supporting details of a story. You may list the main idea as well as the supporting details as shown in the following paragraph:

A little bird sang a song day after day. The old man had heard it so many times that he knew the tune by heart. Even the children who played nearby could sing it.

Main Idea: A little bird sang his song day after day.
Supporting Details: The old man had heard it many times.

The old man knew it by heart.

Even the children who played nearby could sing it.

Another way of bringing out the main idea of a paragraph and of showing the supporting details is to draw the paragraph as a diagram. In doing this type of exercise you will note that most paragraphs could be classified using one of five to perhaps as many as ten different forms. It is suggested that you let students develop the forms based on the information in each paragraph. After it is discovered that most paragraphs take one of five to ten forms that are essentially the same, you may then wish to have students name or classify the various types of forms. For example, the paragraph concerning various brands of soap could be labeled the "Sales Pitch." It is more meaningful to students to let them develop the various forms and then name them than it is to tell them in the beginning that there are "X" normally used types that have names previously given to them.

A little bird sang his song day after day, after day.
The old man had heard it many times.
The old man knew it by heart.
Even the children who played nearby could sing it.

Other paragraphs may have two main ideas.

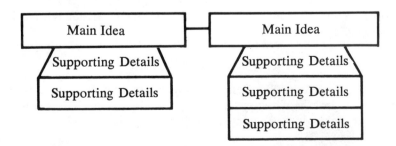

Other types of paragraphs may look like the following.

The Civil War . . . .
It was fought because . . . .
Another reason was . . . .
A third reason was . . . .
The final reason it happened . . . .

"X" brand of soap cleans well . . . .
"X" brand leaves no ring in the bathtub . . . .
"X" brand acts as a deodorant . . . .

therefore
You should always buy it.

Many people eat too much . . . .
Many people drink too much . . . .
Many people watch TV too much . . . .

But on the other hand there are the people who . . . .
Even some of these do not . . . .
Some do not even . . . .
Sometimes there are those who . . . .

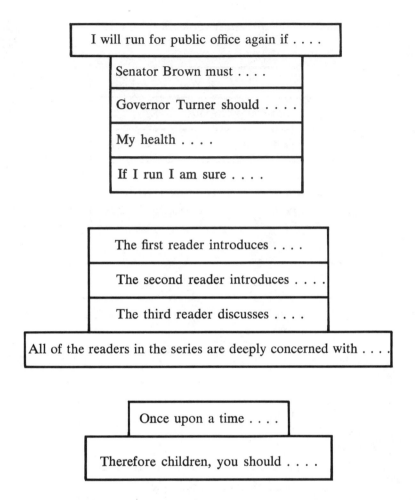

When drawing paragraph diagrams with the children, do not expect to find complete agreement on how they should look. Keep in mind that the important thing is to get the students to think about paragraph structure. When using this system, you may want to have the students suggest names for certain common structure patterns, for example, the logical conclusion, the sales pitch, and the conditional. However do not try this technique in the early stages of pattern development as the students will try to fit new structures into old forms.

B. Read the introduction or title to the story or a chapter and then anticipate with the children what the author is going to say.

C. Select appropriate titles for paragraphs, chapters, or short selections. You might also have the children select the best title from several listed.

D. After the children read a paragraph, have them tell in their own words what the author has said.

E. Many writers use subheadings to help students organize the text. Turn these subheadings into questions and then have children read specifically to answer those questions.

F. Use a series of three pictures, one of which represents the main idea of a paragraph. Have the pupils pick the picture that best represents the main idea. Or you could have the students illustrate a paragraph and put the pictures on cards, i.e., one paragraph and three pictures on a card.

G. Have the pupils underline the sentences in paragraphs that best represent the main idea. Make sure there *is* a best sentence, and also make sure the paragraph has a main idea.

H. Find stories in the newspaper and remove the original captions from each of them. Give these to students and have them read each story and then write their own captions. Compare the students' captions with those of the original stories. Discuss reasons for differences and if captions written by the students are appropriate.

I. Have each student write a paragraph and place an identifying number at the top of the paper. Then pass the paragraph to another student who reads it and writes the main idea or a caption for it on the back of the paper. Then read the various paragraphs and discuss the appropriateness of each caption or main idea sentence.

J. Have students write paragraphs with one sentence being the main idea of that paragraph. Pass these paragraphs around and have other students try to identify the sentence that the writer of the paragraph thought represented the main idea.

Ability to Recognize Important Details

A. Discuss with the children the important details in several paragraphs. Children often focus on minor dates and details that are not really important. Perhaps the testing often used encourages this type of reading.

B. Help the children to find the main idea, then ask them to find significant details that describe or elaborate upon the idea.

C. Ask the children to write down all the details from a selection. Have them classify the details from their list as (1) important, (2) helpful, but not essential, and (3) unnecessary.

D. Have the children answer questions or complete sentences that require a knowledge of the important details.

E. Have the children draw a series of pictures to illustrate the details, for example, the description of a scene.

F. Write three or four paragraphs about a picture and then have students read each of the paragraphs to see which one best describes the picture. The picture may be placed at the top of an 8½″ × 11″ piece of paper with each of the paragraphs arranged below it.

G. Have students read stories in newspapers and magazine articles and then have them attempt to answer the following: Who? What? When? Where? and Why?

Ability to Develop Visual Images

A. For children to visualize a certain setting or image effectively, they must have actually or vicariously experienced it. Review the setting of a story with children before they begin. You could also supplement their information with a film or filmstrip or have children bring pictures from books and magazines.

B. As a child reads a selection, you might stop him from time to time and ask him to describe images gained from the reading. Also the student might be asked questions combining the images from the passage and his own imaginings. Two examples of questions are What color coat do you think the person is wearing? and Was it a big tiger or a little tiger?

C. Discuss figures of speech such as *big as a bear, black as pitch* or *as cold as a polar bear in the Yukon.* Help the children to see that figurative language can either add meaning to a story or in some cases be misleading. Ask the children to listen for and collect various figures of speech.

D. Ask the children to draw pictures of certain settings they have read about. Compare and discuss.

Ability to Predict Outcomes

A. Show a series of pictures from a story and ask the children to tell, either in writing or orally, what they think the story will be about.

B. Read to a certain point in a story and then ask the children to tell or write their versions of the ending.

C. Ask the children to read the chapter titles of a book and predict what the story will be about. Read the story and compare versions.

D. Encourage the children to make logical predictions and to be ready to revise their preconceived ideas in the light of new information.

Ability to Follow Directions

A. Make students aware of key words that indicate a series of instructions, such as *first, second, then,* and *finally.* Discuss the fact that, in this case, there were actually four steps, although the writer only used the

terms, *first* and *second.* As students read directions, have them reinforce this knowledge by having them make lists of words that were
used to indicate steps.

B. Write directions for paper folding, etc., which the students can do at
their seats. Have the children read and perform these directions step
by step.

C. Write directions for recess activities on the chalkboard. Try to get the
students in the habit of following these directions without oral
explanation.

D. Ask the children to write directions for playing a game. Have them
read their directions and analyze whether or not they could learn to
play the game from a certain child's written directions.

E. Encourage the children to read written directions such as those in
workbooks and certain arithmetic problems without your help.

F. Write directions for certain designs to be drawn on a certain size of
paper, for example the following directions may be given:

1. Make an X on your paper halfway between the top and bottom
edges and one-half inch from the left-hand side.

2. Make a Y on the same horizontal plane as the X but one-half inch
from the right-hand side of the paper.

3. Make a Z directly below the Y one-half inch from the bottom edge
of the paper.

4. Draw a line to connect the X and Y.

5. Draw another line to connect the Y and the Z.

After these are completed, have students examine their pictures in
relation to one drawn correctly and shown on the overhead projector
or on the chalkboard. Discuss reasons for some common mistakes.

G. Use commercially prepared material designed for improving ability to
follow directions. (See appendix R.)

Ability to Recognize the Author's Organization

A. Discuss the fact that all authors have some form or organization in
mind when writing. Look over chapter titles and discuss other possi-
bilities for organization. Do the same with shorter selections including
paragraphs.

B. Discuss the author's use of pictures, graphs, charts, and diagrams to
clarify certain concepts.

C. Discuss the use of introductory material, headings, study questions,
and summaries.

D. Explain the value of "signal" words and phrases in showing organi-
zational patterns.

E. Make the children aware of "signal words" and "signal phrases" in selections: *to begin with, next, not long after, then, finally, several factors were responsible for, these led to, which further complicated it by.*

F. Write down a sequence of events from a story the children have read and ask them to number the events in the order in which they happened. Explain before they read the story what they will be expected to do.

G. Write each of the sentences from a paragraph on a separate (small) piece of paper. Ask the pupils to arrange these sentences in a logical sequence in order to form a paragraph that makes sense.

H. Cut up comic strips or pictures of sequential events and have the children assemble them in their correct order.

Ability to Do Critical Reading
(A higher level reading skill)

A. Discuss the use of *colored* or *loaded* words and have students search through editorials or transcripts of speeches of political candidates for these words. Some examples of these words are *left-wing, reactionary, rightist, playboy,* and *extremist.*

B. Examine advertisements for cigarettes to see how they are designed to appeal to various age groups. Note statements that are made about such products and examine if these statements have merit.

C. Examine advertisements for various products in men's and women's magazines to see how they are designed to appeal to different audiences.

D. Find accounts of a political event as reported by two or more newspapers or magazines. Note ways in which the information differs.

E. Examine political cartoons and discuss if they are designed to show the candidate in a positive or negative way.

F. Examine various advertisements to see how they attempt to get the buyer to infer information about the product, which, in reality, may be quite meaningless. For example, a claim for "X" brand of aspirin may say, "Nine out of ten doctors surveyed recommended the ingredients in 'X' brand." What this may mean is that at one time in the speaker's career nine out of ten doctors recommended that someone take an aspirin!

G. Analyze editorials to determine if the writer of the editorial used biased statements or if the writer wished the reader to make certain inferences. Also discuss why a certain writer may be biased in certain areas.

H. Write or have students write paragraphs. Then have the students write statements about the paragraphs, based on the information in those paragraphs, which may or may not be true. Discuss various statements and determine if they are true or if statements made about those paragraphs could logically be inferred.

I. Read reports of interviews with political candidates and note if a candidate had taken certain stands on issues before, or if the candidate's views on a subject tended to change to take advantage of a situation.

GAMES AND EXERCISES FOR COMPREHENSION SKILLS

Story Division

Purpose: To provide practice in comprehension and oral reading skills for pupils who lack self-confidence

Materials: A basal reader for each pupil

Procedure:

You first divide a story such as the following into parts:

1. Toddle was Pam's pet turtle.
   He liked to crawl.
   He got out of his pan of water and crawled all around the house.
2. Toddle bumped into things.
   Bang! Bang! Down they went.
   Mother did not like this.
3. She said, "Please, Pam, put Toddle back into the water, and do make him stay there."

Each child studies *one* part of the story and reads it orally. After a whole story is read, the children are given a comprehension check.

This type of procedure gives the children confidence because they know the part they will be required to read, and they can practice reading it silently before reading it orally.

A Matching Board

Purpose: To provide practice on the various components of comprehension

Materials: A piece of ½" plywood the same size as a sheet of ditto paper
             Shoestrings

Procedure:

Drill two columns of holes (1½" apart) down the center of the piece of plywood as shown following. Make holes the entire length of the board, spacing them the same vertical distance as four spaces on a typewriter. The holes should be just large enough to let the shoestrings pass through them quite easily. Attach shoestrings through the holes in the left column. Tie a knot on the back side, so they will not be pulled through. Make sure each string in the left column is long enough to thread through any hole in the right column.

Ditto various exercises such as sentence completion, missing words from the context of a sentence, word opposites, sentence opposites, etc. Make each set of opposites four vertical typewriter line spaces, so they will correspond with the holes on the board. Use a thumbtack or transparent tape at the top and bottom of each column of questions and answers to hold the dittoed material in place. Use these boards with individual children to provide practice in areas in which they need special help. Various kinds of exercises are illustrated following.

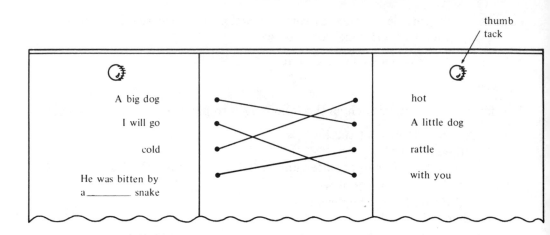

Main Ideas

Purpose: To improve students' ability to concentrate and locate the main idea in a selection

Materials: Basal readers, science or social studies textbooks

Procedure:

Before giving the children a reading assignment, show them a list of true-false questions concerning the material on the reading assignment. Construct the questions so they test for the main ideas of paragraphs from the reading material. This test will give the students an idea of what they are expected to gather from the assignment, and it will improve their ability to recognize main ideas in future reading. Make sure students understand that the questions test for main ideas and not for details.

Directions: Some of the statements below are true and some are false. Write *T* after the true statements and *F* after those that are not true.

1. Carlos did not really want to race his car. ____

2. The weather was just right for racing. ____

3. Someone had been fooling around with Carlos's car. ____

4. Most of Carlos's friends felt that he could win the race if he wanted to. ____

Picture Puzzle

Purpose: To help children recognize, evaluate, and describe various situations

Materials: Pictures clipped from magazines or old discarded readers mounted on tagboards
Word cards
Flannel board

Procedure:

Display a picture on a flannel board. Allow the children to select from a large number of word cards the ones they feel best describe the given picture. Place these word cards on the flannel board with the picture and discuss their appropriateness to the situation.

Variation in Procedure:

Use the same procedure as above except substitute sentence strips for the individual word cards or make sentences from the individual cards.

Riddles

Purpose: To provide practice in the comprehension of descriptive details

Materials: Tagboard

Procedure:

Write a series of short stories describing a particular object or animal. Have the children read the story and decide what the object or animal is. In the bottom corner, under a flap of paper, place the correct answer. The children may check their answers after they have made their decisions. See the example.

> My home is in the country.
> I live on a farm.
> The farmer's children take care of me.
> They give me grain and water.
> I give them eggs.
> I am a good friend of yours.
> What animal am I?
>
> Answer
> is here

What Do You See?

Purpose: To develop picture-word description relationships

Materials: Pictures cut from magazines
              Tagboard
              Flannel board

Procedure:

Place pictures of objects on a flannel board. On tagboard write some questions about the pictures and some questions that will act as distractors. Have the children answer the questions about the pictures posted.

Do you see a frog?
Do you see a hopping rabbit?
Do you see a fat pig?
Do you see a door?
Do you see an open window?
Do you see a red ball?

The Wizard

Purpose: To provide practice in reading for specific questions

Materials: A basal reader for each child

Procedure:

One pupil is chosen as The Wizard. The student asks a question relating to the reading lesson and calls on a classmate to answer. If that child answers correctly, he is The Wizard, and he makes up the next question. Those children who do not answer a question correctly have another chance to be The Wizard with further play.

Classification Game

Purpose: To develop the ability to classify related words

Materials: Pocket chart
Word cards
Envelopes

Procedure:

Divide the pocket chart into four columns. In the first three columns in each row place three related word cards. Leave the fourth column blank and have the children select a word card from their envelopes that belongs in the same class as the other three words in that row.

car	boat	airplane	_____
ball	top	doll	_____
Susan	Bill	Lassie	_____
walk	gallop	skip	_____
red	blue	green	_____

Variation in Procedure:

Instead of filling in the missing word as described above, use four words in which one word does not fit the category represented by the other three words. Have children find and remove the "misfit."

As I See It

Purpose: To provide children with an opportunity to express the visual images they gain from reading or hearing a story

Materials: A story (preferably one with vividly described scenes)
Drawing paper and paints or colors

Procedure:

After the children have heard or read a story, have them illustrate various scenes as they perceived them. After drawing the scenes, mix the illustrations up in a box and have one child stand in front of the room and pull out pictures. After he has chosen a picture, he will try to reconstruct the story on a bulletin board from the many pictures that are in the box. Discuss various differences in drawings and discuss why some pupils interpreted things differently. At times you will want to reread parts of the story to see if material was interpreted incorrectly.

Furnish the Empty Room

Purpose: To develop the ability to recognize appropriate visual images

Materials: Flannel board
Pictures of specific objects cut from magazines or old books

Procedure:

At the top of the flannel board place printed subject headings such as *kitchen* or *playroom*. Have the children select object pictures that are appropriate to the given headings.

My Image

Purpose: To encourage the building of sensory images

Materials: Various materials to create sounds that are very familiar, somewhat familiar, and less familiar to children

Procedure:

Have the children close their eyes and listen as you or another child makes a noise. Have the children open their eyes and write words or phrases that describe the noise. Then have them draw pictures to represent the noise. Encourage them to use a varied vocabulary in their descriptions.

That Makes Sense

Purpose: To develop the ability to associate objects with their sources and to develop the ability to logically complete a given idea

Materials: Pocket chart
             Word cards
             Envelopes

Procedure:

A series of incomplete statements is placed on the pocket chart. Word cards containing the appropriate missing words or phrases are provided for the children. From these they will select the correct answer and place it in the pocket chart next to the incomplete idea.

A dress is made from	in the ground
Fish usually	flour
Cocoa is made from	fly
Oil can come from	seeds
Cabbage grows	beans
Parrots can	on the ground
Strawberries have	swim in water
Cakes are made from	whales
Potatoes grow	wool

Ordered Phrases

Purpose: To provide practice in skimming and in determining sequence (comprehension)

Materials: Cards with phrases copied from a story, book, or basal reader

Procedure:

Have the children read the passage and place the phrases on the cards in columns in the order that the phrases occurred on the page.

You should also write the number order on the back of the cards. Such numbering will enable a child to correct his own work.

Sentence Puzzles

Purpose: To help children see a sequence of ideas

Materials: Envelopes
Paragraphs or short stories that are written in a logical order

Procedure:

Cut up the stories or paragraphs into sentences and paste each sentence on a small rectangular piece of paper. Place one story or paragraph in each envelope. Pass these envelopes out to the children and have them assemble the stories in a logical order. Number the envelopes and have the children keep a record of the stories or paragraphs (by envelope number) they have assembled. The children continue to exchange these envelopes until all have had a turn at each envelope. In some cases you may want to have stories or paragraphs graded according to the reading level of a particular group. In such a case reading group B will do only those envelopes marked *1-B, 2-B,* and so forth.

It Does—It Doesn't

Purpose: To help children classify words according to descriptive specifications

Materials: Pocket chart
Envelopes
Word cards

Procedure

Divide the pocket chart into two columns. Place a statement and its opposite next to each other at the top of the chart. Provide each child with an envelope of word cards containing current vocabulary words. Have the children classify the words found in their envelopes according to the given statements. Use a great variety of statements and word cards that will require careful thought. Vocabulary and classification sentences will vary with grade levels.

It can walk	It cannot walk

Word Cards

boy	top	boat
cup	rabbit	cow
dog	girl	pan
car	bucket	plane
coat	horse	duck

What Did It Say?

Purpose: To develop phrase recognition and the ability to follow directions

Materials: Flash cards

Procedure:

Write specific directions on individual flash cards. As the cards are flashed before the class, call on certain students to respond. Examples of directions are the following:

1. Close the door.
2. Give a pencil to a brown-eyed boy.
3. Stand up. Turn three circles. Touch the desk behind yours.
4. Draw a circle inside of a triangle on the board.

Story Pantomime

Purpose: To provide practice in reading for information and following directions

Materials: Cards on which are printed directions for acting out a certain activity

Procedure:

The cards are passed out to all the pupils in the class. One pupil is selected to act out each set. The other pupils watch critically for the complete acting of every detail in the directions.

Example: Pretend you are washing dishes. Stop up the sink, open the doors under the sink, and get the soap. Put the soap in the sink, turn the faucet on, test the water, put the dishes in the water, and then wash and rinse three dishes. Put the dishes in the dish rack to dry.

A story pantomime might also include such things as the following:

drawing water from a well
making the bed
rocking the baby
picking flowers for a bouquet
singing a hymn
winding the clock
watering the flowers
ironing
picking and eating apples
playing baseball

Good Words–Bad Words

Purpose: To provide practice in critical reading, especially concerning the purpose the author had in mind when the material was written

Materials: Various written or tape-recorded advertisements

Procedure:

Have the children locate and circle or make a list of words they can classify as either "good" words or "bad" words. Good words might include such words as *freedom, well-being, Number One rating,* and *delicious.* Bad words might include words such as *disease, cracks, peels,* and *odor.* Discuss how the use of these words influences our thinking about a certain product. Carry this exercise into the study of characters in books about whom the author wishes to convey a good or bad impression.

19

Vocabulary Inadequate

RECOGNIZED BY

Lack of comprehension or poor performance on tests of vocabulary knowledge

DISCUSSION

As in the case of comprehension, the most common method of testing students' knowledge of word or overall vocabulary is the use of standardized achievement tests. In examining the students' scores, examine the raw scores to see if they are above that which could have been made by chance guessing. A number of standardized reading achievement tests will allow a student who may essentially not read at all to score well into the norms and to have a vocabulary achievement score well above the student's actual vocabulary achievement.

If you know a student you wish to test for vocabulary knowledge is lacking in word attack skills and thus does poorly on a standardized achievement test, it may be best to give the student an oral vocabulary test. If the student does much better on the oral vocabulary test, you can then assume that a lack of proper word attack skills is contributing to the student's low score on the standardized test.

Another method of testing students' knowledge of vocabulary is to ask them the meaning of several words that appear in their textbooks (at their grade level). This will give you a general feel for their vocabulary knowledge; however, it will not allow you to compare the general achievement of your students with those in the country as a whole. In the case of a teacher in a school with a large group of students from a low socioeconomic level, this method of testing vocabulary knowledge within the class may tend to give the teacher "tunnel vision" since a student, with only a near normal vocabulary, may appear very good in comparison to other students in the class.

RECOMMENDATIONS

Most of the words a child or adult knows have been learned as a result of either hearing them used or reading them in the context of a sentence. For students with a limited English vocabulary, much practice in oral language is essential. For students who come from an English-speaking background, the single best way of increasing their vocabulary is to encourage them to read about a number of subjects. The importance of this cannot be overemphasized. Some other suggestions follow.

A. Students of all grades can benefit from the use of semantic feature analysis. To use this technique, pick a theme somewhat familiar to a number of students, such as *speech communication*. First, discuss various ways in which we communicate through speech and list them; for example, seminar, congress, forum, debate, dialogue, conversation, symposium, lecture, homily, testimony, caucus, interview, sermon, and hearing (used as a noun). If students are at an age where they are familiar with the use of a thesaurus, they can quickly find synonyms for words first mentioned.

After the list has been completed, discuss characteristics of several of the items on it. Commenting on the list in the preceding paragraph, students may note such characteristics as *one-way, two-way, no control over who speaks, one person controls who speaks, anyone can speak, formal,* and *informal.* After a logical set of characteristics has been developed, construct a matrix (on an overhead transparency or on the chalkboard) such as the one at the top of page 137.

When the matrix is complete, ask students to decide whether to place a plus (+) or a minus (−) in each blank space of the matrix, depending upon the characteristic of the item in the column. For example, for *seminar* one would be likely to place a plus in the blanks for *two-way, one person controls who speaks, anyone can speak,* and, perhaps, *informal.* On the other hand, a minus would be likely to appear after *one-way, no control over who speaks,* and *formal.*

Semantic feature analysis provides students with a much better understanding of terms than definitions from a dictionary. Encourage students to discuss the merits of placing a plus or a minus after various items. Also allow them to place both a plus and a minus in certain blanks. For example, a seminar might be formal or informal, depending, to some extent, on who is conducting it as well as on its purpose.

After students have completed marking each item with a plus or a minus, have them ask each other questions such as "Jim, what is the difference between a debate and a dialogue?" This will, of course, make students more active participants, and they will be much less likely to forget the meanings of various words. The discussion following the

Semantic Feature Analysis
for
Speech Communication

	One-Way	Two-Way	No Control Over Who Speaks	One Person Controls Who Speaks	Anyone Can Speak	Formal	Informal
Seminar	----	----	----	----	----	----	----
Congress	----	----	----	----	----	----	----
Forum	----	----	----	----	----	----	----
Debate	----	----	----	----	----	----	----
Dialogue	----	----	----	----	----	----	----
Conversation	----	----	----	----	----	----	----
Symposium	----	----	----	----	----	----	----
Lecture	----	----	----	----	----	----	----
Homily	----	----	----	----	----	----	----
Testimony	----	----	----	----	----	----	----
Caucus	----	----	----	----	----	----	----
Interview	----	----	----	----	----	----	----
Sermon	----	----	----	----	----	----	----
Hearing	----	----	----	----	----	----	----

completion of the matrix should be considered as an essential part of the use of this technique for vocabulary development.

B. Semantic word maps also can be fun and challenging to students. Using semantic word maps together with a dictionary and a thesaurus will enable students to learn words that are not in the speaking-listening vocabularies of the students involved in making the map. In using this technique, first pick a topic familiar to students, such as *house*. Then ask them simply to list a number of things that come to mind when hearing this word. Examples might include stone, wood, ice, concrete, electricity, dishwasher, carpenter, mason, skins, and concrete.

After a fairly comprehensive list has been developed, ask students if they see logical categories into which they could fit each of the items. For example, logical categories for this list might be as follows: *equipment* (electricity, dishwasher, garbage disposal), *building materials* (stone, wood, ice, concrete, skins), and *workers* (painter, carpenter, and mason).

Show the development of the semantic map as follows:

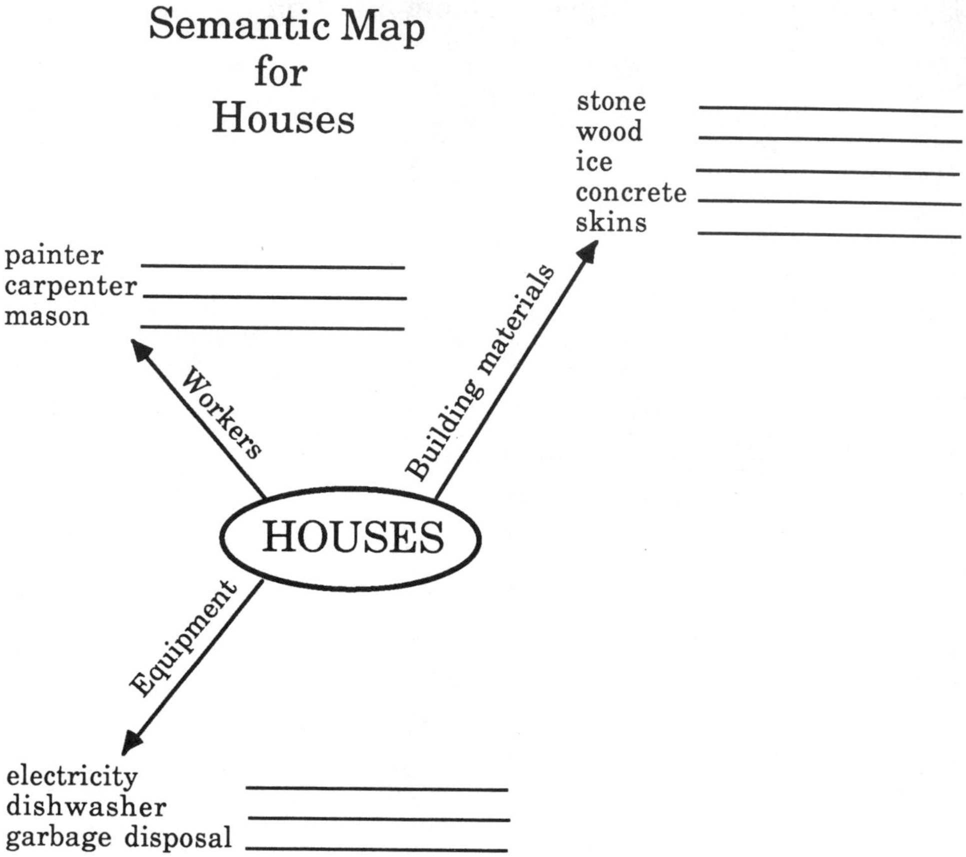

Semantic Map
for
Houses

stone   _____
wood   _____
ice   _____
concrete _____
skins   _____

painter _____
carpenter _____
mason   _____

Workers

Building materials

HOUSES

Equipment

electricity   _____
dishwasher   _____
garbage disposal _____

In doing something as common as a house there would, of course, be more categories than those shown in the figure. After the map has been developed, draw lines beside each word in the various categories, as shown. Then have students use a thesaurus to find a word, or, preferably, more than one word, that could possibly be a synonym of each listed word. Also, depending upon the ages of the students involved, you may wish to use words that are synonyms of the roots of words used in each category. Place these words in the blanks. Examples of words that might be used in the illustration would be *painter* (*tint, dye, pigment, stain*); *carpenter* (*cabinetmaker, builder, producer*); *mason* (*bricklayer, plasterer, cement worker*); *electricity* (*current, juice, power*); *dishwasher* (*cleaner, cleanse, filter, purify*); *garbage disposal* (*dirt, filth, muck, slime*); *stone* (*boulder, gravel, pebble, rock*); *wood* (*forest, lumber*); *ice* (*freeze, chill, refrigerate*); and *concrete* (*cement*).

C. Whenever new words come up in lessons, stop and discuss them in sufficient detail so that all students develop a concept of their meaning.

D. Appoint a *vocabulary committee* to review each new lesson prior to class reading to select all words for which they do not know the meaning. Use these words as a guide to the new vocabulary in addition to the vocabulary given in the textbook.

E. Develop picture files for each unit in the students' textbook. Use the pictures to show the meaning of new words and concepts. These pictures may be placed on a bulletin board or shown and discussed as you introduce each new unit.

F. Place pictures on the bulletin board and have students try to find as many words as possible to describe the pictures. If students are old enough to use a thesaurus, allow them to do so. Place the words under the picture and discuss them regularly.

G. Develop word awareness by showing students how they often skip words for which they do not know the meaning. Promote awareness of new words by getting students to look for new words that they or other students may not know the meaning of. Write the new word on the chalkboard along with the name of the student who found it.

Carlos's new word—*idealism*
Frank's new word—*afterthought*

Discuss these words daily until most students know them. Keep adding new words to the bottom of the list and gradually erase the ones from the top after they have been discussed several times.

H. Encourage students to use vocabulary cards. As students read assignments or any other reading material, have them search for new words. When a new word is found, the student writes it on a vocabulary card. Then she copies the sentence in which it was used and underlines the word. (Encourage the use of context to derive meaning.) After the student completes her reading, she locates the new word in the dictionary and writes its meaning on the card. File the new vocabulary cards in a shoe box and review them periodically.

I. Discuss the use of figurative language and have students look for idiomatic expressions, such as "Our teacher was a bear today," "She was as quiet as a mouse," or "He lost his cool."

J. Encourage students to discuss and do exercises such as the *Reader's Digest's* "It Pays To Increase Your Word Power."

K. Provide a wide background of experiences for students. This can be done, to a certain extent, by taking students on field trips, by showing films and filmstrips, and by discussing a wide range of topics in the classroom. After returning from field trips or using films or filmstrips, discuss any new words and concepts. Also, encourage students to write down any unfamiliar words as they listen to the narration of a film, filmstrip, or video recording. After viewing the filmstrip, film, or video recording, ask students to list their words on the chalkboard or overhead projector and discuss them. A thorough discussion of the meaning of one word is more worthwhile than having students look up several words in the dictionary, write the meanings of the words, and then use the words in sentences. In presenting each word, discuss its meaning with the class and use it in a sentence. Then have several members of the class use the word in sentences they made up. Follow that procedure with all unknown words. Finally, have students write a summary of the field trip, the film or filmstrip, or the class discussion, and use all of the new words that were presented. The author and an elementary principal once checked students' knowledge of 20 words that they had just completed writing the meaning of and using in a sentence during a one-hour period. The average number of words known by each student was two out of the 20, or 10 percent of the words. And, this was immediately after completing the lesson! This would indicate that a little more time spent in discussing each word and making sure that it was *well known* by each student would be much more productive than attempting to introduce many words, in a less thorough manner.

L. Encourage students to use the dictionary to derive a word's meaning. Although only a small percentage of one's total meaning vocabulary comes from the use of the dictionary, all students should learn how to use the dictionary in order to derive word meaning as well as the accompanying skills such as understanding a word's first, second, and third meaning.

M. Encourage students to use books marketed for the purpose of building vocabularies. These are constantly being updated, and new ones appear on the market each year. To find them, look under the subject of *vocabulary development* at a local bookstore. These books present many words, and most teachers can learn much about the teaching of vocabulary by using such books.

N. Prepare lists of words that have synonyms and discuss the words. Have students match the synonyms with the words just discussed. After students have completed the exercise, discuss the various synonyms and encourage students to use them in their conversations.

O. Teach students to use affixes as clues to word meanings. Although research indicates that the study of prefixes and suffixes (collectively called affixes) is somewhat questionable, a knowledge of affixes is highly useful in understanding words in subject areas such as science where a student might encounter such prefixes as *bio-, sub-,* and the like.

P. Teach students how to use a thesaurus and constantly encourage them to use it in their writing.

Q. Many commercial materials have been designed for vocabulary development. A list of these appears in appendix R. Also, a number of software programs have been designed for computer use. A list of companies that distribute computer software programs appears in chapter 30, *Using the Computer in Locating and Correcting Reading Difficulties*.

R. A good sourcebook for teachers on the teaching of vocabulary is one written by Dale D. Johnson and P. David Pearson. The reference for it is as follows: Johnson, Dale D. & Pearson, P. David. *Teaching Reading Vocabulary*. New York: Holt, Rinehart & Winston, 1977.

GAMES AND EXERCISES FOR VOCABULARY DEVELOPMENT

Matching Words and Definitions

Purpose: To enrich vocabulary

Materials: Envelopes that contain slips of paper with words printed on them. The envelopes should also contain a larger second set of slips with a definition of each word.

Procedure:

Have students each take an envelope and empty it on their desks. They should then place the word slips in a column in numerical order.

1. candid
2. slipshod

Students try to match the definition slips with the words. The definition slips should have a number that corresponds with the word slip; however, the number should appear only on the back. This way students can check the accuracy of their work when they have finished. Number each envelope and give students a number sheet corresponding to each envelope. Have them check off each number as they do the words in each envelope. Thus, each student will be sure to do each envelope.

Homonym Concentration

Purpose: To enlarge vocabulary

Materials: Set of word cards (about eight to ten) with a corresponding set of homonym cards (total of 16 to 20)

Procedure:

Play the game the same as "Concentration." Shuffle the cards and place them facedown in rows on a table or on a "concentration" board with squares on it. Two students play. One begins by turning over a card. Then she tries to find its homonym by turning over another card. If the words are not homonyms, she turns both cards facedown, and the next student takes her turn. Whenever a student turns over a pair of homonyms, she gets to keep the cards. The student with the most cards at the end of the game is the winner. (This same exercise may be done with antonyms and synonyms.)

Phrase It Another Way

Purpose: To enrich vocabulary

Materials: Phrase cards or phrases written on the chalkboard

Procedure:

On the chalkboard each day place a new phrase that is commonly used by students or you in daily conversation and activities. Opposite the phrase, write another way of saying the commonly used phrase. Each day you and the students concentrate on using the phrase in a new way. You may wish to place the phrases on chart paper and display them as the number grows.

Old phrase	*Phrasing it another way*
is done	is completed
runs fast	is a rapid runner
couldn't get it	was deprived of it

Drawing New Words

Purpose: To build vocabulary and improve dictionary skills

Materials: A number of 3" × 5" cards with new vocabulary words written in a sentence (underline the new word)
             Dictionary

Procedure:

The cards are shuffled and placed facedown on the table. Students then take turns picking up a card, reading the sentence, and defining the underlined word. Another student looks up the word in the dictionary to see if the definition was correct.

New Word for the Day

Purpose: To enrich vocabulary

Materials: Word cards for new and old words

Procedure:

Decide on a new word that can be substituted for one that is commonly used each day (see example). Place the old and new word in a chart holder. During the day attempt to use the new word instead of the old word. This should be done by you as well as by students. Discuss how doing this type of activity will enlarge vocabularies and make students' talk sound more mature.

Old word	*New word*
talk	discuss
hate	dislike
do better	improve

20

Voicing-Lip Movement

Pupil reads with visible lip movement and/or voicing of words.

DISCUSSION

A pupil who continually voices words while reading silently is not likely to gain any speed until she can be taught that it is not necessary to pronounce each word as it is read. Many people unconsciously pronounce words to themselves even though they do not actually move their lips. Much voicing and lip movement can be detected by watching for visible signs that are apparent when someone speaks. Other students may voice words and yet show no visible signs of doing so. One way to determine whether students are voicing words is to ask them. Very slow, silent reading is also a sign that a pupil may be voicing words. That in itself, however, is not enough evidence to support such a diagnosis. Remember that voicing or lip movement is often an indication that a student is reading material that is too difficult for her. By giving her material that is considerably easier and then noting whether the voicing and lip movement continues or stops, you can determine whether the cause is habit or an indication that the student has been reading at or near her frustration level.

RECOMMENDATIONS

A. As strange as the technique may seem, the single most effective way the author has found to alleviate this problem is to ask the student to hum a *familiar* tune as she reads. While doing this, the student can neither subconsciously nor consciously voice the words being read. The student may first find it distracting and complain about a lack of comprehension; however, if she continues, the student will soon find that her reading speed is not only considerably faster, in most cases, but that her comprehension will also have been improved. The methods that follow are somewhat effective but will usually not work as well as the method just described. This method works exceptionally well with students who wish to practice speed reading.

B. Have the students pace their reading with their hands. Make sure the rate they use is faster than their normal speaking rate. Do not attempt to do this with children in first, second, or third grade.

C. Use controlled reading devices that require reading at a rate too fast for voicing words. (See appendix P.) Do not attempt to do this with children in first, second, or third grade.

D. As the student reads, have her hold her mouth shut with the teeth firmly together. Tell the student to hold her tongue against the roof of her mouth.

21

Low Rate of Speed

RECOGNIZED BY

Pupil is unable to read as many words per minute as would be normal for a pupil of his age on a certain kind of reading material.

DISCUSSION

You can determine if certain pupils are slow readers by giving a timed reading exercise to an entire class. The various reading speeds listed in words per minute can be graphed or charted to determine which students are considerably below average on a particular kind of material for their class. When giving timed exercises, you should choose several pages that are normal reading material in story reading. You should not use pages containing questions, lists, etc. Timed exercises from two to five minutes should be sufficient. You seldom need to worry about achieving a very rapid reading rate in the elementary grades. Therefore, the suggestions listed under items (A), (B), and (C) are more appropriate for junior- or senior-high-level students.

RECOMMENDATIONS

A. Have the pupils pace their reading with their hands. They should attempt to move across the page slightly faster than their comfortable reading speed normally allows. It should, however, be emphasized that the hand paces the eyes and the reading speed, and not the opposite.

B. Focus on speed by using material that can be read fast. Give timed reading exercises followed by comprehension questions. Let the student keep his own chart on speed and comprehension. See appendix P for sample chart.

C. For the older students, assign or let them pick short paperback novels that are meant to be read rapidly. Use these in conjunction with hand pacing to practice for speed.

Timed Stories

Purpose: To encourage rapid reading while still focusing on improving comprehension

Materials: A number of envelopes with short stories on them along with sets of questions over each story

Procedure:

Before doing this, you should have given speed reading tests to your class and grouped them accordingly; i.e., one group that reads from 75–100 words per minute, one group that reads from 100–125 words per minute, and so on. Cut a number of short stories from old basal readers. Put one of these stories along with approximately ten comprehension questions in an envelope. Develop norms for each story; for example, a certain story for the 100–125 group may be labeled as an eight-minute story. Label the envelopes under headings such as *Dog Stories, Family Life Stories,* and *Science Stories.* Let the students choose the stories they want to read. From the labeling, the students will know that they should read the story in a certain number of minutes. This technique is a change from the timed test in which each student is reading the same subject matter. It also avoids having the faster readers waiting for the slower readers; when they finish a story, they can get an envelope and begin another one. Have the children keep a record of the stories they have read and their percent of comprehension on each story.

22

Inability to Adjust Reading Rate to the Difficulty of the Material

RECOGNIZED BY

The student reads at the same rate regardless of the *type* of material he is reading.

DISCUSSION

Many people are in the habit of reading all kinds of material at one speed. They read a newspaper or novel as though it were a science book or a set of directions. This is a habit that can be overcome easily if the student is shown how varying his reading rate can save time and improve comprehension.

To determine whether a student is reading all kinds of material at the same speed, give him a speed test on several kinds of material. The first material should be of the type found in novels or in a newspaper. Then give another speed test on material that would require more careful reading, such as the expository writing in a science book. If the student reads all of the material at approximately the same rate, he is having problems adjusting his reading rate to the difficulty of the material.

To determine reading rate, find the total number of words in the passage and the length of time, in seconds, that students take to read that passage. Divide the number of words by the number of seconds. Multiply the resulting figure by 60. The result will be *words per minute*.

RECOMMENDATIONS

A. Discuss various types of reading material and show the students how rates should vary on these materials. You may wish to construct a chart to explain this idea.

How We Read Different Kinds of Materials

Skim
1. Telephone book
2. Newspaper (when looking for one thing)

Fast
1. Novels
2. Normal reading of newspaper

Medium
1. Our history assignments

Slow
1. Procedures for experiments in science
2. Our mathematics book
3. Explanations in our English books

B. Time an entire class on a reading passage from a novel, and then time them on a reading passage from a mathematics book, preferably one that explains a process. Compare the average amount of time that was taken to read each passage or the number of words read in a certain amount of time. Emphasize that comprehension is necessary in both cases.

C. Check the students' comprehension on easy and difficult material when each is read fast and when each is read slowly. Determine proper reading speeds for adequate comprehension of each type of material.

D. Much of the material in science and social studies is set up with a number of dark headings within the chapters. The student should study this material in the following manner:

1. Turn the first dark heading into a question; for example, the heading may state **The New World.** The student would then make a question of this by saying, "Where was the New World?"

2. The student would read to answer that question.

3. When the student has read down to the next dark heading, he should stop and try to answer the question he has just posed. If he cannot answer it, then he should read the material again. If he can answer it, then he should proceed to the next dark heading and do the same with it.

E. Discuss when it is not necessary to read every word, such as in a descriptive passage of scenery in a novel or details in newspaper articles. Have students underline only those parts that would be necessary for adequate comprehension. Then have students exchange articles or pages of a novel and read only the parts that other students have underlined. Discuss information derived by various students by reading only the underlined material. Ask the students who underlined the material to comment on the adequacy of the second reader's comprehension.

F. If the reader's rate is much too slow, then discuss when it is desirable to skim. If the reader cannot do this, then see the suggestions under *Inability to Skim,* chapter 24.

23

High Rate of Reading at the Expense of Accuracy

RECOGNIZED BY

Pupil finishes reading assignments before the rest of the class and consequently lacks comprehension of what he has read.

DISCUSSION

Reading at a high rate of speed is desirable at times. There are, however, certain types of reading material that should be read more slowly than others. For example, mathematics and much of the science reading matter requires slow, careful reading. Many students are not able to adjust their reading rate downward as the reading material becomes difficult. This situation is especially true of the student who constantly reads novels or the newspaper and is then required to read material that requires considerable concentration.

You may occasionally find a student in the lower elementary grades who reads at a rate that impairs his accuracy. The problem is more prevalent, however, with older students who have become accustomed to reading material that requires little concentration.

RECOMMENDATIONS

A. Have the student react to each paragraph using a code similar to that suggested on ideas for using metacognition, shown in item *C* in chapter 18.
B. Ask the student to use the SQ3R or similar techniques in which he is required to react to each dark heading.
C. Discuss the various reading speeds that are desirable for certain types of material. Show the students as well as tell them.

D. From material found in a reading passage, give oral and written questions that require accurate answers. Let the student know ahead of time that he will be required to answer questions over the reading passage.

E. Give the students worksheets that contain reading passages and questions about subject matter in the reading passages. Ask them to underline the answers to questions as they read them.

F. Give the students study-guide questions over material they are to read. Many books contain questions over a unit or chapter at the end of that unit or chapter. Encourage the students to read these questions before they begin reading the material in the chapter or unit.

24

Inability to Skim

RECOGNIZED BY

Pupil is unable to spot certain phrases, facts, or words rapidly while skimming or scanning reading material.

DISCUSSION

One of the causes of the inability to skim is that the students have not felt a need for this skill. People who actually need to learn to skim and who are shown how to do so, soon become adept at this skill. Teachers who are attempting to improve the ability to skim need to show students how to skim as well as test their ability to do so.

Those pupils who are not adept at skimming can usually be found by using the following procedure. List five to ten facts, dates, sentences, or the like that appear in a lesson and then ask students to find the material within a reasonable time limit. Watch for those students who have done only a little when the faster ones have finished.

There has been no attempt to differentiate between the terms *skim* and *scan* in this book.

RECOMMENDATIONS

A. Hold a class discussion on how skimming can be beneficial to persons such as the student and the businessman. Try to determine when it is appropriate for the student to skim. A list of times when skimming may be appropriate might be similar to the following:

    1. Looking for a name in a telephone book

    2. Looking for a date in a history book

3. Looking for a certain number of factors to solve a problem

4. Reading the newspaper and searching for a certain article

5. Wanting an idea of what an article or book will be about

6. Looking for a word in a dictionary

B. Show the pupils how to move their hands down a page in a telephone directory to find a certain name. After they have practiced and have become proficient with their hands, they can usually do as well without the use of their hands.

C. Give the students copies of newspapers and have them skim them to find things such as the article about the president, or about a baseball pitcher. Another good exercise with a newspaper is to have the students find a phrase on a certain page that describes something or tells a certain fact. After the students have found the phrase, ask them to paraphrase the author.

D. Give study questions on a reading assignment that can be answered by skimming the material. Keep in mind that this is not always the type of reading one wants to encourage.

E. Have the students skim to find a certain word in the dictionary.

F. Have the students skim to find a certain word (name of a city, etc.) or date in a history book.

G. Tell what a certain paragraph is about and then have the pupils skim to find the topic sentence of that paragraph. (Make sure there is one!)

H. Show the children that it is possible to get the meaning of some material when many words are missing. Make paragraphs in which some words *unnecessary* for comprehension are missing. Make sure they understand that they are not to try to supply the missing words. Another variation of this exercise is to give the children paragraphs and have them underline only the words that are really necessary for comprehension. See the example.

The *superintendent* of *schools* in *Huntsville* spoke to a large audience. She *discussed reasons* for the *new building program.* To *some extent, she covered methods* by which *new revenue* might be made *available.* Everyone thought her *speech was excellent.*

GAMES AND EXERCISES

Skim and Sort

Purpose: To provide practice in skimming

Materials: Old textbooks with stories in them that are somewhat varied
Envelopes

Procedure:

Cut three stories from a book and then cut each story into either paragraphs or fairly short passages. Make sure each paragraph or passage contains some subject matter that gives a clue to which story it came from. Mix all of the paragraphs or passages together and place them in an envelope. Write the names of the three stories on the outside of the envelope. Give the children these envelopes and have them sort through them rapidly, putting each paragraph or passage in one of three piles to match the story title. Number each paragraph or passage. When a child has finished sorting these, give him the number key to check his work. (For example, numbers 1, 3, 5, 7, 9, 13, 15, and 16 may belong in the first story, numbers 2, 6, 8, 14, 17, and 18 may belong in the second story, and numbers 4, 10, 11, 12, 19, and 20 may belong in the third story.)

Finish It

Purpose: To provide practice in skimming

Materials: A book of which all children in the game have a copy

Procedure:

Give students the number of a page from which you are going to read. You then begin reading somewhere on that page. After reading a few words you stop, and those who have found the place continue to read to the end of the sentence.

Skimming Race

Purpose: To provide practice in skimming

Materials: Any book that is available to every child in the game

Procedure:

Divide the children into two groups or let captains choose sides. Either you or alternating captains ask a question and tell the children in both groups the page where the answer can be found. The first child to find the answer stands by his seat. The first person standing is called upon to read the answer. A correct answer scores one point for that side. The object is to see who can get the most points in a specified amount of time or in a specified number of questions. If a child stands and then gives a wrong answer, take away one point from his side.

Rapid Search

Purpose: To provide children with practice in skimming

Materials: Several copies of the same articles in magazines, basal readers, or newspapers

Procedure:

One child finds a part of the story that represents some action. He then pantomimes this action, and the rest of the children skim rapidly to try to find the sentence in the story that describes the actions of the child doing the pantomiming.

25

Unable to Locate Information

RECOGNIZED BY

Pupil is unable to locate information in encyclopedias, *Reader's Guide to Periodical Literature,* the card catalog of the library, the *World Almanac,* and other sources.

Pupil is unable to use cross-references and parts of books such as the table of contents, index, and appendix.

DISCUSSION

It is almost a necessity for pupils in the intermediate grades and up to be able to use some of the sources of information listed previously; however, students often lack the skills needed to locate information. Even at the high-school level many pupils are unfamiliar with the use of the index and table of contents in their own textbooks.

Teachers can locate the types of difficulties students are encountering by giving an informal test similar to the following:

Name the part of your textbook that tells the beginning page number of the chapter on atoms.

Where would you look in your textbook to locate the meaning of the word *negotiate?*

Where in your textbook would you find some reference to the subject of atomic reactors?

Find the name of the magazine that published the following article:"_____."

Explain how you would locate the following book in the library:_____

How would you locate something on the subject of whales in the following set of encyclopedias: _____

What city in the United States has the largest population?

What is the purpose of the appendix of a book?

RECOMMENDATIONS

A. Discuss with the students the types of information found in encyclopedias. Also give exercises in which the pupil is required to locate certain volumes and then certain pieces of information using the letter and/or word guides provided.

B. Teach the use of cross-references. Ask the students to find information on certain subjects that are covered under several headings.

C. Explain the use of the library card catalog. (See appendix O.)

D. Teach the pupils how to locate information in the *Reader's Guide to Periodical Literature*. Assign reports that require its use for finding a number of references on a certain subject.

E. Explain the use of the *World Almanac*. Give exercises in its use; for example, ask specific questions such as: What city has the largest population in the world? and What city covers the most square miles?

F. Explain the use of the table of contents, index, and appendix. Do not take it for granted that older students know how to use these. Ask specific questions over their use; e.g., What chapter explains the use of maps?, What page contains an explanation of photosynthesis?, or Where would you find tables showing the relationships between weights and measures in the English and metric systems?

GAMES AND EXERCISES

Student Travel Bureau

Purpose: To provide practice in research and map study skills

Materials: Globes
Road maps
Travel folders
Various encyclopedias

Procedure:

When the pupils are studying a unit on map study, or any other time you desire, arrange the room as a travel bureau. Advertise the class's service much the same as a travel bureau would. If pupils bring in information concerning future trips their family will be taking, you can

1. Present the traveler with a well-marked road map after studying maps from several companies and after corresponding with state highway departments.
2. List places they may wish to visit along the way.
3. Provide a history of landmarks along the way.
4. Provide other specific information as called for.

Thesaurus Puzzles

Purpose: To help children increase their vocabularies through the use of synonyms and antonyms and to use a thesaurus

Materials: Pocket chart
Word cards
Envelopes

Procedure:

Divide the pocket chart into two columns. In the left-hand column, place a list of words that have synonyms or antonyms. Each child is given an envelope of word cards containing synonyms and antonyms of the word list. Each child then selects a word, which is either the synonym or antonym of one of the given words from his envelope, and places his word card on the right-hand side of the chart. A more advanced arrangement of this game can be made through the use of a thesaurus. Given a word in Column One, the children can use the thesaurus to make their own word cards for Column Two.

play	
white	
eager	
rare	
easy	
pleasant	
healthy	
cleanse	
guess	
clear	
dwarf	

List Completion
(For upper grades of junior high school only)

Purpose: To provide practice in the use of the thesaurus

Materials: A thesaurus
The materials shown

Procedure:

Provide lists of words for the children to complete.

Directions: Complete the lists with words that mean almost the same thing.

1. decide	1. erratic	1. charge
2.	2.	2.
3.	3.	3.

1. deck	1. cage	1. charm
2.	2.	2.
3.	3.	3.

Detective

Purpose: To provide practice in locating information and skimming

Materials: Copies of paragraphs from the basal reader, social studies book, or science book the children are using. (From one copy you then can make a spirit master and make multiple copies of a certain paragraph if you desire.)

Procedure:

Copy a certain paragraph from a book that the child has in his desk. Make sure the paragraph gives enough information to let the reader know from what kind of book it is taken; e.g., a paragraph about clouds would be from a science book. Also you should use paragraphs that give a clue that can be found in the table of contents or in the index of the book. Tables and graphs are appropriate if the book has a list of them. Put one of each of these paragraphs, graphs, or tables in an envelope along with a blank sheet of paper. Each child is given an envelope and the assignment to find where the paragraph came from by using the table of contents, index, list of tables and graphs, or appendix. When the student finds the answer (the same paragraph in his textbook), he writes the information on the blank piece of paper and hands it back to you. Number the envelopes and have the child keep records of which envelopes he has completed.

26

Lacks Knowledge of the Alphabet

RECOGNIZED BY

The student is unable to recognize the letters of the alphabet when shown the letters, is unable to point to the letters of the alphabet, is unable to match uppercase and lowercase letters, or is unable to match one uppercase or lowercase letter with another letter that looks exactly the same.

DISCUSSION

Students who, when given an informal reading inventory, know very few words, or students that appear to be severely disabled in reading, should be given a test for letter knowledge. Keep in mind that there are various levels of difficulty in testing for letter knowledge. The materials listed in appendix B will enable you to determine whether the student has difficulty with the alphabet and, if so, the level of difficulty at which the student is weak. For example, it is more difficult for a student to name letters in random order than it is to point to the letters named by the teacher.

RECOMMENDATIONS

A. Teach the child the alphabet song. Then as the student sings the song, have a copy of the alphabet (in alphabetical order) and ask the student to point to each letter as it is sung.

B. Present a few letters each day (perhaps four or five) and discuss their characteristic shapes, such as the fact that they are as high as the letter *a*, or that they have ascenders as the letter *h* or descenders as the letter *p*.

C. Make a list of the first third of the alphabet such as the one that follows:

1. A	5. E
2. B	6. F
3. C	7. G
4. D	8. H

Then make a recording for the student to take home or work with in the classroom. The tape-recorded script can be as follows: "Look at the letter by number one. This letter is *A*. Point to it and say "*A*." Look at it very carefully and say "*A*" again. The next letter by number two is *B*. Point to it and say "*B*." Look at it very carefully and say it again," and continue through the list. You may wish to modify this script to have the student also write the letter. In this case the script would be as follows: "Look at the letter by number one. This letter is *A*. Point to it and say "*A*." Look at it very carefully and say it again. Now write the letter and say "*A*" as you write it," and so on.

D. If some letters are reversed or if the student seems to have a difficult time in learning them, you may do the following: Take a piece of overhead transparency film, approximately 3" × 8", and run it through an unthreaded sewing machine. Run the film through the machine, so the needle has punched holes in it in rows spaced about two millimeters apart. After finishing, cut a piece of cardboard the same size as the transparency film. Then place the transparency film over the piece of cardboard, so the rough side of the transparency film (the bottom when it was placed on the sewing machine) is facing upward. Use book-binding tape (3" long by 1" wide) to form a hinge on the left side, so the transparency film can be lifted up from the cardboard like a page would be opened in a book. Place a fairly large letter you wish to teach between the cardboard and the transparency film, so it may be viewed through the film. Then have the student trace the outline of the letter over the film as he says the name of the letter. The film will be rough, and as the student traces the letter, he will feel the shape of the letter. This can also be done with sandpaper letters or with three-dimensional letters; however, using the film and cardboard system described above will allow you to print the letter with a felt-tip marking pen and place it under the transparency film. This is much easier than having to cut each letter separately from sandpaper.*

E. Place a thin layer of salt or fine sand in the bottom of a shoebox lid and ask the student to trace letters in the sand or salt.

F. When teaching the alphabet, teach one-third of it at a time rather than attempting to teach it all at one time. Place the first third of the

*From Dwyer, Edward J. and Flippo, Rona F., "Multisensory approaches to teaching spelling." *Journal of Reading,* November, 1983, 27, 171–72

alphabet on a chart where it can constantly be seen by children, such as in the example shown.

a b c d e f g h i

Work with students until they can instantly tell you which letter comes before or after any other letter. For example, if you say, "Which letter comes before *g?*" and point to a child, he should instantly say *f*. Most adults can instantly give the letter that immediately *follows* another; however, they usually pause a few seconds before they tell which letter *precedes* another. Knowing the order of the letters will save time later when using the dictionary.

When the students have mastered the first third of the alphabet, replace the chart with another one showing the second third of the alphabet. Students should reach the same level of proficiency as they did with the first third. Then practice the first and second thirds together. Finally, give students the last third of the letters and practice the above-mentioned skill with the entire alphabet.

27

Written Recall Limited by Spelling Ability

RECOGNIZED BY

Student is unable to spell enough words correctly to express her answers on paper.

DISCUSSION

Discovering that a pupil makes a great number of mistakes in spelling is not difficult for the teacher. However, there is a reasonably high correlation between reading and spelling ability. The types of errors made in one may indicate that the same types of errors are present in the other. The pupil who is a phonetic speller may tend to mispronounce words that are phonetically irregular. Similarly, the pupil who uses almost no phonetic word attack skills may also lack the ability to spell. By carefully observing the way a student reads and spells, you may note certain problem areas that will be helpful in determining specific kinds of suggestions for help.

A student who is not able to learn as many words as would be normal for her age/grade level should be taught a mastery list or the most commonly used words. If the student must cut down on the total number of words learned, then the words sacrificed should be those of less utility. Be sure that in *all* subject matter you emphasize spelling. This strategy will help in motivating the children to improve their spelling and will give them the feeling that it is important to spell correctly all the time and not just during the spelling period. Try to determine the mode of learning in which each child is most successful (visual, oral, aural, aural-oral, kinesthetic) and place her in a group to be taught in that particular manner. Furthermore, teach spelling rules inductively and provide for use of newly learned words.

RECOMMENDATIONS

A. Pronounce the word clearly, then have the child pronounce it. Use the word in a sentence and have the child use it in a sentence. Write the word on the chalkboard; or when working with a single child, write it on a piece of paper. Have the child write the word on a card (8½" × 3"). Underline syllables and discuss letter combinations. When underlining syllables, it may be more effective to use different colors for different syllables. The child can use the card for further study. These cards should be kept in a file such as in an old shoe box.

B. When working with children whose spelling is too phonetic (e.g., *nees* for *knees,* or *wun* for *one*), you should concentrate on showing the child the whole word picture rather than focusing on sounds within words.

C. It is important that the student *never* spell the word wrong if it can be avoided because this will tend to reinforce a *wrong* response. It is better to do more work on words prior to the student's attempting to spell them; so when they are written, they are spelled correctly.

D. Keep increasing the spelling vocabulary by adding previously missed words to new lists as well as some words with which students are more familiar. Most children can learn more words than those normally assigned to them in a spelling book.

E. Teaching the following spelling rules will be helpful; however, keep in mind there will be numerous exceptions to rules in the English language. Whenever possible, teach spelling rules inductively. An example of teaching rules inductively would be to list a number of words that exemplify a particular generalization and then let students develop the rule for themselves. This will take time, but students are more likely to remember the rules. Also, it is better to show students certain exceptions to a rule when they learn it than to let them discover exceptions for themselves. At least make clear that there will be exceptions to nearly all of the rules:

   1. Write *ie* when the sound is /ee/, except after *c,* or when sounded as /a/ as in *neighbor* and *weigh.*

   2. When the prefixes *il, im, in, un, dis, mis,* and *over* are added to a word, the spelling of the original word remains the same.

   3. When the suffixes *ness* and *ly* are added to a word, the spelling of the word remains the same. Examples: *mean + ness = meanness; final + ly = finally.*

   4. When a word ends in a consonant + *y* change the *y* to *i* before adding all suffixes except those beginning with *i.* Do not change the *y* to *i* in suffixes beginning with *i* or those that begin with a vowel + *y.*

5. Drop the final *e* before a suffix beginning with a vowel. Examples: *care + ing = caring, write + ing = writing.* (Exceptions: *noticeable, courageous, dyeing. Dyeing* is spelled as it is to prevent confusion with *dying.*)

6. Keep the final *e* in a suffix beginning with a consonant. Examples: *care + ful = careful, care + less = careless.* (An exception is *argue + ment = argument.*)

7. In one-syllable words that are accented on the last syllable and that end in a single consonant + a single vowel, the final consonant should be doubled when adding a suffix beginning with a vowel. (Examples: *beginning, fanning*)

Note: Keep in mind that not all children learn effectively by the use of rules.

F. Make lists of common prefixes and suffixes, as well as *families of sounds.* (See appendix N.)

G. Teach students how to use the dictionary in locating unfamiliar words. Practice this usage on difficult words that can be found by the sounds of the first few letters. Discuss possible spellings for certain words and sounds. Also teach the use of the diacritical markings in the dictionary.

H. Let the children exchange papers and proofread each others' written work. The habit of proofreading will carry over into their own writing.

I. Let the children correct their own papers after taking a spelling test. Some children are much more adept at correcting their own work than other children are. You will need to make periodic checks to determine if the students are having difficulty finding and correcting their own errors.

28

Undeveloped Dictionary Skills

RECOGNIZED BY

Pupil is unable to locate words in a dictionary, to use diacritical markings in determining the correct punctuation of words, or to find the proper meaning for a word as used in a particular context.

DISCUSSION

In addition to the most common errors listed in the "Recognized By" section, there are a number of other dictionary skills with which the student needs to become proficient in order to make the dictionary a useful tool. The following is a list of other skills the students should learn.

1. The use of guide words
2. The use of accent
3. The use of syllabication
4. Interpreting phonetic respellings
5. Using cross-references
6. Determining plurals
7. Determining parts of speech
8. Determining verb tense

The dictionary can be the most useful tool the child will ever possess for independent word analysis. Some students are able to become quite adept at using a dictionary in the second grade; however, most students learn in the third grade, and the skill should be learned no later than the fourth grade.

RECOMMENDATIONS

A. Follow the steps listed for teaching students to locate a word in the dictionary according to alphabetical order. Make sure the pupils are adept at each skill before beginning the next one.

   1. Make sure the child knows the sequence of the letters in the alphabet.

   2. Give several letters to be arranged alphabetically: *a, g, d, b, h,* and *m.*

   3. Give several words that have different first letters to be arranged alphabetically: *bat, game, calf, dog,* and *man.*

   4. Give several words that have the same beginning letters but different second letters to be arranged alphabetically: *pie, pliers, poker,* and *pack.*

   5. Give several words that have the same beginning and second letters but different third letters: *pig, pie, pile,* and *picnic.*

B. Explain the purpose of the guide words at the top of the pages in a dictionary. Have the children write the beginning and ending guide words on pages that contain the words they are looking for.

C. Give students two guide words printed at the top of a piece of paper. Then list a number of words and give students a short amount of time to tell whether the words listed would be found on the same page as the two guide words (five to seven seconds). Time them and have them place a plus (+) after each word that would come on the same page as *key* and *kick* and a minus (−) after each word that would not come on the same page. This assignment will enable students to learn to use guide words rapidly.

key	**kick**
keyway	+
kill	−
khan	+
kibe	+
kidney	−

D. Teach the use of diacritical markings. Almost all dictionaries contain a pronunciation key at the bottom of each page that serves as a guide for teaching this skill.

E. Give students lists of words that they are not likely to be able to pronounce. Have them look up their phonetic respellings and write them beside each word. Have students then take turns reading the pronunciation of each word and let other students agree or disagree with each pronunciation.

F. Give students lists of words that have their accent in two places depending upon the part of speech in which they are used (such as *research*). Let students look the words up in their dictionaries and inductively decide where like words are usually accented as nouns and where they are usually accented as verbs. Other examples are *combat* and *contract*.

G. Have the children use the dictionary to find the proper meanings for the way in which certain words are used in sentences. Use words that are clearly defined by the context of the sentences. Have them write the definitions and then use the words with the same meanings in other sentences.

GAMES AND EXERCISES

Today's Words

Purpose: To provide practice in the use of the dictionary and to increase vocabulary

Materials: A dictionary for each child

Procedure:

Each morning place three or four new words on the chalkboard. Use words that the children have not previously studied. Later in the day ask the students questions using the new words. For example, "Miguel, does *pollution* affect our city?"

Synonym Race

Purpose: To provide practice in using the dictionary to find synonyms. This assignment will increase the child's vocabulary and improve his comprehension in silent reading.

Materials: A basal reader
A dictionary for each student

Procedure:

You select sentences from the current reading lesson that include words you wish the students to study. Write these sentences on the board, underlining the words for which the class is to look up synonyms. The pupils race to see who can supply the most synonyms from their dictionaries.

The starfish does not *please* him.

1. satisfy   3. attract
2. amuse   4. gratify

Water ran in a puddle all over his *clean* house.

1. pure	3. unsoiled
2. spotless	4. immaculate

Written Directions

Purpose: To provide practice in following directions and in the use of the dictionary

Materials: A dictionary for each student in the game
A set of cards or pieces of paper with directions written on them

Procedure:

Give each child a piece of paper on which there is a set of directions. Be sure that the directions are simple, but also include at least one new word that the child will need to find in the dictionary before he can follow the directions. As the children find the meanings of words they have looked up in the dictionary, they then can take turns pantomiming the action described by the directions. The other children try to guess what they are doing and try to guess the word or a synonym for it. If they guess a synonym for a new word, then both the word and the synonym may be written by each child. This practice will help the whole class to remember the meanings of new words. Some examples of directions for the game are as follows:

1. Pretend you are a vagabond.
2. Pretend you are wicked.
3. Pretend you have a halo.

Categories

Purpose: To provide practice on word meaning

Materials: Envelopes
Cards with words on them that the children do not know well
8½″ × 11″ paper or tagboard

Procedure:

At the top of a number of sheets of tagboard write three categories in which words may fall (see the following examples). Place each sheet of tagboard in a manila envelope along with approximately 30 words that will fit the categories listed. Pass the envelopes out to the children and have them use their dictionaries to group the words on the small word cards under the proper categories. Number the envelopes and have the children keep a list of the envelopes that they have completed.

What animals do	*Things that grow*	*Things that are not alive*
fight	trees	rocks
run	cats	books
play	people	paper
jump	weeds	chalk
eat	frogs	chairs
sleep	elephants	pencils
walk	flowers	magnets

Matching Word Meanings

Purpose: To increase vocabulary through the use of the dictionary or thesaurus

Materials: A word sheet similar to the example given
A dictionary or thesaurus for each child

goodness	stoop	helpfulness	waning	amiability
kind	philanthropy	senile	cambered	knobby
bias	hooked	charitable	inelegant	arch
vulgar	elder	unsmooth	look	rough
aged	rippling	bowlike	chunky	curved
elderly	choppy	geriatrics	turn	

BENT	COARSE	BENEVOLENCE	OLD

Procedure:

Have the children place words from the word list under the capitalized word that would be the best category for them.

29

Useful Teaching Methods and Counseling Techniques for Students With Reading Difficulties

In this chapter you will find information on the use of the language-experience approach, the neurological-impress method, and counseling techniques that are especially helpful with students with reading difficulties. Although the language-experience approach is just as appropriate for students without reading difficulties as it is for students with difficulties, certain procedures are emphasized here that may not be emphasized to such a degree in using it with students in a regular developmental reading classroom. The neurological-impress method has been researched by this author, as well as others, and found to be highly successful with students with a rather small sight vocabulary. However, it may not be especially appropriate for a student who is making normal progress. The counseling techniques presented are those the author has found especially useful when counseling students, as well as the parents of students, who have reading difficulties.

USING THE LANGUAGE-EXPERIENCE APPROACH

The language-experience approach combines all of the language arts, i.e., reading, writing, speaking, and listening. The author can say, without reservations, that it always works with students with reading difficulties. When using the language-experience approach, one need not be concerned about whether the material being read is in the background of the learner and will be too difficult to comprehend or whether the student will be interested in the subject. One also need not be concerned about whether or not the reading material will appear too "babyish" for the student. This is, of course, because in the language-experience approach, the reading material is generated by the student.

The language-experience approach can be used with a single student or with a group of students. Much has been written on the use of the language-experience approach, and varying procedures for its use have been suggested. The material that is presented here indicates how it might be used with an individual and with a group. Certain procedures are also stressed that may seem, at first, to be unimportant. However, certain aspects of the language-experience approach are extremely important for its success, and the author recommends little variation from these specific procedures. The material that follows is divided into four sections: (1) The theory behind the success of the language-experience approach, (2) Using the language-experience approach with individual students, (3) Using the language-experience approach with small groups of students, and (4) Important procedures and information about the use of the language-experience approach.

THE THEORY BEHIND THE SUCCESS OF THE LANGUAGE-EXPERIENCE APPROACH

The language-experience approach uses the language of the students as the basis for writing materials that will later be read by those same students. When a student dictates something to the teacher or writes something herself, it will naturally be something in which the student is interested and will also be something that the student will understand with no difficulty. Furthermore, it will be written at a reading level appropriate for the student, and its content will not insult the student regardless of age.

USING THE LANGUAGE-EXPERIENCE APPROACH WITH INDIVIDUAL STUDENTS

In using the language-experience approach with individual students, the teacher should follow this general procedure:

1. Tell the student that you would like to have her dictate a story to you, so she will have something to read immediately. Spend some time discussing topics that interest the student and about which she would like to talk or write.
2. When a subject is found, ask the student what she would like to use as a title for the story. You may wish to make suggestions; however, it is *much better* to attempt to get the student to use her own language. The student may wish to write about some experience that she has had lately, or she may wish to write about a favorite pet or a brother or sister. There are often hands-on experiences that have taken place within the setting of the classroom about which the student may wish to write—a science experiment or something the student is making as a combination of an art project and a social studies assignment.
3. When an appropriate title has been decided, begin to write it. Use either manuscript or cursive writing, depending upon the age-grade level of the student and what she has previously been taught. If the student has done very little writing of any kind, then you should use manuscript writing. As you write each word, make sure the student is watching. Say each word as you write it. As soon as you have finished writing the title or any sentence, stop and bring your finger down on

each word and read it back to the student. It is important to bring your finger down on each word for two reasons. First, it will help the student understand that each set of letters stands for a particular word, and second, it will set a pattern for the student to follow when she begins to read. It is also important that you read the material first, so that the words will again be emphasized. This will give the student a second chance to learn each written word.

4. Ask the student to read the title to you. Make sure that the student brings her finger down on each word as she reads it. This will ensure that the student again notes each word carefully and sees each word as a part of the overall title or sentence. A student will, in most cases, be able to read the title or a sentence back to you without carefully looking at what has been written. Having the student bring her finger down on each word will also ensure that she is actually looking at the word being pronounced and that she is not saying one word while looking at another. If the student is allowed to slide her finger under the words as she reads, there is a tendency to read ahead of or behind where her finger is pointing. Students are hesitant to do this at times; they may have had a teacher who told them not to point to words as they were reading. A student may also resist raising her finger up and bringing it down on each word. Insist that it be done this way and you will, in most cases, find that any initial resistance is quickly overcome.

5. Continue to do the rest of the story as you did with the title. Stop after each sentence is written and point to each word as you reread the sentence. Bring your finger down on the word and read it at exactly the same time as your finger comes down on the word. After reading the sentence, have the student do it in the same manner. Then add a sentence at a time until you have finished the story.

6. After finishing the story, point to each word and read the entire story. Then have the student do the same. If a student miscalls a word, quickly correct her and continue. Depending upon the student and her ability to remember, reading the story several times may be advisable.

7. The length of each story will depend on the characteristics of the student who is dictating it. However, in the beginning stages, be careful not to make the stories too long. The student will lose accuracy in rereading a particularly lengthy story, thus defeating the purpose of having her create her own material. As students continue to improve their reading, you are likely to find that they begin to dictate longer stories.

8. At this point you may let the student illustrate the story or apply stickers or appropriate pictures from other sources.

9. It is suggested that you then type the story using primary or pica type, whichever is appropriate to the age-grade level of the student. The student should have the ability to transfer knowledge of words from manuscript or cursive writing to printed type.

10. After a period of time, such as would elapse after doing another activity, have the student reread the original story and then the type-written copy. You may wish to have the student take the original story, which was illustrated, home and practice reading it to someone in her family. Some students will show a tendency to lose their stories, and having a typed copy will ensure that all stories remain intact.

11. When next meeting with the student, ask her to again read the story that was written in the previous session. If it is read without errors, then write another story and use the same procedure. Continue this sequence, i.e., rereading all previous stories and writing another one each time you meet.

12. After the student has written a number of stories, you may bind them into a booklet and let the student illustrate the cover.

13. After the student has built up a considerable sight vocabulary and has developed some beginning word attack skills, you may have her gradually begin to read basal readers or trade books.

USING THE LANGUAGE-EXPERIENCE APPROACH WITH SMALL GROUPS OF STUDENTS

In using the language-experience approach with small groups of students, you may wish to follow a sequence such as the following:

1. Find some event or subject of interest to the group, and tell them that you would like to help them write a story about the event or subject.

2. Ask students to decide upon a title for the story. When they have agreed upon a title, write it using the exact words given by the students. As you write it, say each word. After finishing the title, instruct the students to watch carefully as you read it. Point to each word as you read it. Be careful to bring your finger down on each word and read it only as your finger touches the word. Then ask the students to read the title as you point to each word. You may have several students read it individually.

3. When writing the story, use these general guidelines:

   ☐ Use the type of writing to which the students are accustomed; i.e., either manuscript or cursive.

   ☐ Use the language that the students suggest and make very few, if any, changes.

☐ Write on something that can be saved for future use. Use 24" × 36" lined chart paper if it is available.

☐ Use a felt-tip pen or marker that will make broad, readable lines.

☐ In the beginning stages, use one-line sentences and gradually increase the length of the line as students' reading improves.

☐ Emphasize a left-to-right movement.

☐ Make sure students see all words as they are written.

4. After the story has been finished, read it to the class, being careful to point to each word as it is read.

5. Have the students read the story as a choral exercise as you point to each word.

6. After the students have read the story as a choral exercise, have individual students come to the chart and read the story. The student should point to each word as she reads it, exactly as you have been doing.

7. Use a typewriter to duplicate the story after it is finished. Also have the children copy the chart in its exact form.

8. After a period of time, ask students to reread the story. You may have children take turns reading a sentence at a time.

9. After duplicating the story, give each student a copy to take home to practice reading to someone in her family.

10. After the students have practiced reading the story a number of times, you may also duplicate the story on a large piece of tagboard. The tagboard may then be cut into strips with one sentence on each strip. Either you or the students may then place the strips in a pocket chart to recreate the original story. At this time you should make sure each student can read each sentence in isolation. After you have done this, you may cut the strips of sentences into words and recreate the original story by placing each word in the pocket chart.

11. Each time you meet with the group, read the previously written story and then write another one. Let this process continue until stories have been read many times and students know all, or nearly all, of the words as sight words.

12. As students grow in their ability to read, let them begin to write and illustrate their own stories. Then bind these into booklets and let the students illustrate the covers. Let students exchange booklets and read each others' stories.

13. Let students begin to read commercially written materials as their sight vocabulary and word attack skills permit.

IMPORTANT PROCEDURES AND INFORMATION ABOUT THE USE OF THE LANGUAGE-EXPERIENCE APPROACH

A. Teachers should remember these important procedures about the language experience approach:

1. When students dictate stories, attempt to use the exact language of the students.

2. Make sure that both you and the students point to each word as it is being read. Doing this in the beginning stages of using the language-experience approach ensures that each word is memorized as a separate entity as well as a part of an entire story.

3. Keep words clearly spaced, so children will soon understand the difference between *words* and *letters*.

4. In the beginning stages, be sure to use only one-line sentences and then gradually expand the length of the sentences as the students become more adept at reading.

5. Emphasize a series of events, if possible, so students will see the development of the story.

6. Use 24" × 36" chart paper, so capital letters are two inches high and lowercase letters are one inch high.

7. Make sure students see the words as they are being written.

8. Duplicate the chart, so children can take the materials home to be practiced with another member of the family.

9. Emphasize left-to-right direction and the return sweep in the writing and reading of the stories.

B. Keep in mind that there are certain limitations in the use of the language-experience approach. For example, a teacher using this approach almost exclusively is not likely to follow a sequential step-by-step program in teaching word attack skills. Many studies have shown that structured programs tend to produce better overall achievement from students. For this reason, you would probably want to use the language-experience approach in conjunction with a basal reader program or as a supplemental program for students with reading difficulties.

C. Different types of charts may be written in essentially the same manner as has been described in the preceding material. Some types of charts and their uses are as follows:

1. *Summarizing charts.* This chart shows a series of events on a field trip or a step-by-step procedure for doing an experiment in science.

2. *Story charts.* This chart describes an event in the life of a group or an individual.

3. *Planning charts.* This chart lists plans for such things as an anticipated trip, or some other event in which the entire class will participate.

4. *Direction charts.* This chart gives specific directions for the assembly of a toy or perhaps paper folding exercises.

5. *Dictionary charts.* This chart lists new words that have been learned in science, social studies, or other subject areas.

D. There has been considerable controversy over the shaping of the language of students who are using the language-experience approach. One of the premises upon which the language-experience approach is based is that what a student can say they can also read. Anyone who has used this approach will know that even a student who has experienced very little success in reading will nearly always be able to read back to the teacher what she has dictated and what has been written by the teacher. For students whose language is somewhat divergent from what might be considered standard English, the question sometimes arises as to whether or not the teacher should correct certain usage errors made by the student. It is the author's belief that in the beginning stages of reading, the teacher should use the exact language of the student, and when the student has reached a certain degree of sophistication in her reading, an attempt might then be made to correct grammatical errors. It is the author's experience that if an attempt is made to reword what the student has originally dictated to the teacher, then the student, when reading the material back to the teacher, is highly likely to read what was originally dictated rather than to read the material in its corrected form.

E. It should be remembered that unless students begin to read trade books and other types of materials after they have developed a reasonable sight vocabulary, their vocabularies will, of course, be limited to only those words in their speaking vocabularies. Therefore, students using the language-experience approach should be encouraged to read other materials as soon as it is feasible.

USING THE NEUROLOGICAL-IMPRESS METHOD

The use of the neurological-impress method was explained some years ago by R. G. Heckelman.* It has been extremely successful with students with reading difficulties, and it is easy to use. The neurological-impress method is, in fact,

---

* Heckelman, R. G. Using the neurological-impress remedial reading technique. *Academic Therapy Quarterly,* Summer 1966, 235–39.

so easy to use that teachers are often hesitant to do so. A procedure for its use is as follows:

1. Sit the student slightly in front of you, so you can point to the material the student is reading and so you can read directly into the student's ear.
2. Begin reading material that is at an easy instructional or independent reading level. As you continue to work with the student, you can increase the level of difficulty of the material.
3. Tell the student that you are going to read the material and that she is to read along with you as you point to the words. Then begin to read at a slightly slower than normal rate for you. While reading, be sure to point to each word as it is read. *This part of the procedure is extremely important.* The student may complain, at first, that she is unable to keep up with you. This should not, however, keep you from using the procedure. Explain to the student that she will become a better reader and will probably soon be able to keep up with you.
4. As you work with the student, you are likely to notice a sharp improvement in her ability to read. Begin to increase your rate of reading as the student's reading improves.
5. Read for periods of five to fifteen minutes two to four times per day. This method can be explained to parents, so they may use the same procedure while the student is at home. Heckelman suggests that it is common to cover from ten to twenty pages of materials in one session.
6. Heckelman suggests that if periods of approximately fifteen minutes are used, then the procedure should be continued until the student has read for an accumulated total of eight to twelve hours.

Heckelman has emphasized that in using this method you will probably see a great increase in the student's ability to read. He cautions that one of the teacher's most frequent mistakes is to spend too much time reading material written at low levels of difficulty because the teacher does not expect the student to learn so rapidly. For example, Heckelman says that if a student is started at the first-grade level, she might be expected to be reading in materials at the third-grade level after an accumulated total of two hours and that after an accumulated total of six hours, the student might be reading materials at the fifth- or sixth-grade level of difficulty.

Heckelman suggests that one of the reasons for the tremendous success that students often experience with the neurological-impress method is that the student is exposed to many words, many times, in a relatively short period of time. For example, a student reading for a period of approximately fifteen minutes may be exposed to from one to two thousand words.

Studies have been done in which teachers have tried to duplicate the neurological-impress method using tape-recorded materials and telling students to follow along with the tape-recorded reading. However, this has not produced results that are comparable to those obtained when working with a student in a one-to-one setting. This is probably because when a student is reading in conjunction with a tape recorder, you have no way of ensuring that the student is actually looking at the word being read. If the student is not actually looking at the word being read, then the student is not likely to benefit any more than if she were only listening to the passage.

COUNSELING TECHNIQUES THAT MAKE A DIFFERENCE

A number of studies have shown that the counseling aspects of working with students with reading difficulties contribute nearly as much to their gain in achievement as the teaching of the reading skills that are lacking. In the text that follows, some especially important aspects of the counseling program are presented. You need not be an "expert" to use these procedures. They have all been proven to be extremely beneficial. Various counseling procedures are broken down into the two categories of (1) interviewing the parent and (2) interviewing and counseling the student.

INTERVIEWING THE PARENT

Interviewing the parent or parents of a student with reading difficulties is important for several reasons. In the interview you will often be able to discover certain things that they may hesitate to put in writing. For example, in an interview parents will often give information concerning their perception of their child's capabilities. If the parents have other children, they will be able to give important information on their feelings concerning the student's ability to learn compared with their other children. This will provide the teacher with important information, not only about the student but also about the parents' feelings of the capabilities of the student. It is important that parents believe that their child *has* the ability to learn and that they are willing to do their part in carrying out a program of remediation in the home.

Parents can also provide accurate information on when they first noticed the reading problem. For example, if the student has had problems from the very beginning of school, it would indicate that the reading difficulties may be severe and take longer to remediate. However, if the student suddenly started having reading problems at a later grade level, then it might indicate that the student has developed some emotional problem because of a divorce, a death in the family, or some other traumatic event. The development of a reading problem might also indicate that there was an onset of a physical problem such as a need for glasses or the development of a lethargic feeling which could be caused from taking antihistamines for an allergy.

The initial interview should also reveal, to some extent, if counseling is needed. The parents may need guidance to help them make the child feel confident in her ability to learn. The parents, either consciously or unconsciously, may have given their child the impression that she does not have the ability to achieve at a normal rate. The parent interview can also provide important information on whether or not the parents have been consistent in dealing with the child. For example, do the parents tell their child to do something and then not carry through with requiring it to be done, or is the child allowed to find excuses for not performing certain tasks?

In the initial parents' interview, it is also important that you get a verbal commitment from the parents that they are willing to do such things as the following:

1. Set aside a *specific time* each evening when the student is required to do homework assignments or recreational reading.
2. Provide a reading environment in which the student sees her parents reading.
3. Provide a quiet place where the student can concentrate on homework or recreational reading without being interrupted by brothers or sisters or without interference from a television.
4. Check to see that homework is done.
5. Take the student to the library and learn techniques for selecting books to be read for pleasure.

INTERVIEWING AND COUNSELING THE STUDENT

In the initial interview of the student, it is important to determine if the student is aware of or will admit that she has a reading problem. This might be likened to the technique used in the organization of Alcoholics Anonymous. That is, a student who is not truly aware of her problem or who believes that she does not have a problem is going to be much more difficult to work with than a student who recognizes the presence of a problem.

In the beginning stages of the interview, the interviewer should first establish rapport with the student by talking about some neutral subject or by giving some kind of test that does not reflect on the intelligence of the student, such as an eye test. After the student has warmed to the interviewer, the following request might be made of the student, "Tell me about your reading." To reply, the student will not be able to give a short answer such as Yes, No, or I don't know. In some cases it may be necessary to ask more open-ended questions to get the student to respond. Ultimately, the interviewer wants to know if the student is aware of her reading problem.

If the student is aware of the problem and, after diagnostic testing, her perception of the problem is confirmed, then this part of the interviewing and counseling may be terminated. If the student is not aware of her problem or will not admit to having a problem, then counseling should be done to make the student aware of the problem. For example, if a student has a problem with word attack skills, you may wish to tape-record the reading of a passage and mark the student's oral reading errors. Then play the recording back to the student and point out the errors. In years past it was often believed that teachers should not point out problems that a student may have but only emphasize the good. The emphasis on the good is certainly a worthwhile procedure; but the author has found that once students admit to having a problem, they are more likely to be cooperative in correcting it.

Some students may take several sessions to actually admit having a reading problem. The goal of getting the student to admit to having a problem can be considered as met when the student verbalizes the nature of the problem when asked. Once you believe the student has recognized her problem, then wait for a period of time—for example, after doing some activity that may last for ten to twenty minutes. Then say to the student, "Now what do you think the problem with your reading really is?" After this, ask such questions as, "What do you think should be done about it?" When the student is able to verbalize the problem and has some idea as to what should be done about it, this part of the counseling procedure is complete.

The second important part of the counseling procedure is to find something upon which the problem can be blamed that does not reflect on the intelligence of the student. For example, when talking with the student, you may learn that she missed a month or two of schooling during the first or second grade; or that during the second or third grade, it was found that the student needed glasses because of an eye problem. If this is the case, you can tell the student that when a number of days of school is missed in the early grades, it often causes the student to have problems with her reading. It is not necessarily important that you actually find the cause of the problem but that you find something to blame it on that does not reflect on the intelligence of the student. It is also suggested that you make the student aware of the many things with which she has been successful. For example, the student may be good at playing video games or might have been very successful in assembling a new bicycle. Doing this will help the student overcome the fear that she is not intelligent and, therefore, has failed to learn and cannot learn now.

30

Using the Computer in Locating and Correcting Reading Difficulties

INTRODUCTION*

The use of computers for instruction is widely accepted today in American elementary and secondary schools. Historically, computer-related teaching has been applied in the natural sciences (especially mathematics and laboratory sciences). The primary emphasis of instructional computing in the latter part of this decade now lies in the area of language arts. As awareness of reading literacy in America gains momentum, technological discoveries highlighting the role of the computer in facilitating reading and writing become important.

LANGUAGE ARTS TEACHERS AND TECHNOLOGY

The priorities of language arts teachers in the use of computers in education differ from those of other classroom teachers, school administrators, and members of the community. These priorities are quite different than those of colleagues in the laboratory sciences, social studies, and special education, but are very similar to the priorities of mathematics teachers.

For example, language arts teachers desire teacher training that would lead to the use of computers in several areas (teaching, grade-reporting, testing, etc.) of classroom use. They also wish to participate in selecting specific goals for the use of computers in the classroom. However, language arts teachers do not feel that mandatory computer literacy instruction for both teachers and students should be a high priority. By contrast, special education teachers do not see the same level of importance for the first priority (computer integration). Science and business education teachers do not agree with the second priority (goal selection). Lastly, community members want more importance placed on computer literacy issues than do language arts teachers.

---

*The text on pages 189–192 has been written by Dr. Brent E. Wholeben of the Department of Educational Leadership and Counseling, University of Texas at El Paso. Dr. Wholeben is a nationally known authority on computer education.

You will also find that the needs of language arts teachers for computer use vary from elementary to secondary school. Elementary school reading teachers, for example, will desire that all students have an equal opportunity to use the computer for facilitating learning. However, secondary school language arts teachers will be more concerned with potential benefit than they will with equity; that is, students who will benefit more from classroom computer use will be afforded more opportunities to use computers than will other students.*

SELECTING AND ACQUIRING SOFTWARE AND HARDWARE

Regardless of your approach to the use of computers for teaching, and regardless of its potential benefit for the student, computer-assisted reading instruction will be seriously compromised if inappropriate courseware is used on inadequate hardware. Valid and reliable procedures must be followed to select the most useful instructional programs and machines.

Unfortunately, many schools today continue to select instructional computing equipment (especially hardware) because of special price discounts levied by vendors or manufacturers. A typical scenario would have the school *(1)* purchasing hardware because of a good price, *(2)* selecting from whatever instructional software is available for that particular machine, then *(3)* dropping everything into the lap of the classroom teacher as a packaged instructional module without providing specialized training to ensure its proper use. Such an approach to selection and acquisition prepares a fertile environment for possible misuse of the vast potential of the instructional computer. As an alternative to this more traditional approach, we suggest the following steps be followed.

Teacher Training

Before you do anything else, learn about the architecture of computers (especially microcomputers) in general, and about the use of computers in the classroom in particular. Read magazines, attend short courses at your local college or university, interview other teachers in your geographic area who use instructional computers, write your professional education association(s) for further information, and, finally, write to authors who have written on the subject of instructional computers (especially for teaching reading). If you do not have any foundation for the application of computers to classroom teaching,

---

* For a technical discussion of teachers' perceptions of priorities for educational computing policy related to instructional discipline of the teacher and grade-level of instruction, see: Wholeben, B. E. (1987). Policy profiles for ethics and equity in educational computing: Contrasting policy initiatives for strategic planning in social sciences (pp. 107–125). *Proceedings of the 1987 conference of the National Social Sciences Association.* El Cajon, CA: National Social Sciences Association.; and, Wholeben, B. E. (1987). Policy profiles for ethics and equity in educational computing: Contrasting middle school policy initiatives for strategic planning. *Research Annual: 1987 Selected Studies* (pp. 101–114). Columbus, OH: National Middle School Association.

you will be unable to fully comprehend the role instructional computers might play to satisfy your own needs.

Needs Assessment

Next, and possibly with the help of your colleagues and specialists at your district office, learn what your teaching needs encompass. Basically, this will include addressing *(1)* how you desire to utilize computers in the teaching of reading (e.g., introducing a topic, teaching a particular lesson, or evaluating individual student progress), *(2)* where such computer-assisted instruction might intervene (e.g., lesson plans that will include computerized methods), and *(3)* how computer-assisted techniques would complement other teacher-assisted tools (e.g., workbooks). The needs assessment is not simply an hour or two of reflective reasoning, nor is it coffee-break conversation with your colleagues. Most needs assessments have been known to require a large expenditure of time, and must be prepared well in advance, as you select and acquire your required materials and equipment. Without an accurate assessment of your instructional computing needs, you run the risk of seriously compromising the effective use of computers for the teaching of reading.

Software Selection

Once you have your needs firmly in mind, it is time to survey what instructional software (viz., courseware) is available on the market, at what price, and to what extent it fits your assessed needs. Surveying the variety of courseware packages on the market is becoming easier with the publication of massive software catalogs by many of the major educational software vendors. Finding out the price is always easy. Discovering the degree to which a software package fits your needs can, unfortunately, be an ordeal.

First, few courseware advertisements provide a detailed profile of the specific instructional objectives that dominate a particular courseware package. The few paragraphs on the back of the package are meant to draw attention to the product, show that this particular software does *everything* imaginable, and thereby increase the reader's interest in purchasing. However, remember that these are advertisements, not critical reviews, of a product that is on the market first, for profit, and second, for assisting teaching. Unless you actually experiment with the package yourself, you will learn little from the scant, written documentation accompanying the diskette or firmware module.

Selecting a computer-assisted instruction package is like selecting a textbook. You would never order a textbook for your class without first evaluating its contents and assessing the degree to which the text fits your instructional needs. Be prepared to learn that few software packages exist that will satisfy all of your individualized needs. In fact, it is quite common to discover two or three software programs that together satisfy your needs, but separately are insufficient. Finally, be wary of independent critiques of available software packages that are published in magazines or professional education journals—

you will note that every review sounds positive. Few, if any, of the negative reviews are ever published for subscribers.

Hardware Selection

Let us assume that you now recognize the utility of computer-assisted instruction in fulfilling some aspect of your objectives in teaching reading. After becoming somewhat computer-literate yourself, you might perform an extensive needs assessment of your reading program and your students. Next, and with the detailed results of your needs assessment in hand, you discover that no single courseware package will do everything that you want to do; rather, a combination of available software programs satisfies your needs adequately. And beyond this awareness that you seem to require more than one software package, you recognize that the particular software you want runs on different computer systems. You are now faced with the ultimate dilemma: which courseware packages will *best* suit your needs, assuming you will purchase only a single hardware system.

This is no different than the selection and purchase of any instructional tool. You will have to settle for the best mix of satisfied personal and instructional objectives that is available to you. Finally, you will have to temper your selection with the funds available for purchasing the necessary hardware *and* software.

CHOOSING PREVENTION OR CURE

You may now feel that the selection of instructional computing materials and equipment is a nightmare; it appears that some of your needs may never be satisfied, no matter how hard you work at it. You may be right. You could, of course, choose the more traditional path: buying first and asking questions later. You could also choose to ignore the opportunities of computer-assisted instruction, and decline to learn how computers might satisfy your professional objectives. But investing some time and *possible* frustration in selecting instructional computer materials will bring unimaginable rewards.

IMPORTANT POINTS TO REMEMBER WHEN USING THE COMPUTER IN LOCATING AND CORRECTING READING DIFFICULTIES

A. As mentioned in the introduction, whether educators like it or not, choice of whether or not we are to use computers is clear—they are here to stay. However, the technology in this field is changing so rapidly that what is written today will, in many cases, be outdated tomorrow. There is no doubt that the computer, with its ability to constantly provide instant feedback and interact with each student for each response, is such an overwhelming advantage in teaching that its use will continue to increase. However, the fact that the computer has appeared in both school and home settings so rapidly is already creating problems and will, no doubt, continue to do so. For example, the fact that so many programs have appeared so rapidly with little, and in some cases no, review and trial, has caused and will continue to cause disenchantment among those who are using them. Few textbooks used by students are marketed without going through some type of review process before they are printed in their final form. Yet, software continually appears on the market with little or no review or trial to ensure its usefulness.

B. Materials for the teaching of reading can be classified into three categories: those that *teach*, those that *test*, and those that provide *reinforcement*. A student is taught from a book that gives an explanation of how to do something that he wants to accomplish. Also, when a teacher explains a concept to students who knew nothing about that concept, then they have been taught. However, if students are given a workbook page over a lesson either on something that has not first been covered by the teacher or on something that they know nothing about, then the workbook page is simply a test. If the teacher had discussed the concept prior to assigning the page in the book, and the student was somewhat familiar with the subject matter, then the material would serve as a reinforcement for the concept that had just been taught. In working with materials (software) designed for use with computers, it is important to keep these three classifications in mind since many of the materials that now appear on the market, at best, serve as a reinforcement for concepts previously taught.

C. It is also important to keep in mind that many of the skills that are commonly tested in reading need to be tested in a situation that is the same as, or analogous to, actually using that skill in reading. In many cases this cannot be done in any other way than by the student giving an oral response. Since computer technology, at this time, does not allow the broad interpretation of students' oral responses, then many reading skills cannot be accurately tested with a computer. An example of this type of reading skill would be in testing students' knowledge of basic sight words. If you wish to know if a student knows how to pronounce a certain group of words, then you would need to show the student the words and have him pronounce them. In the testing of certain areas of phonics knowledge, the student must also make an oral response for the teacher to know if he really understands and can use phonics knowledge. This is explained fully in appendix K in the section that describes methods of testing phonics knowledge. Therefore, in using the computer in locating and correcting reading difficulties, one might want to ask such questions as the following:

1. Does the lesson *teach, test,* or *reinforce?*

2. If the lesson is expected to teach, does the student have the necessary background information and sight vocabulary for reading the lesson, so he will be able either to make the proper responses or to read responses that are corrected by the computer?

3. Is the student able to respond in the same manner he would in actually reading? Keep in mind that reading is *decoding,* and when a student writes an answer or chooses a number designating an answer, the student is *encoding.* The author has done considerable research that shows students who may be able to encode by using a certain skill would not be able to decode by using the same skill. Conversely, the student who may be able to decode using a certain skill may not be able to encode by using the same skill.

SPECIFIC WAYS OF USING COMPUTER-ASSISTED INSTRUCTION IN READING

As teachers and students in reading education become more familiar with computer hardware and software, they will develop more ways to use their knowledge in teaching reading. Here are some specific ways in which teachers and students can effectively make use of the computer.

FOR THE TEACHER

Administration or Record Management

One example of very useful programs available are those designed for record management and report writing for individual educational plans, as required by Public Law 94–142. Using this type of program can greatly facilitate an otherwise tedious job. Record management programs are also available for simply keeping an accurate inventory of books, of student attendance, or of materials available on specified subjects, and for managing data concerning students' progress through certain programs.

For the reading supervisor or reading consultant, the computer can assist in tracking funds allotted for specific purposes. It can record the names of teachers who are interested in in-service education on a specific subject and record the number of times they visit each classroom. At any time, the reading consultant or supervisor can then call up those names to invite the teachers to various in-service education sessions on the teaching of comprehension, word attack skills, vocabulary development, or whatever area in which the teacher expressed an interest.

Electronic Grading

Using the microcomputer for grading enables the teacher to generate many different types of reports easily, including somewhat detailed individual reports for parents. Electronic gradebooks usually allow the teacher to summarize the performance of the class on all or on specified tests. They also simplify many of the necessary calculations that were necessary in the past.

The Use of Readability Formulas

The use of the computer to determine the readability level of reading materials is already being widely used and will continue to be used even more in the future, especially as more reliable readability formulas become available.

Reading specialists who have used formulas now on the market are becoming aware of the varying results they receive in the application of more than one formula to the same reading passage. It is not uncommon to find that a passage may be rated as 7.5 by one formula while another may rate it a 3.0. These do not, of course, make the formulas any less valuable; however, they do tell us that there are more factors that we must consider in determining the readability level of a passage than sentence length or number of "hard" words. For example, the knowledge and interest that the reader brings to the passage is extremely important, but cannot be measured by readability formulas. The syntax, or way a writer chooses to string her words together, is also an important factor in determining the difficulty of a reading passage. However, syntax and a number of other variables are very difficult to measure.

Test Construction or Authoring Programs

Although teachers have generally had neither the time nor the inclination to learn programming languages, the use of software for test authoring has become feasible. There are now a number of software programs on the market that will enable the teacher to construct her own multiple-choice questions, cloze materials, as well as other designs such as true-false.

Materials are available for the development of various teaching procedures, including more elaborate branching programs. These can be extremely valuable to the reading teacher, but most teachers at this time will still find that the number of hours required to develop instructional materials makes the use of these programs somewhat impractical. This does not, however, imply that the technology is not available to anyone who wishes to pursue this avenue.

Word Processing

Many teachers will, of course, find that if the computer served no purpose other than that of being a word processor, it would still be an extremely valuable piece of equipment. Typing can be a great deal of pleasure when errors are so easily corrected. And because a number of printers will accept only mimeo stencils or ditto masters, the computer allows the teacher to print tests after she has written and proofread them and is relatively sure they are error-free.

FOR THE STUDENT

In an analysis of materials for teaching reading and the other language arts, you are likely to find that materials designed for student use can be classified under the following categories: alphabet, comprehension (including critical reading), placement testing, speed reading, spelling, study skills, vocabulary development, word attack, and writing.

Alphabet

There are computer programs to cover many aspects of learning and using the alphabet. Programs include those for matching uppercase and lowercase letters, learning alphabetizing skills, writing the letters properly, practicing visual discrimination of numbers and letters, and learning sounds through the use of voice synthesizers.

Comprehension

In working with materials in the area of comprehension, as well as in other areas, one should be aware that some materials teach, some test, and others reinforce. In the author's opinion, the best types of materials are those that actually teach. Unfortunately, in the area of comprehension all too many of the available programs only test or, at best, reinforce. For example, there are quite a number of programs that make use of the cloze procedure for the improvement of comprehension. Research on the use of the cloze procedure indicates that it is usually beneficial to students and will, if used enough, improve their overall ability to comprehend. Other programs ask the student to make choices about cause and effect or various answers concerning critical reading. Most of these, however, do not actually teach the student *how* to do these skills. For the most part, one has to assume that if the student answers enough of these types of questions, then she will learn to read critically and learn cause and effect on her own. In many cases, this may be a false assumption.

Critical Reading

In reviewing materials for the development of critical reading, as stated in the previous section, you should take note of whether the materials actually teach the student how to read critically or whether the student is simply expected to learn these skills from repeated questioning. Because critical reading is usually considered to be a higher-level skill than simple recall, one might assume that students using this type of program would be the more proficient readers. It is, of course, easier to develop materials for students who read well since they can read *why* their answers are or are not correct.

Placement Testing

The computer can be helpful to the teacher in testing some types of skills. However, you should keep in mind that when a student is tested for a skill, she should be doing the same thing in the testing situation that she would be doing when actually using the skill. For example, the best way to test a student for knowledge of the /b/ sound is to show her a *b* in some configuration (see the El Paso Phonics Survey) and ask her to give the sound that *b* represents. Testing many reading skills with the computer is difficult because the student is able only to encode and cannot decode. There are, of course, computer testing situations in which the student can respond similarly to the ways she would in a normal testing situation. For example, the student can read a passage and then answer questions just as she would do on a standardized reading achievement test. The computer, of course, has the advantage of being able to score the test immediately with little or no room for human error.

Perhaps the most important point to keep in mind when using the computer for placement of students is whether the information derived will place the student in a certain level, or in a certain set of skills, that will ultimately make her a better reader. A test should never be given unless the results of that test will ultimately affect the type of instruction the student is to receive.

Speed Reading

The computer is an excellent device for presenting material at a rapid pace to the student for the purpose of increasing reading speed. Students receiving this type of practice usually raise their reading speed. However, various research studies done over the years have shown that tachistoscopic devices were no more valuable, and in most studies less valuable, than simply telling the student to pace her reading with her hand. That is, when students were told to move their hand across each line slightly faster than they would normally read and to allow the hand to pace the eye, they were soon able to increase their reading speed. In fact, this type of instruction allows the student to pace herself, which is often desirable in this type of practice. On the other hand, the computer can serve as an excellent motivator. In evaluating this type of program, note whether the speeds are easily adjustable and whether the flow of the print seems to be natural. Some speed reading programs, depending on the format, tend to break in places other than natural phrasing or thought units.

Spelling

One of the major advantages of using the computer in the teaching of spelling is that it can take a student, at a comfortable pace, through as many words as she can master in a given amount of time. For those students who need extra drill, the computer can also present many repetitions of words in various formats. Some people believe that the computer does not lend itself to a phonetic approach in spelling. The use of more and better voice synthesizers in the future should, to some extent, allow the computer to present spelling more phonetically.

Study Skills

Computer programs are available for teaching, testing, and/or reinforcement of such study skills as alphabetizing, learning to use a table of contents and index, using guide words in the dictionary, outlining, using the library card catalog, learning to read schedules or timetables, and learning to select the best reference or word meaning in the dictionary.

Vocabulary Development

There are many programs available for testing, teaching, and/or reinforcement of vocabulary. Many of these use homonyms, antonyms, and synonyms as well as drill on prefixes and suffixes. Some programs focus on abbreviations, contractions, plurals, and word families. Words are presented in context as well as out of context. We know that vocabulary words are learned best when they are presented in a meaningful setting such as a field trip. In purchasing software, you should look for vocabulary development programs that present words in many settings or in a variety of activities.

Word Attack

Many computer programs are now available for improving students' ability to use word attack skills. However, very few of these programs actually teach students to become more adept at word attack. Perhaps a term that would be more appropriate for many of the programs would be *electronic workbooks*. There are, however, a number of programs that appear to be worthwhile, and students who are disabled readers can benefit from the use of them. A definite advantage of using the computer in this area is that students are given instant feedback.

Writing

A number of programs are now available for helping students develop their ability to write. Programs designed for word processing enable students to edit their material easily and develop their writing style. Programs stress such things as sentence logic, proofreading, correction of phrases frequently misused, creative writing, sentence mechanics, parts of speech, and punctuation skills. Some of the programs that present sentence combining exercises are also helpful in developing students' ability to comprehend.

A look at a computer software directory will reveal that a great deal of material is available. However, keep in mind that the use of poor quality materials not only wastes the students' time, but also usurps time that could have been spent more wisely. For this reason it is extremely important that you, as a potential or practicing teacher, learn how to evaluate both computer software and computer hardware. Both of these topics are covered in the material that follows.

THE EVALUATION OF COMPUTER SOFTWARE

You are likely to want the same features in computer software that you would want in any good program for locating and correcting reading difficulties. However, in order to make an intelligent decision, it is necessary to know some of the capabilities of a computer in relation to traditional reading materials. The information that follows should help you to understand some of the capabilities and limitations of the computer in relation to the teaching of reading.

Computer software could logically be divided into three categories—*(1)* for management or record keeping, *(2)* as a supplement to the regular reading program, or *(3)* as the main reading program. Remember that there are essentially three main kinds of reading materials—those that teach, those that test, and those that reinforce. In evaluating computer software, you should first decide whether you are considering the purchase of the materials for managing your reading program, for supplementing it, or for using it as a main curriculum (which will be doubtful, in the case of locating and correcting reading difficulties). In reading the description of the materials, or more likely in evaluating materials as you use them on a computer, you should decide how you might use them—to *teach,* to *test,* or to *reinforce.*

Following are some characteristics you may wish to consider, as well as questions you may wish to ask in evaluating reading software.

PURCHASING OF SOFTWARE

1. The cost of the materials is, of course, an important factor. If the materials are quite expensive, then you would want to spend more time evaluating them. However, regardless of cost, an inexpensive program that is of little value should never be considered as an alternative to a more expensive program that meets all or most of the characteristics of an excellent teaching program.
2. In addition to the cost, you should consider whether or not the distributor will allow you to return materials that you do not deem worthwhile.
3. A number of writers suggest that most programs you purchase (especially the more expensive ones) should have been on the market for at least a year.
4. It is best to purchase from software companies that are well-known and have been in business for a considerable length of time.
5. When purchasing a major program, make sure the dealer will either allow you to return older versions of the program or give you a discount on the purchase of updated ones as they become available.

6. Purchase only programs that have been tested and proven worthwhile.
7. Purchase only materials for which you can either make a backup copy or purchase a second backup copy at a considerable discount.
8. Was the material developed by someone well-known in the field of reading, or was the material developed by a team of reading and computer consultants? Most programmers do not have adequate knowledge in the field of reading, and many people in reading do not have adequate experience in programming. A program that combines the skills of a programmer, a reading expert, and an instructional expert would therefore be ideal.

Teacher's Manual or Directions

1. Are the objectives for the program listed, so you will know exactly what is to be covered?
2. Is information given on the entry level of the student in terms of grade level or previous skills that the student should have acquired?
3. Are some sample frames shown, so that you will have some idea of the general format?
4. Are the directions for use of the materials clear and understandable?
5. Is information provided on minimum and maximum times that students will need to complete various lessons?
6. Are the directions for the student clear and at a reading level appropriate for the grade level of the skills taught? (This refers to any written materials that accompany the program. This same question should be asked of the material that appears on the screen—see Program Characteristics.)

Program Characteristics

1. If the program is linear, is the material in proper sequence? Most programs currently on the market are programmed in a linear sequence. In this type of programming, a student must go through a certain sequence of lessons or steps regardless of how well he performs on each step.
2. If the program is of the branching type, does it provide for a number of options? (For example, a program that is of the branching type should allow the student to move ahead into more difficult material or move back into easier material as needed.)
3. If some type of written material is necessary as a follow-up, is it provided with the program?
4. Does the lesson provide prompts or hints for answers with which the student is experiencing difficulty?
5. Are the contents free of any racial or sexual bias?

6. Is this program a more effective way of presenting the information than other materials that may be less costly and more easily obtained?
7. Can the student load (boot) the program without having an extensive knowledge of the use of microcomputers?

User Control

1. Can the student determine the entry point, in terms of difficulty, of the materials being presented?
2. If the student cannot determine the entry point, can the teacher realistically determine the proper entry point?
3. Can the student skip over material that he already knows or increase the rate at which it is presented? (Keep in mind that this option exists with a book and that this, along with the ability of the computer to interact with the student, should be two of the most important features of a computer.)
4. Can the student exit the program and reenter at another time?
5. Can the student review the directions if necessary?

Feedback Characteristics

1. Feedback should be designed so that the student knows whether he has made the right or wrong response; and if it would be helpful, depending upon the concept being taught, the student should be told why a certain response is wrong.
2. Feedback should be positive; i.e., the student should be given praise for right answers but should not be scolded for those answers that are not right.
3. Praise or reinforcement should come only periodically, for best results. If the student is praised after each correct response, it will become somewhat meaningless.
4. Is the type of feedback appropriate for the age-grade level of the student?

User Friendliness

1. Can the student easily understand the directions on the screen?
2. Can the student move from one part of a program to another without going through long, elaborate directions? (For example, a user friendly program might ask the student, "Do you wish to go to an easier question?" At this point the prompt *Y/N* might appear. If the student had been answering a number of questions wrong, he might then go to an easier part of the program by pressing the *Y* key for *yes*.

Graphics

1. Do the graphics add to or detract from the presentation of the material being taught?
2. Are the graphics in color?
3. Are the graphics appropriate for the grade level of the student?
4. Graphics *should not be* such that a wrong response will bring forth a more colorful or interesting display than a correct response.
5. Is the program free from violence or imitation of violent games used in arcades? (It should be.)

Evaluation System

1. Does the program have its own evaluation system?
2. Is there a record of student performance that will be useful to the teacher?
3. Does the program collect and store data and then prescribe appropriate lessons based on the student's performance?
4. What are the criteria for successfully completing the material?
5. Can the teacher transfer certain information to other programs to keep an overall record of a student's performance?
6. Can a particular student's record of performance be printed?

Compatibility

1. Will the software operate on your computer?
2. Does your computer have sufficient memory for the program? (A program designed for a 64K computer will not run on a computer with less memory.)
3. Does the program run on a computer using the same language as yours?

Peripheral Requirements

1. Does the program require a printer?
2. Does the program require a voice synthesizer?
3. Does it require one or two disk drives? (Some computers use a cassette to store information. Information stored on a cassette is more difficult to retrieve than information stored on a disk because of the tape recorder's slow speed; therefore, it is highly recommended that cassettes not be considered for serious instructional programs in the school setting.)

THE EVALUATION OF COMPUTER HARDWARE

Probably the worst mistake a user can make is to purchase a computer and then find that there is very little computer software available for that computer. For this reason the author would emphasize that before considering the purchase of a computer, you should look at one of the more comprehensive software directories listed under *Educational Software Directories* to see what software is available for whatever you wish to teach. It will take only a minute or so to decide that most of the educational software that is available is for use on only a few brands of computers. After deciding what software you would like to use, you should then consider some of the following factors in choosing a computer:

1. Is the dealer reputable and how long has the company been in business?
2. Does the dealer have a service plan?
3. What is the memory capacity of the computer? Will it handle all of the programs that you are likely to use?
4. Do you need one disk drive or two disk drives? Many programs require two disk drives, and in some cases, it would be difficult to duplicate disks without two disk drives.
5. If any programming is to be done, it is important to know what languages the computer uses.
6. What peripherals are available for each computer, and which are you likely to need?
7. How large is the screen display? Most computers range in width from twenty to eighty characters, and the length of the display tends to run from 16 to 32 lines. However, on word processors the screen display length may be up to 54 lines or more.
8. Do you need a color monitor? If most of the programs you will run are in color, you will need a color monitor. However, if most of the programs are in black and white, you may actually get a better image quality with a black and white or other monochrome monitor.
9. What is the quality of the graphics on the monitor? The greater the number of dots on the monitor screen, the better your image will be.
10. Does the computer have built-in sound or music available? On some programs this is a necessity.
11. What is the cost of the computer in relation to that of comparable models?

After looking at numerous computers, you may wish to make an evaluation sheet for each computer to help you make your decision. Different factors will be worth different weights, depending upon which factors you think are most important. Using the factors listed above, your evaluation sheet for a particular computer might appear as follows.

COMPUTER EVALUATION SHEET

Brand of Computer _____ Dealer _____ Date _____

Factors	Factor Number†	X	Computer Rating*	=	Weighted Score
1. Dealer reputation	3		2		6
2. Dealer service plan	4		4		16
3. Memory capacity	5		5		25
4. Number of drives	5		5		25
5. Languages	3		2		6
6. Peripherals available	4		2		8
7. Screen display	3		1		3
8. Color monitor	3		3		9
9. Graphics	2		1		2
10. Sound/Music	3		3		9
11. Cost	5		3		15
			Final Score ____		124

†The factor number used in this case was arbitrarily picked between one and five with five being extremely important and numbers less than five being of less importance. The factor number would have to be derived by the user depending upon his needs.

*The computer rating is your rating based on what you can determine about each of the eleven factors listed. Again, a rating scale of 1–5 was used with five being an excellent or superior rating and one being the lowest possible rating.

In evaluating the final score you may find that two or three brands of computers have nearly the same score. On the other hand, you may find that others vary by 20 to 30 points. If the final scores are within a very close range (perhaps 2–6 or slightly more), you may wish to reexamine various factors in relation to the numbers assigned to them as well as the computer rating and the numbers assigned to this category. Your ultimate decision will, of course, need to be made on the basis of the factors and computer ratings that you feel are most important in your own teaching situation.

COMPUTER TERMINOLOGY

Access Time   The amount of time it takes a computer to retrieve a word or other information from memory.

Applications Software   Software written to perform a specific task; for example, mailing list, spelling checker, or inventory.

Back Up   A second copy of information in a program or of information generated by a computer.

Bit   The contraction of Binary Digit. A bit always has the value of zero or one. Bits are universally used in electronic systems to encode information, orders (instructions), and data. Bits are usually grouped in nybbles (four), bytes (eight), or larger units. Computers are classified by bits, e.g., 8, 16, 32 bits.

Byte A byte on a computer would be the same as any one piece of information that you might find on a typewriter keyboard. Therefore, a byte would be a number, a letter, or some type of symbol.

CAI Computer aided instruction.

Central Processing Unit This is the brain of the computer. The central processing unit contains tiny chips that enable the computer to process information.

Character Any number, symbol, letter, etc., that can be transmitted as output by the computer.

Character Printer A printer that prints whole characters such as numbers, letters, punctuation marks, etc. Character printers usually print in a good quality similar to a typewriter.

Command An order given to a computer to enable it to process information. A command might be in the form of typing *Y* for *yes, N* for *no, escape,* or *return.*

Computer Memory Computer memory can be classified into two main categories—*internal* memory and *external* memory. Internal memory is put there by the manufacturer and is ready to operate when the machine is turned on (booted). The computer may be designed to hold a certain amount of information that is programmed into its memory after it is turned on (booted). For example, a computer may be designed to run on Applesoft Basic when it is turned on. It may also be programmed for other computer languages by the use of a disk. Memory that is put there by the manufacturer is referred to as *read only memory* (ROM). It cannot be changed or added to by the user. Memory may be stored in a computer until the computer is turned off. This type of memory is referred to as *random access memory* (RAM). Unless this information is stored on an external device before the computer is turned off, it is lost. External memory is usually stored on disks or diskettes. Information may be on a disk when you purchase it, or it may be put on a disk by the user. Disks with information on them when you purchase them are referred to as *software programs.*

CP/M (Control Program/Monitor) One of a number of computer operating systems.

CPU (Central Processing Unit) The brain or processing unit of a computer.

Daisy Wheel Printer A printer that uses a round wheel with spokes like those on a typewriter, at the end of which are characters.

Data The information that is processed by a computer.

Data Base This usually refers to a computer program designed to keep track of and manipulate various kinds of data.

Dedicated A computer used for a specific purpose. For example, some computers are designed to be used mainly for word processing. This usually enables them to be operated more efficiently than computers used for a myriad of purposes.

Disk This usually refers to a memory storage device that looks much like a thick record album. Most disks are designed for large business computers and will hold considerably more information than a diskette. (Disks are usually considered to be *hard,* and diskettes are referred to as *soft* or *floppy* disks.)

Diskette This also is a memory storage device that looks somewhat like a 45-rpm record album. Diskettes may be either *hard* or *floppy.* A hard disk, as the name implies, would not bend easily. On the other hand, a diskette that is floppy is flexible and will bend rather easily. At the present time most diskettes are either $3\frac{1}{2}$, $5\frac{1}{4}$, or a few are 8 inches in diameter.

Dot Matrix This is a type of printer that imprints images using a matrix of dots. A better-quality printer would have more dots per square inch than one costing less.

File A set of information contained on a storage device such as a hard disk or a diskette; similar to a manila file folder that separates information from that in another file folder.

Hard Copy Material printed on paper (as contrasted with material stored electronically).

Hardware This term refers to all of the larger (hard) parts of the system, such as the printer, keyboard, disk drives, voice synthesizer, telephone modem, monitor, and the like.

K This refers to one thousand bytes of information. Thus, a 64K computer will hold 64,000 numbers, letters, or symbols.

Keyboard This is a device, much like the keyboard of a typewriter, that sends commands to the computer.

Kilobyte One thousand bytes—more precisely, 1024 bytes.

LCD Liquid crystal display.

LED Light emitting diode.

Letter Quality Printer A printer that is said to have the quality one would generally expect from a good quality typewriter. Most printwheel printers would be considered to be letter quality.

Light Pen A device designed to read electronically encoded symbols or to record emission of light from a source such as a computer screen.

Menu A listing of commands available for a certain program. A menu for a computer program for readability might be as follows: Do a New Passage? Show Statistics? Use Different Formula?

Modem A device that receives or sends audible tones from/to a telephone line and transforms them into electrical impulses to then send/receive to/from the computer.

Monitor This is a device that looks much the same as the screen of a television. However, monitors that are made for computers will usually be of better quality, especially in terms of the print that appears on the screen.

Music Synthesizer A device that reproduces musical tones from the output of a computer.

Nybble Usually four bits, or one-half byte.

Output This is the information that comes out of a computer. It may be displayed on a monitor that looks much like a television screen, it may be printed, or it may go out over a telephone line using a modem.

Peripherals These are pieces of hardware that may be added to a computer, such as a printer, disk drives, a telephone modem, and the like.

Permanent Storage Storage device in which records would not be lost by shutting down a computer. Hard disks or diskettes would be considered as permanent storage for information, although they could be erased.

Program Language Computers operate by using a base two, or binary, number system. (In the United States we use a base ten system which, of course, contains the numerals 0–9.) In order to make communicating with computers easier because of long numbers that would be involved in a base two number system, we use program languages. The most common one used in school software is some form of BASIC. The acronym BASIC stands for Beginner's All-Purpose Symbolic Instruction Code. It should be stressed that there are several forms of BASIC; one company's computer that used BASIC might not be compatible with another company's computer that also uses BASIC. Other computing languages arc COBAL, PASCAL, and FORTRAN.

Random Access Memory (RAM)   *See Computer Memory.*

Read Only Memory (ROM)   *See Computer Memory.*

Software   A program, usually on a disk or diskette, that is designed to teach, test, or reinforce a concept. Occasionally, cassettes (the same type used to record music) are still used for program storage. Information is retrieved much more slowly from a cassette, however, than from a disk. Therefore, the use of a disk or diskette is highly preferred over the use of cassettes.

User Friendly   This refers to a program that enables someone new to its operation to function without making serious mistakes or becoming frustrated because of the program's inability to communicate easily with the user.

Voice Synthesizer   A device designed to reproduce a likeness of the human voice from the output of a computer.

SOURCES OF SOFTWARE REVIEWS

Chime Newsletter
Clearinghouse of Information
On Microcomputers in Ed. OSU
108 Gunderson
Stillwater, OK 74078

Courseware Report Card
150 West Carob Street
Compton, CA 90200

The CUE Card
Software Reviews, Teacher
1314 Normandy Drive
Modesto, CA 95351

Curriculum Review
517 South Jefferson
Chicago, IL 60607

EPIE Micro-Courseware PRO/FILES
P.O. Box 839
Water Mill, NY 11976

The Journal of Reading
(Computer Software Reviews)
International Reading Association
800 Barksdale Road, P.O. Box 8139
Newark, DE 19714–8139

Media & Methods
1511 Walnut Street
Philadelphia, PA 19102

MicroSIFT Courseware Evaluation
Northwest Regional Ed. Lab.
101 S.W. Main Street, Suite 500
Portland, OR 97204

The Reading Teacher
(Computer Software Reviews)
International Reading Association
800 Barksdale Road, P.O. Box 8139
Newark, DE 19714

School Library Journal
P.O. Box 1978
Marion, OH 43305

SECTOR
Exceptional Children Center
Utah State University
Logan, UT 84321

Software Reports
Trade Service Publications
10996 Torreyana Road
San Diego, CA 92121

Teaching and Computers
Scholastic
P.O. Box 2038
Mahopac, NY 10541

Whole Earth Review
27 Gate Five Road
Sausalito, CA 94965

COMPANIES THAT PUBLISH OR DISTRIBUTE COMPUTER SOFTWARE MATERIALS FOR USE IN EDUCATION

Academic Hallmarks
P.O. Box 998
Durango, CO 81301

Advanced Ideas, Inc.
2902 San Pablo Avenue
Berkeley, CA 94702

Agency for Instructional Technology
P.O. Box A
Bloomington, IN 47402

Ahead Designs
699 North Vulcan
Encinitas, CA 92024

Apple Computer, Inc.
Customer Relations
MS 18-F
220525 Mariani Avenue
Cupertino, CA 95014

Aquarius Instructional™
P.O. Box 128
Indian Rocks Beach, FL 33535

Avalon Hills
Microcomputer Games
4517 Hartford Road
Baltimore, MD 21214

A/V Concepts Corporation
30 Montauk Boulevard
Oakdale, NY 11769

A.V. Systems
1445 Estrella Drive
Santa Barbara, CA 93110

B5 Software
Great Western
3355 South Boulevard
Columbus, OH 43204

Bainum Dunbar, Inc.
6427 Hillcroft
Suite 133
Houston, TX 77081

Bantam Software
666 Fifth Avenue
New York, NY 10103

Barnell Loft Publications
958 Church Street
Baldwin, NY 11510

Bede Software, Inc.
P.O. Box 2053
Princeton, NJ 08540

BLS
203 Fairlee Road
Wilmington, DE 19810

R. R. Bowker
245 West 17th Street
New York, NY 10011

Brain Bank, Inc.
220 Fifth Avenue
Suite 408
New York, NY 10001

Broderbund Software
17 Paul Drive
San Rafael, CA 94903

Bytes of Learning
Suite 202
150 Consumers Road
Willowdale, Ontario, Canada M2J1P9

Cardinal Software
14840 Build America Drive
Woodbridge, VA 22191

College Skills Center
Department 875501
320 West 29th Street
Baltimore, MD 21211

Commodore Buyers Guide
P.O. Box 651
Holmes, PA 19043

COMPress
P.O. Box 102
Wentworth, NH 03282

ComputAbility Corporation
The Handicapped's Source
101 Route 46
Pine Brook, NJ 07058

COMPU-tations
P.O. Box 502
Troy, MI 48099

Computer Assisted Instruction, Inc.
6115 28 Street, SE
Grand Rapids, MI 49506

Computer Curriculum Corporation
P.O. Box 10080
Palo Alto, CA 94303

Computer Curriculum Corporation
1701 West Euless Blvd.
Suite 139
Euless, TX 76039

Computer Island
227 Hampton Green
Staten Island, NY 10312

Conduit
The University of Iowa
Oak Dale Campus
Iowa City, IA 52242

Control Data Publishing Company, Inc.
800 Queen Avenue South
Box 1305
Minneapolis, MN 55440–1305

Cross Educational Software
1802 North Trenton Street
P.O. Box 1536
Ruston, LA 71270

CSR Computer Systems Research
Avon Park South
P.O. Box 45
Avon, CT 06001

Cue Softswap
P.O. Box 271704
Concord, CA 94527

Curriculum Applications
P.O. Box 264
Arlington, MA 12174

Dale Seymore Publications
P.O. Box 10888
Palo Alto, CA 94303

Davidson & Associates
3135 Kashiwa Street
Torrance, CA 90505

DC Heath Company
125 Spring Street
Lexington, MA 02173

DEC Computing
5307 Lynnwood Drive
West Lafayette, IN 47906

DLM Teaching Resources
P.O. Box 4000
One DLM Park
Allen, TX 75002

Dormac, Inc.
P.O. Box 752
Beaverton, OR 97075

Dorsett Courseware
P.O. Box 1226
Norman, OK 73070

Educational Activities, Inc.
P.O. Box 392
Freeport, NY 11520

Educational Resources
2354 Hassel Road, Suite B
Hoffman Estates, IL 60195

Educational Software & Marketing
   Company
1630 South State Street
Suite 101
Springfield, IL 62704

Educulture, Inc.
1 CyCare Plaza
Suite 805
Dubuque, IA 52001–9990

EduSoft
P.O. Box 2560
Berkeley, CA 94701

Electronic Learning
Scholastic, Inc.
P.O. Box 2041
Mahopac, NY 10541–9964

EMC Publishing
Changing Times Education Service
300 York Avenue
Saint Paul, MN 55101

Follett Software
4506 Northwest Highway
Crystal Lake, IL 60014

Friendlee Software
6041 West View Drive, Suite G
Orange, CA 92669

Gamco Industries, Inc.
P.O. Box 1862W
Big Spring, TX 79721

George Earl Software
1302 South General McMullen
San Antonio, TX 78237

Grolier Electronic Publishing
95 Madison Avenue
New York, NY 10016

Harcourt Brace Jovanovich, Publishers
1250 Sixth Avenue
San Diego, CA 92101

Hartley Courseware
P.O. Box 431
Dimondale, MI 48821

Hartley Courseware
133 Bridge Street, Box 419
Dimondale, MI 48821

Hoffman Educational Systems
1720 Flower Avenue
Duarte, CA 91010

Houston Independent School District
Center for Educational Technology
5300 San Felipe
Houston, TX 77056

HRM Software
175 Tompkins Avenue
Pleasantville, NY 10570

INET Corporation
8450 Central Avenue
Newark, CA 94560

Instructional/Communications-
    Technology, Inc.
10 Stepar Plaza
Huntington Station, NY 11746

InterLearn
P.O. Box 342
Cardiff by the Sea, CA 92007

Jagdstaffel Software
645 Brenda Lee Drive
San Jose, CA 95123

Kapstrom Educational Software
5952 Royal Lane, Suite 124
Dallas, TX 75230

Laureate Learning Systems
110 East Spring Street
Winooski, VT 05404

The Learning Company
545 Middlefield Road, Suite 170
Menlo Park, CA 94025

Learning Research Associates
P.O. Box 39, Dept. 8
Roslyn Heights, NY 11577

Learning Well
200 South Service Road
Roslyn Heights, NY 11577

Little Shaver Software
267 Bel Forest Drive
Belleair Bluffs, FL 33540

Living Videotext
2432 Charleston Road
Mountain View, CA 94043

Logo Computer Systems
121 Mt. Vernon Street
Boston, MA 02108–9957

MCE, Inc.
157 South Kalamazoo Mall, 250
Kalamazoo, MI 49007

MECC
3490 Lexington Avenue North
St. Paul, MN 55126

Media & Methods
1511 Walnut Street
Philadelphia, PA 19102

Media Basics, Inc.
Larchmont Plaza
Larchmont, NY 10538

Media Materials
2936 Remington Avenue
Baltimore, MD 21211

Merit Audio Visual
P.O. Box 392
New York, NY 10024

Mic-Ed Incorporated
8108 Eden Road
Eden Prairie, MN 55344

Micro Power & Light
12820 Hillcrest Road, #120
Dallas, TX 75230

Micro-Ed, Inc.
P.O. Box 444005
Eden Prairie, MN 55344

Micromedia Software
276 Oakland Street
Wellesley, MA 02181

Microphys Programs, Inc.
1737 West Second Street
Brooklyn, NY 11223

Midwest Educational Software
P.O. Box 214
Farmington, MI 48024

Midwest Publications
P.O. Box 448
Pacific Grove, CA 93950

Mindscape, Inc.
(Educational Division)
3444 Dundee Road
Northbrook, IL 60062

Northwest Regional Educational
Laboratory
101 Southwest Main Street
Suite 500
Portland, OR 97204

Orange Cherry Software
P.O. Box 390
Pound Ridge, NY 10576

PLATO Education Services Marketing
8800 Queen Avenue, South
Minneapolis, MN 55431

Precision Software
3452 North Ride Circle
Jacksonville, FL 32217

Prentice-Hall
Software
Englewood Cliffs, NJ 07632

The Psychological Corporation
555 Academic Court
San Antonio, TX 78204

Queue, Inc.
562 Boston Avenue
Bridgeport, CT 06610

Radio Shack
(Education Division)
1600 One Tandy Center
Ft. Worth, TX 76102

Random House
(School Division)
Department 436
400 Hahn Road
Westminster, MD 21157

Research Design Associates
P.O. Box 848
Stony Brook, NY 11790

Resource Software International
330 New Brunswick Avenue
Fords, NJ 08863

Right On Programs
1736 Veteran's Memorial Highway
Central Islip, NY 11722

Scholastic Book Services
P.O. Box 1068
Jefferson City, MO 65102

Scholastic Software
Scholastic Inc.
730 Broadway
New York, NY 10003

Scholastic, Inc.
P.O. Box 7501
2931 East McCarty St.
Jefferson City, MO 65102

Helen J. Schwartz
English Department
Carnegie-Mellon University
Pittsburgh, PA 15213

Science Research Associates
155 N Wacker Drive
Chicago, IL 60606

Sensible Software
210 S Woodward
Suite 229
Birmingham, MI 48011

Silver Burdett & Ginn
P.O. Box 2649
4343 Equity Drive
Columbus, OH 43216

Society for Visual Education, Inc.
1345 Diversey Parkway
Department VM
Chicago, IL 60614–1299

SOFTSWAP
San Mateo Office of Education
333 Main Street
Redwood City, CA 94063

Software Reports
A Division of Trade Service
10996 Torreyana Road
San Diego, CA 92121

Softwriters Development Corporation
4718 Harford Road
Baltimore, MD 21214

South Coast Writing Improvement
Project
University of California
Santa Barbara, CA 93106

Southwest Ed Psych Services
P.O. Box 1870
Phoenix, AZ 85001

Speco Educational Sales
3208 Daniels, Suite #6
Dallas, TX 75205

Spin-a-Test Publishing Company
3177 Hogarth Drive
Sacramento, CA 95827

Springboard Software, Inc.
7807 Creekridge Circle
Minneapolis, MN 55435

Sunburst Communication, Inc.
Room HG 31
39 Washington Avenue
Pleasantville, NY 10570–9971

Teach Yourself by Computer Software
2128 Jefferson Road
Pittsford, NY 14534

Teacher Support Software
P.O. Box 7130
Gainesville, FL 32605–7125

Teacher's College Press
TC, Columbia University
New York, NY 10027

The Teaching Assistant
22 Seward Drive
Huntington Station, NY 11746

Thinking Networks, Inc.
P.O. Box 6124
New York, NY 10128

Treehouse Publishing Company
P.O. Box 35461
Phoenix, AZ 85069

Triton Products Company
P.O. Box 8123
San Francisco, CA 94128

Troll Associates
100 Corporate Drive
Mahwah, NJ 07498

Tyson Educational Systems, Inc.
P.O. Box 2478
Miami, FL 33055

Weaver Instructional Systems
6161 28th Street, SE
Grand Rapids, MI 49506

Whole Earth Software Catalog
Quantam Press/Doubleday
Garden City, NY 11530

Zephyr Services
306 South Homewood Avenue
Pittsburgh, PA 15208

MAGAZINES WITH INFORMATION ABOUT COMPUTERS AND SOFTWARE

A+
Ziff-Davis Publishing Company
One Park Avenue
New York, NY 10016

ACADEMIC COMPUTING
Academic Computing Publications, Inc.
200 West Virginia
McKinney, TX 75069

Apple II Review
Redgate Communications
3381 Ocean Drive
Vero Beach, FL 32968

The CAD/CAM Journal
For the Macintosh Professional
Koncepts Graphic Images, Inc.
16 Beaver Street
New York, NY 10004

COMPUTE
Compute Publications, Inc.
324 West Wendover Avenue
Suite 200
Greensboro, NC 27408

COMPUTE
Compute Publications, Inc.
P.O. Box 10955
Des Moines, IA 50347–0955

COMPUTER WORLD
375 Cochituate Road, Route 30
Framington, MA 01701

EDUCOM
(Bulletin)
Computer Literacy Project
777 Alexander Road, P.O. Box 364
Princeton, NJ 08540

ELECTRONIC LEARNING
Scholastic, Inc.
730 Broadway
New York, NY 10003–9538

Family Computing
730 Broadway
New York, NY 10003

Family Computing
P.O. Box 2508
Boulder, CO 80321

INSTRUCTOR
P.O. Box 6099
Duluth, MN 55806–0799

MACAZINE
ICON Concepts Corporation
P.O. Box 1936
Athens, TX 75751

The Macintosh Buyers Guide
Redgate Communications Corporation
660 Beachland Boulevard
Vero Beach, FL 32963

MacTutor
P.O. Box 400
Placentia, CA 92670

MacUser/Macintosh
MacUser Publications
25 West 39th Street
New York, NY 10018

MACWORLD
PCW Communications, Inc.
555 DeHaro Street
San Francisco, CA 94107

NIBBLE MAC
Micro SPARC, Inc.
45 Winthrop Street
Concord, MA 01742

SIERRA On-Line, Inc.
P.O. Box 485
Coursegold, CA 93614

TEACHING and Computers
Scholastic
730 Broadway
New York, NY 10003–9538

EDUCATIONAL SOFTWARE DIRECTORIES

Addison-Wesley Book of Apple Software
Addison-Wesley Publishing Co., Inc.
Jacob Way
Reading, MA 01867

The Book of Apple Computer Software
The Book Company
6711 Valjean Avenue
Van Nuys, CA 91406

The Complete Macintosh Sourcebook
Info Books
P.O. Box 1018
Santa Monica, CA 90406

INSTRUCTOR
Computer Directory for Schools
545 Fifth Avenue
New York, NY 10017

The Software Encyclopedia, 1988
R. R. Bowker Company
245 W. 17th Street
New York, NY 10011

Swift's Educational Software Directory
D C Heath Co.
2700 North Richardt
Indianapolis, IN 46219

TESS-The Educational Software
   Selector
EPIE Institute
P.O. Box 839
Water Mill, NY 11976

TRS Educational Software
Sourcebook, RADIO SHACK
Education Division
1400 One Tandy Center
Ft. Worth, TX 76102

Whole Earth Software Catalog
Quantum Press/Doubleday
Garden City, NY 11530

A

Code for Marking in
Oral Diagnosis

This section, as explained under the section entitled "How to Use This Book," is to teach the beginning reading-education student a shorthand method of marking oral-reading errors. You should find it helpful to read the following information, which should then enable you to use this code effectively.

PREPARATION FOR USING THE CODE FOR MARKING IN ORAL DIAGNOSIS

It is suggested that you make yourself familiar with the shorthand method of marking students' oral-reading errors before attempting to use it. You will note there are ten items or ten notations that are to be made to indicate errors or characteristics that readers are likely to make in oral reading. Each of these notations, of course, denotes a particular kind of error or characteristic of the reader. Once they have been coded and studied, you will find that they will become a blueprint for instruction.

Study each of the ten notations, so you feel relatively comfortable that you understand what is meant by such things as an omission, a reversal, a pause, and the like. If you were to analyze the coded passage that follows using the "Code for Marking in Oral Diagnosis," you would find the following types of errors made by the students who read this demonstration passage.

Tom drove his automobile to the county fair. He saw no place to park. He drove up and down between the rows of cars. Finally he decided to go home.

1. Circle all omissions.
2. Insert with a caret (∧) all insertions.
3. Draw a line through words for which substitutions or mispronunciations were made and write the substitution or mispronunciation over the word. Determine later whether the word missed was a substitution or mispronunciation.

4. If the student reads too fast to write in all mispronunciations, you may draw a line through the word and write a *P* over the word for partial mispronunciation or a *G* over the word for gross mispronunciation.

5. Use a dotted or wavy line to indicate repetitions.

6. Mark reversals in the same way as substitutions and later determine whether the mistake was really an inversion or a substitution.

7. Use an arched line to connect words in which the student disregarded punctuation. (See line connecting *fair* and *he* in the paragraph example.)

8. Use parentheses ( ) to enclose the words for which the pupil needed help.

9. Make a check (√) over the words that were self-corrected.

10. Make two vertical lines (‖) preceding a word where a pause appeared.

Tom drove his automobile to the county fair. He saw no place to park. He drove up and down between the rows of cars. Finally he decided to go home.

Line 1:   The student inserted *new* between the words *his* and *automobile*.

Line 1:   The student omitted the word *county* between *the* and *fair*.

Line 1:   The student did not stop or pause for the period at the end of the sentence ending with the word *fair* and the next sentence beginning with the word *He*.

Line 1:   The student called the word *saw* as *was*. This could be called a substitution; however, in this case it would be referred to as a reversal or inversion since *was* is *saw* spelled backwards. In some coding systems, the authors recommend using a system of marking inversions or reversals using a mark such as the following: ǀs/a\wǀ. In this case the mark would indicate that the student said *saw* for the word *was*. However, the author has found that, other than the very most common reversals or inversions such as *saw* for *was* or *b* for *d*, it is usually necessary for the person who coded the material to examine the word in some detail to determine whether it was an inversion or reversal or whether it was a mispronunciation or a substitution. Because the person doing the coding is often forced to mark a mistake very rapidly, a determination of this type cannot be made instantly. For that reason, the author suggests that this type of error be marked the same as mispronunciations—i.e., marking a line through the word, and then after the reader has finished, the teacher can determine whether the mistake was an inversion or reversal or whether it was a substitution or a mispronunciation.

Line 1: The student made no attempt or did not say the word *place* after a period of time (usually five seconds) and was, therefore, told or given aid with the word *place*.

Line 1: The student read the word *park* as *pack* and then corrected it without help from the teacher.

Line 2: The student repeated the word *He* at the beginning of the sentence.

Line 2: The student paused before the word *drove* for a longer period of time than the scorer believed was normal; however, the period of time was less than five seconds, or it would have had parentheses ( ) around it to indicate that the student had been told the word.

Line 2: The student repeated the phrase *up and down.*

Line 2: The student substituted the word *among* for the word *between.*

Line 2: The student grossly mispronounced the word *Finally.* In some cases, the teacher might note the improper pronunciation since this might be helpful in analyzing the student's problem with word attack skills. However, when the student reads too rapidly to write in the improper pronunciation, the teacher usually simply writes a *G* over the word indicating that it was grossly mispronounced, which means that the pronunciation was so far off that it did not even sound like the original word.

Line 2: The student partially mispronounced the word *decided.* If possible, it is best to write the incorrect mispronunciation of the word over the correct word. This will then be helpful in analyzing what the student seems to be doing wrong in attacking new words. However, when the student reads too rapidly for the person doing the coding to keep up with the coding, then a *P* over the word means that it was only partially mispronounced rather than grossly mispronounced. In this case, the student might have pronounced the word with a hard *c* or *k* sound. This could also have been quickly indicated by crossing out the *c* and putting a *k* over it.

PRACTICE IN USING THE CODE FOR MARKING IN ORAL DIAGNOSIS

In using the "Code for Marking in Oral Diagnosis," you will need to duplicate something that the student will be reading orally, so you have a copy that reads the same as the one read by the student. It will be helpful if the copy on which you will be doing the coding is double-spaced, so you can more easily write in notations on various oral-reading errors made by the student. You should then seat the student next to you, so you can easily hear the student as the passage is read. It is suggested that you attempt to find a student at a lower grade level who is not a rapid reader when you first begin this procedure since it may become very frustrating to attempt to mark the errors of a student who reads rapidly, especially if the student makes a considerable number of errors.

It is also suggested that you tape-record the student's reading of the passage, so it may be replayed a number of times. This will ensure that your original coding was correct or will give you a chance to make any needed changes from the original reading.

INTERPRETING A CODED PASSAGE

Once the student has read the passage or has read several passages that are near his or her high instructional or frustration level, you can begin an interpretation of the meaning of the various types of errors or miscues. You will note that chapters 1 through 8 deal directly with these kinds of errors and that by studying the error pattern, you will often be able to note whether or not the student has difficulties with the kinds of problems listed in chapters 10, 11, and 9 through 17.

B

Preparation and Use of Materials for Testing Letter Knowledge

PREPARING FOR THE TEST

Before administering the letter recognition inventory, it is suggested that you make multiple copies of the answer sheet on p. 223, so you will have one for each student to be tested. It is also suggested that you remove the stimulus sheet from p. 221 and use rubber cement or tape to fasten it to a 5″ × 8″ card. You may then wish to laminate the card, so it will not become soiled from having been handled.

SPECIFIC DIRECTIONS FOR GIVING THE LETTER RECOGNITION INVENTORY*

Before beginning this test you may first wish to have the student write all of the letters in both upper and lower case. If this is done correctly, then place a plus (+) mark in the blank by TASK #1 on the opposite side of this sheet. If they are not all done correctly, you may wish to note exceptions. (optional)

A. Give the student the *Letter Stimulus Sheet* and ask him or her to read each of the letters in row 1, then row 2, row 3, etc. Mark them as plus (+) if they are answered correctly or you may simply wish to place a plus (+) mark in the blank beside TASK #2 (p. 223) to indicate that they were all given correctly. If they are not answered correctly, then write the answer given by the student in each blank. If the student can do this task, stop the test. If he or she cannot name all of the letters, continue with the tasks listed below:

B. Show the student the *Letter Stimulus Sheet* and ask him or her to point to letters as you name them. Do them in random order from the lower case letters and then do them in random order from the upper case letters. Be sure to do all of them or do enough of them so that you are

---

*The letter recognition inventory is from E. E. Ekwall, (1986). *Teacher's Handbook on Diagnosis and Remediation in Reading,* 2nd ed. (Boston: Allyn and Bacon). Reprinted by permission of the author and Allyn and Bacon.

certain the student can identify all letters when they are named. If the student can do this, then place a plus (+) mark by TASK #3 (p. 223) and discontinue the testing. If the student cannot do this task, then note that on TASK #3 and continue with the tasks listed below:

C. Show the student the Letter Stimulus Sheet and ask him or her to match upper case letters with lower case letters, e.g., point to the *n* in the lower case letters and ask the student to point to the *N* from the letters in the upper case group. You may wish to alternate by first pointing to a letter in the lower case and having the student match it with the corresponding letter from the upper case group; then point to a letter in the upper case and have the student match it with the corresponding letter in the lower case group. Be sure to do all of them or do enough of them so that you are certain the student can match all letters. If the student can do this, then place a plus (+) mark by TASK #4 (p. 223) and discontinue the testing. If the student cannot do this task, then note that on TASK #4 and continue with the task listed below:

D. Show the student the Letter Stimulus Sheet and point to a letter from row #11 and ask the student to point to another letter that is exactly the same as that letter. Do this with all of the letters, i.e., first *b* then *m*, etc., until all pairs have been matched. If the student can do this, then place a plus (+) mark by TASK #5. If the student cannot do this task, then note that on TASK #5.

IMPORTANT POINTS TO REMEMBER

When testing for a student's knowledge of the letters, keep in mind that certain tasks concerning letter knowledge are more difficult than others. For example, note that TASK 2 is more difficult than TASK 3, that is, naming letters in random order from a stimulus sheet is more difficult than pointing to the letters as they are named by the teacher. Likewise, pointing to the letters as they are named by the teacher (TASK 3) is more difficult than being asked to identify a lower case *g* when shown an upper case *G* (TASK 4). Therefore, in giving this test, begin with TASK 1 (if you wish) asking the student to write the letters of the alphabet in both upper and lower case. Then the student will do TASK 2. If he can do that task, then there would be no need to do TASK 3. If the student cannot do TASK 3, then he should be asked to do TASK 4, etc.

LETTER STIMULUS SHEET

1.	e	n	i	p	c
2.	v	x	a	j	z
3.	b	o	s	u	q
4.	k	y	f	l	d
5.	g	t	m	r	h	w

6.	C	J	P	H	K
7.	O	G	N	Q	D
8.	L	R	B	Z	Y
9.	A	S	F	M	V
10.	I	W	T	X	U	E

11. b m g d r p m b g r p d m o

LETTER KNOWLEDGE ANSWER SHEET

STUDENT'S NAME _____   SCHOOL _____

DATE _____

TESTER _____

See directions.

1. e _____ n _____ i _____ p _____ c _____
2. v _____ x _____ a _____ j _____ z _____
3. b _____ o _____ s _____ u _____ q _____
4. k _____ y _____ f _____ l _____ d _____
5. g _____ t _____ m _____ r _____ h _____ w _____
6. C _____ J _____ P _____ H _____ K _____
7. O _____ G _____ N _____ Q _____ D _____
8. L _____ R _____ B _____ Z _____ Y _____
9. A _____ S _____ F _____ M _____ V _____
10. I _____ W _____ T _____ X _____ U _____ E _____

TASK 1: _____ Student can write all lower case letters correctly
         _____ Student can write all upper case letters correctly

Exceptions noted: _____

_____

TASK 2: _____ Student can name all lower case letters correctly
         _____ Student can name all upper case letters correctly

TASK 3: _____ Student can identify all lower case letters when named
         _____ Student can identify all upper case letters when named
         _____ Student cannot identify all lower case letters when named
         _____ Student cannot identify all upper case letters when named

Exceptions noted: _____

_____

TASK 4: _____ Student can match all upper and lower case letters
         _____ Student cannot match all upper and lower case letters

Exceptions noted: _____

_____

TASK 5: _____ Student can match a letter with another one that is exactly the
              same
         _____ Student cannot match letters that are exactly the same

Exceptions noted: _____

_____

C

Preparation and Use of Materials for the *Quick Check* for Basic Sight Words

PREPARING FOR THE TEST

Before administering the *Quick Check for Basic Sight Word Knowledge,* it is suggested that you make multiple copies of p. 227, which is the answer sheet to be used in assessing students' knowledge of basic sight words. It is also suggested that you remove p. 229. This page can then be placed on a surface such as tagboard and fastened with rubber cement or transparent tape. After it is cemented in place, you may wish to laminate it to keep it from becoming soiled from handling.

SPECIFIC DIRECTIONS FOR TESTING BASIC SIGHT WORDS

Have your answer sheet ready and give the student the stimulus sheet. Ask the student to read the words in the same order as they are numbered. Tell the student to read each word carefully and skip any word that is not known, or instruct the student to say "I don't know" when a strange word is encountered. Mark the answer sheet as suggested in the directions. If the student pauses more than approximately one second before saying a word, count it as wrong.

IMPORTANT POINTS TO REMEMBER

The *Quick Check for Basic Sight Word Knowledge* is used as a quick way to test students' knowledge of basic sight words. If there is any doubt in your mind as to whether or not a student should be given an entire basic sight word test, you may give students this list first. If the student does not miss *any* words on this test, then she may not need to take the entire basic sight word test. However, if a student misses even one word on this list, she should be given the entire basic word test.

The *Quick Check for Basic Sight Word Knowledge* was developed by giving Ekwall's basic sight word list to 500 students in grades two through six, using a tachistoscotic presentation. One hundred students were tested at each of these five grade levels. A computer analysis then listed, in ascending order of difficulty, the words students most often missed. From this list 36 words were chosen. The first few words are the easier ones. However, following the first few easier words are the ones students tended to miss more often. The list also includes words commonly confused by many students. When giving this test, you should make sure that the student is exposed to each word briefly (approximately one second). Given more time, the student may use word attack skills instead of his or her knowledge of basic sight words. A student who missed *even one word* in this test should be given the entire basic sight word test in appendix D.

Quick Check For Basic Sight Word Knowledge

Answer Sheet

Name_____ Date_____

School_____ Tester_____

Directions: As the student reads the words from the stimulus sheet, mark those words read correctly with a plus (+) and those read incorrectly with a minus (−) or write in the word substituted. If the student says he or she does not know an answer, then mark it with a question mark (?). (If a student misses any words on this test, then he or she should be given the full list of basic sight words.)

1. I _____
2. the _____
3. was _____
4. down _____
5. these _____
6. saw _____
7. than _____
8. start _____
9. this _____
10. want _____
11. those _____
12. went _____
13. both _____
14. then _____
15. shall _____
16. upon _____
17. while _____
18. draw _____

19. thing _____
20. run _____
21. thank _____
22. once _____
23. wish _____
24. think _____
25. every _____
26. ran _____
27. another _____
28. leave _____
29. should _____
30. there _____
31. sure _____
32. always _____
33. carry _____
34. present _____
35. such _____
36. hurt _____

Quick Check for Basic Sight Word Knowledge

1. I	13. both	25. every
2. the	14. then	26. ran
3. was	15. shall	27. another
4. down	16. upon	28. leave
5. these	17. while	29. should
6. saw	18. draw	30. there
7. than	19. thing	31. sure
8. start	20. run	32. always
9. this	21. thank	33. carry
10. want	22. once	34. present
11. those	23. wish	35. such
12. went	24. think	36. hurt

Preparation and Use of Materials for Testing Basic Sight Words

PREPARING FOR THE TEST

Before administering this test of basic sight words, it is suggested that you make multiple copies of pp. 232–234 the answer sheet to be used in assessing students' knowledge of basic sight words. It is also suggested that you remove pp. 235–241. These pages can be placed on a surface such as tagboard with the use of rubber cement. After they are cemented in place, it is suggested that you laminate them; the pages may become soiled if not protected since they are likely to be handled by a number of students.

SPECIFIC DIRECTIONS FOR TESTING BASIC SIGHT WORDS

Have your answer sheet ready (pp. 232–234) and give the student the stimulus pages (pp. 235–241). Ask the student to read the words in the same order as they are numbered. Tell the student to read each word carefully and to skip any word that is not known. Mark the answer sheet as suggested in the directions. If the student pauses more than approximately one second before a word, count it wrong.

IMPORTANT POINTS TO REMEMBER

In giving any basic sight word test, it is important to remember that you are testing instant recognition of each word. The use of a list, such as the one given in this appendix can be very efficient; however, it can also be misleading. For example, when a student pauses before a word, he or she may not know the word but may use word attack skills and be able to correctly pronounce it. Students may also hesitate before some words and then guess and get them right. It is usually better to count a word wrong if there is any doubt because of a hesitation by the student. After you have finished testing each student, you may wish to go back and point to any words that you think the student may have known. If the student immediately recognizes the word, you may then wish to count it right.

Ekwall Basic Sight Word
Answer Sheet

Name _____ Date _____

School _____ Tester _____

Directions: As the student reads the words from the stimulus sheet, mark those read correctly with a plus (+). Mark those read incorrectly with a minus (−) or write the word substituted. Use a question mark (?) to indicate that the student says he or she does not know the answer. If a student hesitates longer than approximately one second before pronouncing a word, then count it wrong.

PRE-PRIMER

1. a	___	22. look	___	43. can	___	63. time	___
2. did	___	23. run	___	44. good	___	64. after	___
3. have	___	24. water	___	45. in	___	65. came	___
4. know	___	25. be	___	46. not	___	66. he	___
5. one	___	26. for	___	47. this	___	67. now	___
6. to	___	27. his	___	48. who	___	68. she	___
7. and	___	28. make	___	49. come	___	69. tree	___
8. do	___	29. said	___	50. has	___	70. all	___
9. her	___	30. we	___	51. it	___	71. could	___
10. like	___	31. big	___	52. of	___	72. help	___
11. play	___	32. get	___	53. three	___	73. old	___
12. too	___	33. house	___	54. will	___	74. so	___
13. are	___	34. my	___	55. oh	___	75. up	___
14. down	___	35. the	___	56. you	___	76. am	___
15. here	___	36. what	___	57. your	___	77. day	___
16. little	___	37. but	___	**PRIMER**		78. how	___
17. put	___	38. go	___	58. about	___	79. on	___
18. two	___	39. I	___	59. call	___	80. some	___
19. away	___	40. no	___	60. had	___	81. us	___
20. eat	___	41. then	___	61. mother	___	82. an	___
21. him	___	42. where	___	62. see	___	83. find	___

84. is	____	115. sat	____	145. high	____	176. think	____
85. other	____	116. there	____	146. more	____	177. began	____
86. something	____	117. when	____	147. party	____	178. door	____
87. very	____	118. saw	____	148. than	____	179. laugh	____
88. around	____	119. they	____	149. why	____	180. never	____
89. fly	____	120. would	____	150. ate	____	181. shall	____
90. jump	____	121. yes	____	151. cold	____	182. thought	____
91. over	____	**FIRST READER**		152. happy	____	183. better	____
92. stop	____	122. again	____	153. morning	____	184. far	____
93. want	____	123. boy	____	154. pretty	____	185. light	____
94. as	____	124. fun	____	155. thank	____	186. new	____
95. from	____	125. long	____	156. with	____	187. side	____
96. let	____	126. or	____	157. ball	____	188. took	____
97. ran	____	127. soon	____	158. color	____	189. black	____
98. take	____	128. well	____	159. if	____	190. fast	____
99. was	____	129. any	____	160. much	____	191. night	____
100. back	____	130. brown	____	161. pull	____	192. sleep	____
101. funny	____	131. girl	____	162. their	____	193. under	____
102. man	____	132. Mr.	____	163. work	____	194. father	____
103. red	____	133. out	____	164. been	____	195. walk	____
104. that	____	134. stand	____	165. cry	____	196. five	____
105. way	____	135. were	____	166. into	____	197. four	____
106. blue	____	136. ask	____	167. must	____	**2-1 READER**	
107. give	____	137. buy	____	168. rabbit	____	198. always	____
108. may	____	138. got	____	169. these	____	199. does	____
109. ride	____	139. Mrs.	____	170. yellow	____	200. going	____
110. them	____	140. please	____	171. before	____	201. live	____
111. went	____	141. tell	____	172. dog	____	202. pick	____
112. by	____	142. white	____	173. just	____	203. sure	____
113. green	____	143. at	____	174. name	____	204. another	____
114. me	____	144. children	____	175. read	____	205. each	____

206. grow ____	230. hold ____	254. keep ____	277. drink ____
207. made ____	231. next ____	255. our ____	278. sing ____
208. place ____	232. school ____	256. six ____	279. turn ____
209. ten ____	233. told ____	257. which ____	280. off ____
210. because ____	234. box ____	258. cut ____	281. small ____
211. end ____	235. eye ____	259. friend ____	282. use ____
212. hand ____	236. home ____	260. kind ____	283. most ____
213. many ____	237. once ____	261. own ____	284. such ____
214. right ____	238. should ____	262. start ____	285. wash ____
215. thing ____	239. until ____	263. while ____	286. people ____
216. best ____	240. bring ____	264. full ____	287. write ____
217. enough ____	241. fall ____	265. last ____	288. present ____
218. hard ____	242. hot ____	266. still ____	**3-2 READER** ____
219. men ____	243. only ____	267. wish ____	289. also ____
220. round ____	244. show ____	268. gave ____	290. don't ____
221. those ____	245. wait ____	269. left ____	291. draw ____
222. book ____	246. carry ____	270. year ____	292. eight ____
223. even ____	247. first ____	**2-2 READER** ____	293. goes ____
224. head ____	248. hurt ____	271. dear ____	294. its ____
225. near ____	249. open ____	272. seem ____	295. king ____
226. say ____	250. sit ____	273. today ____	296. leave ____
227. together ____	251. warm ____	274. done ____	297. myself ____
228. both ____	252. clean ____	275. seven ____	298. upon ____
229. every ____	253. found ____	276. try ____	299. grand ____

Ekwall Basic Sight Word List

1.	a	28.	make	55.	oh
2.	did	29.	said	56.	you
3.	have	30.	we	57.	your
4.	know	31.	big	58.	about
5.	one	32.	get	59.	call
6.	to	33.	house	60.	had
7.	and	34.	my	61.	mother
8.	do	35.	the	62.	see
9.	her	36.	what	63.	time
10.	like	37.	but	64.	after
11.	play	38.	go	65.	came
12.	too	39.	I	66.	he
13.	are	40.	no	67.	now
14.	down	41.	then	68.	she
15.	here	42.	where	69.	tree
16.	little	43.	can	70.	all
17.	put	44.	good	71.	could
18.	two	45.	in	72.	help
19.	away	46.	not	73.	old
20.	eat	47.	this	74.	so
21.	him	48.	who	75.	up
22.	look	49.	come	76.	am
23.	run	50.	has	77.	day
24.	water	51.	it	78.	how
25.	be	52.	of	79.	on
26.	for	53.	three	80.	some
27.	his	54.	will	81.	us

82.	an	109.	ride	136.	ask
83.	find	110.	them	137.	buy
84.	is	111.	went	138.	got
85.	other	112.	by	139.	Mrs.
86.	something	113.	green	140.	please
87.	very	114.	me	141.	tell
88.	around	115.	sat	142.	white
89.	fly	116.	there	143.	at
90.	jump	117.	when	144.	children
91.	over	118.	saw	145.	high
92.	stop	119.	they	146.	more
93.	want	120.	would	147.	party
94.	as	121.	yes	148.	than
95.	from	122.	again	149.	why
96.	let	123.	boy	150.	ate
97.	ran	124.	fun	151.	cold
98.	take	125.	long	152.	happy
99.	was	126.	or	153.	morning
100.	back	127.	soon	154.	pretty
101.	funny	128.	well	155.	thank
102.	man	129.	any	156.	with
103.	red	130.	brown	157.	ball
104.	that	131.	girl	158.	color
105.	way	132.	Mr.	159.	if
106.	blue	133.	out	160.	much
107.	give	134.	stand	161.	pull
108.	may	135.	were	162.	their

163.	work	190.	fast	217.	enough
164.	been	191.	night	218.	hard
165.	cry	192.	sleep	219.	men
166.	into	193.	under	220.	round
167.	must	194.	father	221.	those
168.	rabbit	195.	walk	222.	book
169.	these	196.	five	223.	even
170.	yellow	197.	four	224.	head
171.	before	198.	always	225.	near
172.	dog	199.	does	226.	say
173.	just	200.	going	227.	together
174.	name	201.	live	228.	both
175.	read	202.	pick	229.	every
176.	think	203.	sure	230.	hold
177.	began	204.	another	231.	next
178.	door	205.	each	232.	school
179.	laugh	206.	grow	233.	told
180.	never	207.	made	234.	box
181.	shall	208.	place	235.	eye
182.	thought	209.	ten	236.	home
183.	better	210.	because	237.	once
184.	far	211.	end	238.	should
185.	light	212.	hand	239.	until
186.	new	213.	many	240.	bring
187.	side	214.	right	241.	fall
188.	took	215.	thing	242.	hot
189.	black	216.	best	243.	only

244. show	263. while	282. use
245. wait	264. full	283. most
246. carry	265. last	284. such
247. first	266. still	285. wash
248. hurt	267. wish	286. people
249. open	268. gave	287. write
250. sit	269. left	288. present
251. warm	270. year	289. also
252. clean	271. dear	290. don't
253. found	272. seem	291. draw
254. keep	273. today	292. eight
255. our	274. done	293. goes
256. six	275. seven	294. its
257. which	276. try	295. king
258. cut	277. drink	296. leave
259. friend	278. sing	297. myself
260. kind	279. turn	298. upon
261. own	280. off	299. grand
262. start	281. small	

Preparation and Use of Materials for Testing Knowledge of Contractions*

PREPARING FOR THE TEST

Before administering the test, it is suggested that you remove p. 244 and duplicate it so that you will have multiple copies to use as answer sheets for testing each student. Also remove p. 245 and use rubber cement or tape to fasten it to a 5″ × 8″ card. It is suggested that it then be laminated to keep it from being soiled from handling.

SPECIFIC DIRECTIONS FOR TESTING FOR KNOWLEDGE OF CONTRACTIONS

Have your answer sheet ready (p. 244) and give the student the stimulus sheet (p. 245). Then read the directions that appear on the answer sheet.

IMPORTANT POINTS TO REMEMBER

A rather high percentage of students have occasional problems with the pronunciation of contractions; however, you are likely to find a greater percentage who do not know what two words each contraction stands for. It should be kept in mind that pronunciation is important for reading purposes, but students will not use a contraction in their writing until they know the two words for which each contraction stands.

---

*Reprinted by permission of Allyn and Bacon from *Teacher's Handbook on Diagnosis and Remediation in Reading,* 2nd edition (Boston: Allyn and Bacon, 1986).

Knowledge of Contractions
Answer Sheet

Name _____ Date _____

School _____ Tester _____

Directions: Say, "here is a list of contractions. I want you to begin with number one and say the contraction and then tell what two words it stands for." Following each contraction are two lines. If the student is able to pronounce the contraction correctly, put a plus (+) in the first blank. If he or she can then tell you what two words it stands for, put a plus (+) in the second blank. Mark wrong answers with a minus (−). The grade-level designation following each blank stands for the point at which the contraction should be known.

1. aren't _____ _____ 1.9	25. there's _____ _____ 2.5
2. can't _____ _____ 1.9	26. we'll _____ _____ 2.5
3. don't _____ _____ 1.9	27. there'll _____ _____ 2.5
4. weren't _____ _____ 1.9	28. what's _____ _____ 2.5
5. couldn't _____ _____ 1.9	29. you'll _____ _____ 2.5
6. didn't _____ _____ 1.9	30. doesn't _____ _____ 2.9
7. wasn't _____ _____ 1.9	31. hasn't _____ _____ 2.9
8. hadn't _____ _____ 1.9	32. you'd _____ _____ 2.9
9. won't _____ _____ 1.9	33. he'd _____ _____ 2.9
10. haven't _____ _____ 1.9	34. you're _____ _____ 2.9
11. isn't _____ _____ 1.9	35. he's _____ _____ 2.9
12. wouldn't _____ _____ 1.9	36. I'd _____ _____ 2.9
13. anybody'd _____ _____ 2.5	37. we've _____ _____ 2.9
14. he'll _____ _____ 2.5	38. I've _____ _____ 2.9
15. it's _____ _____ 2.5	39. they've _____ _____ 2.9
16. here's _____ _____ 2.5	40. she'd _____ _____ 2.9
17. I'll _____ _____ 2.5	41. who'd _____ _____ 2.9
18. let's _____ _____ 2.5	42. she's _____ _____ 2.9
19. she'll _____ _____ 2.5	43. they'd _____ _____ 2.9
20. that's _____ _____ 2.5	44. we'd _____ _____ 2.9
21. where's _____ _____ 2.5	45. they're _____ _____ 2.9
22. they'll _____ _____ 2.5	46. we're _____ _____ 2.9
23. I'm _____ _____ 2.5	47. you've _____ _____ 2.9
24. who'll _____ _____ 2.5	

Knowledge of Contractions

1. aren't	25. there's
2. can't	26. we'll
3. don't	27. there'll
4. weren't	28. what's
5. couldn't	29. you'll
6. didn't	30. doesn't
7. wasn't	31. hasn't
8. hadn't	32. you'd
9. won't	33. he'd
10. haven't	34. you're
11. isn't	35. he's
12. wouldn't	36. I'd
13. anybody'd	37. we've
14. he'll	38. I've
15. it's	39. they've
16. here's	40. she'd
17. I'll	41. who'd
18. let's	42. she's
19. she'll	43. they'd
20. that's	44. we'd
21. where's	45. they're
22. they'll	46. we're
23. I'm	47. you've
24. who'll	

F

Preparation and Use of Materials for Testing Ability to Use Context Clues

PREPARING FOR THE TEST

Pages 251–261 contain materials that you may use to test students' ability to use context clues. Each page contains materials for testing context clues at a level from grade one to grade six. To prepare the materials for testing, remove these pages from this appendix. Cut each page in half along the dotted lines and use rubber cement or magic tape to fasten each half of the page to separate sides of a 5" × 8" card. You may then wish to laminate the card to keep it from becoming soiled with use. In fastening the materials to the 5" × 8" card, make sure that the material on one side of the card is in the same position as the material on the other side, so both you and a student can read the materials at the same time. When all cards are completed, you should place them in grade-level order, so the front of the first card contains the material to be read by a student reading at first-grade level, the second card contains the materials to be read by a student reading at second-grade level, and so on. The other side of the cards (to be read by the tester) will then contain the same passages as those to be read by the student, except that the words omitted on the student's passage will be underlined on the side seen by the tester. This side of the card also shows the grade level at which the material is written.

SPECIFIC DIRECTIONS FOR ADMINISTERING THE TEST

Begin the test at a level at which you are sure the student can function at his or her low instructional or independent reading level. Hold the card so the student can read the material on his or her side. Read the directions printed at the top of the card and then let the student proceed to orally read the passage printed on the other side. It should not be necessary to record the student's errors; however, as the student reads, if you believe you have chosen too difficult a passage to begin with, or too easy a passage to begin with, then move to the next passage that is either easier or more difficult. If the student uses a word that is a logical substitute for the one that is omitted, then count it as correct. No norms have been developed for how well students should do in using context clues; however, the author suggests that, in the following passages, you use the following criteria in determining student performance:

No error.....................Excellent
One error ....Good
Two errors ....Fair
Three or more errors .... Poor

IMPORTANT POINTS TO REMEMBER

It is often taken for granted that students will automatically attempt to use context clues even though they have not been told how to do so. This is probably true since most experienced adult readers constantly use context clues, both for word recognition and word meaning, and probably assume that students will do the same. It should be emphasized that most beginning readers will improve somewhat in their ability to use context clues simply by urging them to do so.

In the pages that follow, there are materials for testing students' ability to use context clues. It should be stressed that most students will be unable to use context clues effectively unless they are reading at a level that is rather easy for them (their independent or easy instructional level). Therefore, in using the materials, be sure to use only passages that the student would be able to read fairly easily if no words were omitted. If you wish to develop materials for testing students' ability to use context clues, other than those presented on the following pages, then the section that follows will be helpful.

DEVELOPING YOUR OWN MATERIALS FOR TESTING STUDENTS'
KNOWLEDGE OF CONTEXT CLUES

In constructing materials for testing context clues, you should first keep in mind that students must be aware of context in their oral language. Depending upon the age-grade level of the students with whom you are working, the following sequence is suggested:

1. Make a tape recording of a passage in which certain words are omitted. Replace words that are omitted with the sound of a bell or tone of some type. When the bell or tone sounds, ask the student to give orally the word that he or she feels should have appeared in place of the tone. In making either a tape recording or a written type of exercise for testing context clues, make sure the words that are omitted are ones that could

be gotten from the context of the sentence. The tape recording might be as illustrated in the following script:

> Lori was going to (beep) a party.
> It was going to (beep) on Saturday.
> She invited some of (beep) friends to come.
> She was (beep) happy.

2. Progress to written materials in which the word omitted is replaced with the first letter of the word omitted, and the rest of the letters are replaced with a blank line as follows:

> Lori was going to h ____ a party.
> It was going to b _ on Saturday.
> She invited some of h _ friends to come.
> She was v ____ happy.

3. Progress to written materials in which the word omitted is replaced with a ____ for each letter omitted as follows:

> Lori was going to _ _ _ _ a party.
> It was going to _ _ on Saturday.
> She invited some of _ _ _ friends to come.
> She was _ _ _ _ happy.

4. Lastly, progress to written materials in which the word omitted is replaced with a line. At this point, be sure to make all lines equal length.

> Lori was going to ____ a party.
> It was going to ____ on Saturday.
> She invited some of ____ friends to come.
> She was ____ happy.

Teacher reads these directions: Here is a story with some words left out. Each time a word is left out, it has been replaced with a line. When you come to a line, try to figure out what word should be in that blank. Ready—begin.

Jan has a cat.

The cat's <u>name</u> is Tab.

Tab does not <u>like</u> dogs.

One day <u>a</u> dog ran after Tab.

<u>Tab</u> ran up a tree.

The dog could not go <u>up</u> the tree.

Then <u>the</u> dog went away.

Grade one reading level

Jan has a cat.
The cat's _____ is Tab.
Tab does not _____ dogs.
One day _____ dog ran after Tab.
_____ ran up a tree.
The dog could not go _____ the tree.
Then _____ dog went away.

Teacher reads these directions: Here is a story with some words left out. Each time a word is left out, it has been replaced with a line. When you come to a line, try to figure out what word should be in that blank. Ready—begin.

One day Sam was going to school.
He was riding with his father in their car.
He looked out of the window and saw an elephant.
He said, "Look, father, there goes an elephant."
Sam's father did not even look because they were
  in a large city.
That day Sam's father heard that
  an elephant had escaped from a circus.
That evening Sam's father said, "I'm sorry, Sam,
  you did see an elephant this morning."

One day Sam was going to school.
He was riding with _____ father in their car.
He looked out of the window and _____ an elephant.
He said, "Look, father, _____ goes an elephant."
Sam's _____ did not even look because they were
  in a large city.
That day _____ father heard that
  an elephant had escaped from a circus.
That evening Sam's father said, "I'm sorry, Sam,
  you did _____ an elephant this morning."

Teacher reads these directions: Here is a story with some words left out. Each time a word is left out, it has been replaced with a line. When you come to a line, try to figure out what word should be in that blank. Ready—begin.

Ann and her brother Mike like to play basketball in a park that is far from their home. When they want to play, they usually take a bus to get <u>to</u> the park. There are other boys and girls <u>that</u> play there, too. Sometimes when they <u>go</u> to the park, their father and mother go with them. Their father and mother like to take some food and <u>have</u> a picnic while they are at the park.

Grade three reading level

Ann and her brother Mike like to play basketball in a park that is far from their home. When they _____ to play, they usually take a bus to get _____ the park. There are other boys and girls _____ play there, too. Sometimes when they _____ to the park, their father and _____ go with them. Their father and mother like to take some food and _____ a picnic while they are at the park.

Teacher reads these directions: Here is a story with some words left out. Each time a word is left out, it has been replaced with a line. When you come to a line, try to figure out what word should be in that blank. Ready—begin.

Most kinds of dogs make excellent pets. They <u>can</u> learn fast, <u>and</u> they also <u>have</u> an excellent memory. An intelligent <u>dog</u> can learn <u>to</u> respond to many commands. Many dogs that have been taught <u>well</u> can learn more <u>than</u> 100 words and phrases.

Grade four reading level

- -

Most kinds of dogs make excellent pets. They _____ learn fast, _____ they also _____ an excellent memory. An intelligent _____ can learn _____ respond to many commands. Many dogs that have been taught well can learn more _____ 100 words and phrases.

257

Teacher reads these directions: Here is a story with some words left out. Each time a word is left out, it has been replaced with a line. When you come to a line, try to figure out what word should be in that blank. Ready—begin.

Fire is very important to all of us today. Wherever ruins of early man have been found, there has always been evidence of fire in that civilization. It is thought that early man may have first found fire when lightning struck trees and caused them to burn. Some people think that man might have been able to start fires by getting them from active volcanoes.

Grade five reading level

Fire is very important to all of us today. Wherever ruins of early man have _____ found, there has always been evidence _____ fire in that civilization. It is thought _____ early man may _____ first found fire when lightning struck trees and caused _____ to burn. Some people think that man might have been able _____ start fires by getting them from active volcanoes.

259

Teacher reads these directions: Here is a story with some words left out. Each time a word is left out, it has been replaced with a line. When you come to a line, try to figure out what word should be in that blank. Ready—begin.

One of the most famous eagles in the entire world is not the one we see on stamps or coins. It was <u>an</u> eagle caught by an Indian named Blue Sky who lived in Wisconsin. Blue Sky sold <u>the</u> eagle to a man that sold <u>him</u> to a soldier in the Civil War who named him Old Abe. Before the eagle died, <u>he</u> had been through four years <u>of</u> war and had survived twenty-two battles.

Grade six reading level

One of the most famous eagles in the entire world is not the one we see on stamps or coins. It was _____ eagle caught by an Indian named Blue Sky _____ lived in Wisconsin. Blue Sky sold _____ eagle to a man that sold him to a soldier _____ the Civil War who named him Old Abe. Before the eagle died, _____ had been through four years _____ war and had survived twenty-two battles.

G

Preparation and Use of the *Quick Survey Word List* and the *El Paso Phonics Survey*

PREPARATION OF THE *QUICK SURVEY WORD LIST*

The author suggests that you remove p. 264 (*Quick Survey Word List*) and rubber cement or tape it on a 5″ × 8″ card. After placing it on the card, you may wish to laminate it since it will be handled by students and in the process of usage may become soiled if not laminated.

DIRECTIONS FOR ADMINISTERING THE *QUICK SURVEY WORD LIST*

The *Quick Survey Word List* is designed to enable the tester to determine quickly if a student has the necessary word attack skills to read material written at an adult level successfully. It may be given to students at approximately the fourth grade level or above to determine if it is necessary to administer the *El Paso Phonics Survey*. The student is simply given the word list and asked to pronounce each word. The student should be told, however, that the words that he or she is about to attempt to pronounce are nonsense words or words that are not real words. The student should also be told that the words are very difficult, but that you would like to know if he or she is able to pronounce them. If the student can pronounce each of the words correctly, it would not be necessary to administer the *El Paso Phonics Survey* since the ultimate purpose of learning sound-symbol correspondence is to enable the student to attack new words. On the other hand, if it becomes apparent after one or two words that the student is not able to pronounce the words on the *Quick Survey Word List,* then it should be discontinued; and the *El Paso Phonics Survey* should be administered.

The correct pronunciation of the words on the *Quick Survey Word List* are shown on p. 265. This key shows the correct pronunciation as well as the part of each word that should be stressed. It should be remembered, however, that accent rules or generalizations pertaining to the English language are not consistent; therefore, if the words are pronounced correctly except for the accent or stress shown on certain syllables, they should be considered as correct. It is also suggested that the page with the correct pronunciation of the *Quick Survey Word List* should be removed, rubber cemented or taped to a 5″ × 8″ card, and placed in your diagnostic kit.

QUICK SURVEY WORD LIST*

wratbeling	twayfrall
dawsnite	spreanplit
pramminciling	goanbate
whetsplitter	streegran
gincule	glammertickly
cringale	grantellean
slatrungle	aipcid

IMPORTANT POINTS TO REMEMBER ABOUT THE USE OF THE *QUICK SURVEY WORD LIST*

The *Quick Survey Word List* is also designed to test a student's knowledge of such word attack skills as syllabication, vowel rules, rules for *C, G,* and *Y,* and accent generalizations. It should, however, be stressed that students who do not do well on the list should be stopped after the first two or three words. Remember—only if the student is able to pronounce all of the words correctly (except for accent) would you continue through the entire list. Having a student attempt to pronounce the words when he or she is not able to do so without difficulty will only discourage the student. If the student does not do well on the first one or two words, then you should simply say to the student, "Let's stop. These words are usually meant for adults, and you would not be expected to be able to read them."

---

*Reprinted by permission of E.E. Ekwall and Allyn and Bacon from *Teacher's Handbook on Diagnosis and Remediation in Reading,* 2nd edition (Boston: Allyn and Bacon, 1986).

PRONUNCIATION OF QUICK SURVEY WORDS*

răt'-bĕl-ĭng

däs'-nīt

prăm'-mĭn-cĭl-ĭng

hwĕt'-splĭt-tər

jĭn'-kyool

crĭn'-gāl

slăt'-rŭn-gəl

twā'-frăl

sprēn'-plĭt

gōn'-băt

strē'-grăn

glăm'-mər-tĭck-ly

grăn'-tĕl-lēn

āp'-sĭd

PRONUNCIATION KEY

l — litt<u>le</u>

ə — <u>a</u>bout

ä — f<u>a</u>ther

ə — tamp<u>er</u>

hw — <u>wh</u>at

kyoo — <u>cu</u>te

PREPARATION OF THE *EL PASO PHONICS SURVEY*

The author suggests that you remove pp. 271–275 (*El Paso Phonics Survey*: General Directions and *El Paso Phonics Survey*: Special Directions) and rubber cement them or tape them to a 5″ × 8″ card and laminate them, so they will be available for quick and easy reference in administering the *El Paso Phonics*

Survey in the future. You should also remove pp. 281–282 (*El Paso Phonics Survey*: Answer Sheet) and make multiple copies of this material to be used with students when administering the *El Paso Phonics Survey*. These pages should also be protected, so they will be available for duplicating in the future. You should also remove pp. 277–279 and laminate them. These pages are the stimulus sheets for the *El Paso Phonics Survey*; they will be handled by students and if not laminated will become soiled.

DIRECTIONS FOR ADMINISTERING THE *EL PASO PHONICS SURVEY*

As you will note, there are two sets of directions for administering the *El Paso Phonics Survey*—the General Directions and the Special Directions. The General Directions give overall instructions for administering the *El Paso Phonics Survey* and should be read thoroughly before attempting to give it for the first time. The Special Directions give information on specific items that should be helpful for teacher's aides and others not trained in phonics. They should, however, be read by anyone who is administering the *El Paso Phonics Survey* for the first time.

IMPORTANT POINTS TO REMEMBER ABOUT THE *EL PASO PHONICS SURVEY*

At the beginning of the next section on the rationale for using the *El Paso Phonics Survey*, you will find the advantages of using this survey versus other types of phonics tests. Be sure to become familiar with these other commonly used methods and the problems that tend to be encountered in using each of them. By learning this information, you will not be "learning for obsolescence" as newer instruments are developed for use in phonics testing.

In taking the *El Paso Phonics Survey*, the student is shown three easy words: *in, up,* and *am*. The teacher makes sure the student knows each of these words before beginning the test. The student is then shown a stimulus sheet such as the following:

1. p am pam
2. n up nup

The student is told to say the *name* of the first letter, to pronounce the word in the middle, and finally to say the word formed by adding the initial consonant to the middle word. Although the final word is usually a nonsense word, the teacher is not giving the student a nonsense word in isolation. By saying the name of the letter and the small word in the center, the student finds that the only new task is to blend the letter sound with a word already known. (Remember the *El Paso Phonics Survey* should not be given unless the student knows each of the three stimulus words—*in, up,* and *am*—before beginning the test.) You will also note that vowels, vowel pairs, and special letter combinations are all put together with one of the first eight initial consonants tested on the survey. The students who get all of the first eight consonant sounds right prove their knowledge of them and show the teacher whether or not they know the vowel sounds that follow. The *El Paso Phonics Survey* does not have any of the disadvantages of the other six methods of testing phonics knowledge (discussed in the following section). In taking the *El Paso Phonics Survey*, some students give the nonsense word the wrong ending sound, even though they pronounced the sound correctly earlier. Extensive use of the *El Paso Phonics Survey* shows that this can happen with the student who is not sure of the initial consonant sound and expends so much thought in pronouncing it, the student simply does not attend to the pronunciation of the final sound. When this happens, do not count the initial consonant sound as correct, even if pronounced correctly.

RATIONALE FOR USING THE *EL PASO PHONICS SURVEY*

In the past, six methods have commonly been used to test students' knowledge of phonics. The rationale for using a test such as the *El Paso Phonics Survey* becomes quite obvious once one understands the shortcomings of these six methods, as discussed below.

METHOD ONE: *Using real words to test phoneme-grapheme relationships*

With this method, the teacher might ask the student to pronounce the words *dog, do,* and *done* to test the students' knowledge of the /d/ sound. The problem here is that the student probably already knows these words as sight words, and whether he or she knows the /d/ sound is irrelevant. Many disabled readers have a fairly large sight vocabulary but do not know the initial consonant sound of many words. The student may recognize the beginning /d/ sound but be unable to pronounce words such as *dispart* and *displace,* because the student may not know the short /i/, the /s/, the /p/, or other sounds and may make no response at all. Thus, the teacher would receive no useful information, finding only that *something* in the word was unknown.

METHOD TWO: *Using nonsense words to test phoneme-grapheme relationships*

In this case, the teacher might ask the student to pronounce a word such as *dupe* to test for knowledge of the /d/ sound. If the student can pronounce the word, the student probably knows the /d/ sound. However, if the student makes no response, it might mean one of several things:

1. The student does not know the vowel, consonant, final *e* rule (*v c é* as in *cake*).

2. The student may not know the short /u/, /p/, or /d/ sounds.
3. The student may not be able to blend the sounds together even if they are known.

METHOD THREE: *Testing sounds in isolation*

This method lacks inter-scorer reliability and thus cannot be a valid method of testing students' phonics knowledge. To prove this, ask a student to give the sounds represented by the following letters: *f, r, b, w, l, n, m,* and *v,* while you tape-record the responses. Then ask a group of teachers to listen to the tape and mark each response *right* or *wrong.* Next, ask each teacher to tell his or her response for each sound given by the student. In most cases, the considerable disagreement among the teachers indicates that this procedure is unreliable and, thus, not valid.

METHOD FOUR: *Having students write the first letter or letters of a word pronounced by the teacher*

In using this method, the teacher usually pronounces a word such as *shoe* and asks the students to write the first letter or letters that they hear at the beginning of the word on a piece of paper with numbered lines. See the following example:

1. _____
2. _____

When the teacher pronounces the stimulus word, as in *shoe,* the students are to write *sh* in the first blank. Although this method may appear to measure ability to use the *sh* sound in reading, it rarely does so in reality. In a study, the author found that students who hear a certain sound miss different phoneme-graheme relationships than students who see the same sound in a strange word.* Obviously, hearing a word and writing the initial consonant is a different skill than seeing and pronouncing the same word as tested in the *El Paso Phonics Survey,* or as pronounced in isolation. Reading is, of course, a decoding task, and writing a heard initial consonant sound is an encoding task.

---

*Eldon E. Ekwall, "An Analysis of Children's Test Scores When Tested with Individually Administered Diagnostic Tests and When Tested with Group Administered Diagnostic Tests" final research report, University Research Institute, University of Texas at El Paso, 1973.

METHOD FIVE: *Multiple choice*

In using this method, the teacher pronounces a word, and the students underline or circle one of four choices, as in the following example:

1. f g d b
2. r p n k

Actually, this is also an encoding rather than a decoding task; that is, the students make a written response after hearing an oral stimulus, such as they do in spelling. Furthermore, multiple choice testing usually gives students at least one-fourth of the answers right, regardless of their knowledge.

METHOD SIX: *Multiple choice with a stimulus*

This is almost the same as method five, except that the stimulus word is generated by a picture rather than by the teacher. For example, there might be a picture of a fox next to the choices in the first question. The students are told to look at the picture and say the word that stands for the word's initial sound. This is also an encoding rather than a decoding task and is again multiple choice, allowing a student who knows almost nothing about phonics to get at least one-fourth of the answers right.

El Paso Phonics Survey

General Directions

1. Before beginning the test, make sure the student has instant recognition of the test words that appear in the box at the top of the first page of the survey. These words should be known instantly by the student. If they are not, reschedule the test at a later date, after the words have been taught and the student has learned them.

2. Give the student the *El Paso Phonics Survey* stimulus sheet, pages 277–279.

3. Point to the letter in the first column and have the student say the name of that letter (not the sound it represents). Then point to the word in the middle column and have the student pronounce it. Then point to the nonsense word in the third column and have the student pronounce it.

4. If the student can give the name of the letter, the word in the middle column, and the nonsense word in the third column, mark the answer sheet with a plus (+).

5. If the student cannot pronounce the nonsense word after giving the name of the letter and the word in the middle column, mark the answer sheet with a minus (−); or you may wish to write the word phonetically as the student pronounced it. If the student can tell you the name of the letter and the small word in the middle column but cannot pronounce the nonsense word, you may wish to have him or her give the letter sound in isolation. If the student can give the sound in isolation, either the student is unable to "blend" or does not know the letter well enough to give its sound and blend it at the same time.

6. Whenever a superscript letter appears on the answer sheet, refer to the Special Directions sheet on p. 275.

7. To the right of each answer blank on the answer sheet is a grade level designation. This number represents the point at which most basal reading series have already taught that sound. At that point, you should expect it to be known. The designation 1.3 means the third month of the first year.

8. When the student comes to two- or three-letter consonant digraphs or blends, as with the *qu* in number 22, she is to say "*q-u*" as with the single letters. *Remember*: the student never gives letter sounds in isolation when engaged in actual reading.

9. When the student comes to the vowels (number 59), she is to say "short *a*," and so forth, and then the nonsense word in column two. If the student does not know the breve (ˇ) over the vowels means short *a, e,* and so forth, then explain this. Do the same with the long vowels where the macron (¯) appears.

10. All vowels and vowel combinations are put with only one or two of the first eight consonants. If any of the first eight consonants are not known, they should be taught before you attempt to test for vowel knowledge. You are likely to find that a student who does not know the first eight consonant sounds will seldom know the vowel sounds anyhow.

11. You will note that **words** appear to the right of some of the blanks on the answer sheet. These words illustrate the correct consonant or vowel sound that should be heard when the student responds.

12. Only phonic elements have been included that have a high enough utility to make them worthwhile learning. For example, the vowel pair *ui* appears very seldom, and when it does, it may stand for the short *i* sound in "build" or the long *oo* sound in "fruit." Therefore, there is really no reason to teach it as a sound. However, some letters, such as *oe*, may stand for several sounds, but most often stand for one particular sound. In the case of *oe*, the long *o* sound should be used. In cases such as this, the most common sound is illustrated by a word to the right of the blank on the answer sheet. If the student gives another correct sound for the letter(s), then say, "Yes, that's right, but what is another way that we could say this nonsense word?" The student must then say it as illustrated in the small word to the right of the blank on the answer sheet. Otherwise, count the answer as wrong.

13. Stop the test after five consecutive misses or if the student appears frustrated from missing a number of items even though she has not missed five consecutive items.

El Paso Phonics Survey

Special Directions

[a]3. If the student uses another *s* sound as in "sugar" (*sh*) in saying the nonsense word "sup" ask, "What is another *s* sound?" The student must use the *s* as in "sack."

[b]15. If the student uses the soft *c* sound as in "cigar" in saying the non-sense word "cam," ask, "What is another *c* sound?" The student must use the hard *c* sound as in "coat."

[c]16. If the student uses the soft *g* sound as in "gentle" in saying the nonsense word "gup," ask, "What is another *g* sound?" The student must use the hard *g* sound as in "gate."

[d]17. Ask, "What is the *y* sound when it comes at the beginning of a word?"

[e]23. The student must use the *ks* sound of *x*, and the nonsense word "mox" must rhyme with "box."

[f]35. If the student uses the *th* sound heard in "that," ask, "What is another *th* sound?" The student must use the *th* sound heard in "thing."

[g]44. If the student uses the *hoo* sound of *wh* in saying the nonsense word "whup," ask, "What is another *wh* sound?" The student must use the *wh* sound as in "when."

[h]72. The student may either give the *ea* sound heard in "head" or the *ea* sound heard in "meat." Be sure to note which one is used.

[i]73. If the same *ea* sound is given this time as was given for item 72, say, "Yes, that's right, but what is another way we could pronounce this nonsense word?" Whichever sound was *not* used in item 72 must be used here; otherwise, it is incorrect.

[j]81. The student may give either the *ow* heard in "cow" or the *ow* heard in "crow." Be sure to note which one is used.

[k]82. If the same *ow* sound is given this time as was given for item 81, say, "Yes, that's right, but what is another way we could pronounce this nonsense word?" Whichever sound was *not* used in item 81 must be used here; otherwise, it is incorrect.

[l]88. The student may give either the *oo* sound heard in "book" or the *oo* sound heard in "moon." Be sure to note which one is used.

[m]89. If the same *oo* sound is given this time as was given for item 88, say, "Yes, that's right, but what is another way we could pronounce this nonsense word?" Whichever sound was *not* used in item 88 must be used here; otherwise, it is incorrect.

El Paso Phonics Survey

| | in | up | am |

1.	p	am	pam	25.	sl	in	slin
2.	n	up	nup	26.	pl	up	plup
3.	s	up	sup	27.	fl	in	flin
4.	r	in	rin	28.	st	am	stam
5.	t	up	tup	29.	fr	in	frin
6.	m	up	mup	30.	bl	am	blam
7.	b	up	bup	31.	gr	up	grup
8.	d	up	dup	32.	br	in	brin
9.	w	am	wam	33.	tr	am	tram
10.	h	up	hup	34.	sh	up	shup
11.	f	am	fam	35.	th	up	thup
12.	j	up	jup	36.	ch	am	cham
13.	k	am	kam	37.	dr	up	drup
14.	l	in	lin	38.	cl	in	clin
15.	c	am	cam	39.	gl	am	glam
16.	g	up	gup	40.	sk	up	skup
17.	y	in	yin	41.	cr	in	crin
18.	v	am	vam	42.	sw	up	swup
19.	z	up	zup	43.	sm	in	smin
20.	c	in	cin	44.	wh	up	whup
21.	g	in	gin	45.	sp	up	spup
22.	qu	am	quam	46.	sc	up	scup
23.	m	ox	mox	47.	str	am	stram
24.	pr	am	pram	48.	thr	up	thrup

49.	scr	in	scrin	77.	ar	arb
50.	spr	am	spram	78.	er	ert
51.	spl	in	splin	79.	ir	irt
52.	squ	am	squam	80.	oe	poe
53.	sn	up	snup	81.	ow	owd
54.	tw	am	twam	82.	ow	fow
55.	wr	in	wrin	83.	or	orm
56.	shr	up	shrup	84.	ur	urd
57.	dw	in	dwin	85.	oy	moy
58.	sch	am	scham	86.	ew	bew
59.	ă	tam		87.	aw	awp
60.	ĭ	rin		88.	oo	oot
61.	ĕ	nep		89.	oo	oop
62.	ŏ	sot		90.	au	dau
63.	ŭ	tum				
64.	ā	sape				
65.	ō	pote				
66.	ī	tipe				
67.	ē	rete				
68.	ū	pune				
69.	ee	eem				
70.	oa	oan				
71.	ai	ait				
72.	ea	eam				
73.	ea	eap				
74.	ay	tay				
75.	oi	doi				
76.	ou	tou				

El Paso Phonics Survey
Answer Sheet*

Name _____ Sex _____ Date _____

School _____ Examiner _____

Mark answers as follows: **PEK** = Point at which phonic
Pass +   element is expected to be
Fail - (or write word as pronounced)   known

                Answers PEK   Answers PEK

Initial Consonants

		Answers	PEK				Answers	PEK
1. p	pam	_____	1.3	28. st	stam	_____	1.6
2. n	nup	_____	1.3	29. fr	frin	_____	1.6
[a]3. s	sup	_____	1.3	30. bl	blam	_____	1.6
4. r	rin	_____	1.3	31. gr	grup	_____	1.6
5. t	tup	_____	1.3	32. tr	tram	_____	1.6
6. m	mup	_____	1.3	33. br	brin	_____	1.9
7. b	bup	_____	1.3	34. sh	shup	_____	1.9
8. d	dup	_____	1.3	[f]35. th	thup	_____	1.9 (thing)
9. w	wam	_____	1.3	36. ch	cham	_____	1.9 (church)
10. h	hup	_____	1.3	37. dr	drup	_____	1.9
11. f	fam	_____	1.3	38. cl	clin	_____	1.9
12. j	jup	_____	1.3	39. gl	glam	_____	1.9
13. k	kam	_____	1.3	40. sk	skup	_____	1.9
14. l	lin	_____	1.3	41. cr	crin	_____	1.9
[b]15. c	cam	_____	1.3	42. sw	swup	_____	1.9
[c]16. g	gup	_____	1.3	43. sm	smin	_____	2.5
[d]17. y	yin	_____	1.3	[g]44. wh	whup	_____	2.5 (when)
18. v	vam	_____	1.3	45. sp	spup	_____	2.5
19. z.	zup	_____	1.3	46. sc	scup	_____	2.5
20. c	cin	_____	1.3	47. str	stram	_____	2.5
21. g	gin	_____	1.3	48. thr	thrup	_____	2.5
22. qu	quam	_____	1.3	49. scr	scrin	_____	2.5

Ending Consonant

				50. spr	spram	_____	2.5
				51. spl	splin	_____	2.5
[e]23. m	mox	_____	1.3	52. squ	squam	_____	2.9

Initial Consonant Clusters

				53. sn	snup	_____	2.9
				54. tw	twam	_____	2.9
24. pr	pram	_____	1.3	55. wr	wrin	_____	2.9
25. sl	slin	_____	1.6	56. shr	shrup	_____	3.5
26. pl	plup	_____	1.6	57. dw	dwin	_____	3.5
27. fl	flin	_____	1.6	58. sch	scham	_____	3.9

---

*The *El Paso Phonics Survey* is from E. E. Ekwall, *Teacher's Handbook on Diagnosis and Remediation in Reading,* 2nd edition (Boston: Allyn and Bacon, 1986). Reprinted by permission.

Vowels, Vowel Teams, and Special Letter Combinations

Answers PEK

59. a	tam	_____	1.6
60. i	rin	_____	1.6
61. e	nep	_____	1.6
62. o	sot	_____	1.6
63. u	tum	_____	1.6
64. a	sape	_____	1.6
65. o	pote	_____	1.6
66. i	tipe	_____	1.9
67. e	rete	_____	1.9
68. u	pune	_____	1.9
69. ee	eem	_____	1.9 (heed)
70. oa	oan	_____	1.9 (soap)
71. ai	ait	_____	1.9 (ape)
[h]72. ea	eam	_____	1.9 (meat)
[i]73. ea	eap	_____	2.5 (head)
74. ay	tay	_____	2.5 (hay)
75. oi	doi	_____	2.5 (boy)
76. ou	tou	_____	2.5 (cow)
77. ar	arb	_____	2.5 (harp)
78. er	ert	_____	2.5 (her)
79. ir	irt	_____	2.5 (hurt)
80. oe	poe	_____	2.9 (hoe)
[j]81. ow	owd	_____	2.9 (cow or crow)
[k]82. ow	fow	_____	2.9 (cow or crow)
83. or	orm	_____	2.9 (corn)
84. ur	urd	_____	2.9 (hurt)
85. oy	moy	_____	2.9 (boy)
86. ew	bew	_____	2.9 (few)
87. aw	awp	_____	2.9 (paw)
[l]88. oo	oot	_____	2.9 (book or moon)
[m]89. oo	oop	_____	3.5 (book or moon)
90. au	dau	_____	3.5 (paw)

Preparation and Use of Materials for Testing Knowledge of Vowel Rules and Syllable Principles

PREPARING FOR THE TEST

The materials on pp. 287–295 are printed on only one side of the page. You will note that there are 18 rectangles, each with something printed on it. These are meant to be cut out and rubber cemented or taped to 3″ × 5″ cards. They should then be laminated. You will note that the cards are numbered from 1 to 15; however, there is a 1-B, a 7-B, and a 14-B. The 1-B should be cemented to the back of number 1, 7-B should be cemented to the back of number 7, and 14-B should be cemented to the back of number 14. In cementing the materials to the backs of these three cards, make sure that the material on both sides of the cards is placed so that you can read the material on the back of the card while someone is reading the material on the front of the card. When you have finished laminating each card, place them in order, faceup on the table, so that they are numbered from 1–15. You may wish to use a rubber band to keep them in this order when not being used.

You will also note that on pp. 285 and 286 there is an answer sheet for each of the vowel rules and syllable principles. These should be removed from the text and duplicated so that you will have a copy for each student being tested.

SPECIFIC DIRECTIONS FOR TESTING VOWEL RULES AND SYLLABLE PRINCIPLES

Have your answer sheet in front of you, so you can mark it easily as the student responds. Show the student the first card that says *Syllable Principles* on the front. At this time read the material on the back of this card to the student. After reading the directions on the back of this card, show the student the first card with words on it (#2). Take the card marked #1 and put it on the back of the deck and continue in this order. Ask the student to tell you where he or she would divide into syllables each of the nonsense words on the stimulus cards. The student must get all responses correct to show that he or she knows the syllable principle. For example, in principle #1 there are four stimulus words. The student must get all words right to show that the rule is actually known and that the student is not guessing. It is not important that the student can recite the rule, only that he or she knows where to divide the words. If the student responds to all of the words correctly, then mark syllable principle number 1 as correct with a plus (+), or if it is wrong mark it with a minus (−). Continue in this manner until you have tested all of the syllable principles. The testing of the vowel rules is done by the same procedure as the testing of the syllable principles.

IMPORTANT POINTS TO REMEMBER

You should not attempt to test for students' knowledge of vowel rules unless the student is thoroughly familiar with all vowel and consonant sounds. Therefore, if a student has difficulty with phonics and structural analysis one should first, give the *El Paso Phonics Survey*. If the student knows nearly all initial consonants, consonant clusters, and vowels then you could logically proceed with testing his or her knowledge of vowel rules. However, if the student does not know all initial consonants, consonant clusters, and vowel sounds then testing should be delayed until such time as the student has learned these.

When testing for knowledge of vowel rules and syllable principles, remember that the ultimate goal is to enable the student to *use,* not just to *recite,* the rule or principle that applies to each word.

Phonics research in the past two decades has not always been used to the best advantage; too many outdated rules appear in textbooks and teacher's manuals even today. The material on the following pages is designed to test the student's knowledge of phonics rules in terms of using the rules and principles, rather than reciting them.

Answer Sheet for Vowel Rules and Syllable Principles Test

Name of Student_____
(Last)   (First)   (Middle Initial)

Grade in School_____ Sex_____ Date Tested_____

Syllable Principles

Instructions: Make a plus (+) on the line following the number of the syllable principle if the answer is correct. Make a minus (−) on the line following the number of the syllable principle if the answer is incorrect.

1. ____ Divide wherever there are two consonants surrounded by vowels providing there are no consonant clusters between the vowels. al/pil, op/por, bot/nap, and cur/ron

2. ____ When a word ends in consonant-*le,* the consonant preceding the *le* is included in the syllable with *le.* na/ple, fra/ble, da/ple, and sa/ple

3. ____ Divide between compound words and normal places in the words making up the compound words. cow/per/son, dog/leg, and cow/lick

4. ____ Do not divide between consonant digraphs or blends (consonant clusters). In this case treat the cluster as though it were a single consonant and divide the word so that the cluster goes with the second vowel as in #5 below, or as you would in #1 above. ba/chop, ba/shil, and da/phod

5. ____ In vowel-consonant-vowel situations (VCV) first try dividing so that the consonant goes with the second vowel. mo/nan, fa/dop, and da/lop

Vowel Rules

Instructions: Mark vowel rules the same as the syllable principles above using a (+) or a (−).

1. ___ Single syllable words with only one vowel at the end should usually be pronounced so that the vowel stands for its long sound. ra, de, and po

2. ___ A single vowel at the end of a syllable in a multisyllable word should be given the long sound first. molo, gamo, and ralo

3. ___ A single vowel in a closed syllable usually stands for the short sound of the vowel. loc, pid, and dap

4. ___ Whenever *r* follows a vowel, providing it is in the same syllable, it usually changes the sound of the vowel. (They may be grouped as follows: *er, ur, ir* sound as *ur* in *fur*; *ar* sounds like the *ar* in *car*; and *or* sounds like *or* in *corn*.) der, bir, cur, par, and por

5. ___ The letters *w* and *l* influence the vowel sound preceding them making the vowel neither long nor short. This is true more of the time when there is a double *l*. kaw, rall, baw, and kall

6. ___ When a vowel-consonant-final *e* appears at the end of a word, the first vowel will usually stand for its long sound. Although this is not true an extremely large percentage of the time, it is more true than not. nide, lode, and pake

7. ___ A *y* at the end of a single syllable word, preceded by a consonant, usually stands for the long *i* sound. (Note that in this rule the *y* must be preceded by a consonant.) bly and cly

8. ___ A *y* at the end of a multisyllable word preceded by a consonant usually stands for the long *e* sound. (Note in this rule the *y* must be preceded by a consonant and not a vowel.) noply and dalry

9. ___ A *y* at the beginning of a word usually has the *y* consonant sound as in the word *yard*. yamp and yorp

**Syllable
Principles**

1

Syllable Principles

Say, "Here are some nonsense words. In other words they are not real words. Tell me where you would divide them into syllables if they were real words."

Optional

Why?

1–B

---

alpil

oppor

botnap

curron

2

---

naple

frable

daple

saple

3

cowperson
dogleg
cowlick

4

bachop
bashil
daphod

5

monan
fadop
dalop

6

Vowel
Rules

7

Vowel Rules

Say, "I'm going to show you some nonsense words again. This time tell me how you would pronounce each word."

Optional

Why?

7–B

---

ra

de

po

8

---

molo

gamo

ralo

9

---

loc

pid

dap

10

der
bir
cur
par
por

11

kaw
rall
baw
kall

12

nide
lode
pake

13

Rules for "Y"

14

Rules for "Y"

Say, "Here are some more nonsense words. They will help me know if you know how to pronounce the 'Y' sound."

Optional

Why?

14–B

bly

cly

noply

dalry

yamp

yorp

15

Using the Cloze Procedure*

DEVELOPING, ADMINISTERING, AND SCORING CLOZE PASSAGES

In constructing cloze passages, you could omit every third, fifth, or tenth word. However, most of the research that has been done is based on the deletion of every fifth word. Blank lines of equal length are then used to replace each of the words that have been deleted. It should also be stressed that the commonly used percentages for determining students' Free or Independent, Instructional, and Frustration levels are based on the deletion of every fifth word. If every eighth or tenth word were to be deleted, these commonly used percentages would not apply.

Passages may vary in length depending on the grade level of the students; however, for students of ages equivalent to third- or fourth-grade level or above, passages of about 250 words are often used. The entire first and last sentences are usually left intact. If passages of 250 words plus intact first and last sentences are used, and if every fifth word is omitted, then there will be fifty blanks, and every blank or answer will be worth two percentage points.

Cloze passages may be administered in a group situation much as one would do with standardized reading tests. However, in administering cloze passages there are usually no specific time limits for completion of the work.

For passages in which every fifth word has been deleted the percentages for the various reading levels are as follows:

Independent Level   = 57 to 100 percent
Instructional Level = 44 through 56 percent
Frustration Level   = 43 percent or below

*Eldon E. Ekwall, *Teacher's Handbook in Diagnosis and Remediation in Reading,* 2nd ed. (Newton, MA: Allyn & Bacon, 1986). Reprinted by permission of Allyn & Bacon.

In scoring the passages, only the exact word omitted is usually counted as correct—that is, correct synonyms are not counted as being correct. Research has shown that the overall percentages change very little regardless of whether synonyms are counted as correct or incorrect. Furthermore, if words other than the exact word omitted were counted, scoring would be much more difficult—that is, what one teacher might consider as an adequate answer another teacher may not, and we would thus tend to lose interscorer reliability. In scoring cloze passages, however, students are not usually penalized for incorrect spelling as long as there is little or no doubt about which word was meant to be used.

A plastic overlay such as an overhead projector transparency can be made of each cloze passage with the correct answers appearing on the plastic overlay. When this is superimposed on the student's copy, you can readily check the number of right and wrong answers. These can, in turn, be converted to percentages. From these percentages you can then determine whether the material is at the student's Independent, Instructional, or Frustration level.

Using the Cloze Procedure to Place Students in Graded Materials

1. Select six to twelve passages from a book or material that students will tentatively be using. Pick them randomly but equally distributed from the front to the back of the book.
2. Give the tests to 25-30 students in a class in which the text is commonly used.
3. The mean score on each test is calculated and then the mean of the means is calculated (see p. 300).
4. Select the test that is closest to the mean of the means and throw the rest of the scores away.
5. When a test has been selected for each of the texts a teacher is likely to use, the tests can be duplicated and compiled into booklets that can be administered as group tests. When a student's score is 57 percent or higher, the student is reading at his or her Independent reading level. A score from 44 percent to 56 percent is equivalent to the student's Instructional reading level. A score of 43 percent or less is considered to be at the student's Frustration level. (In a textbook, of course, one is concerned with placing the student in the textbook that is represented by the passage in which the student scored at his or her Instructional reading level.)

Using the Cloze Procedure to Meet the Needs of the Students

1. Divide the book into sections and select two or more passages from each section. The same length passages as described earlier can be used.
2. Make a random selection of the students for whom the book will be used.
3. If you are using a great number of students, you may wish to put them into a number of groups and then let each group take some of the tests. (Make sure, however, that the selection of the subgroups is done randomly.)
4. If students are able to score at their Instructional level on the passages from the book, then it would be considered suitable for them. On the other hand, if most students scored at their Frustration level on the passages from the book, it would be considered too difficult for them.

The Reliability of the Cloze Procedure

The reliability of the cloze procedure will essentially depend upon the following four factors:

1. If longer tests are used, the students' scores will probably be more accurate, but it will take longer to correct them.
2. If a larger number of tests is used when selecting the one to represent the material, then the test selected will more accurately represent the difficulty of the material.
3. Some materials are uneven in difficulty. These materials should be avoided, if possible.
4. The procedure outlined herein must be followed exactly or the results will not be accurate.

PROCEDURE FOR DETERMINING THE MEAN OF THE MEANS

The example below illustrates how to find the mean of the means. In this example there were ten passages and five students. (In determining the mean of the means one would, of course, be likely to have more than five students.) Note that there are ten means—52.4, 34.6, etc. These means were added and their total was 480.6. When this figure (480.6) was divided by the number of means (10) the mean of the means was 48.06. This figure was closest to the mean of Passage Number 8 (47.4). Therefore, that passage was most representative of the difficulty of the material; as a whole, Passage Number 8 would then be kept and the rest of the passages would be discarded.

	1	2	3	4	5	6	7	8	9	10
Mary	56	42	84	12	48	34	51	47	75	49
Sam	42	41	83	10	40	30	49	50	74	42
Sally	32	36	74	18	42	41	55	51	75	45
Joe	76	26	66	26	47	31	60	38	69	39
Fred	56	28	54	41	49	33	59	51	72	54
Totals	262	173	361	107	226	169	274	237	365	229
Means	52.4	34.6	72.2	21.4	45.2	33.8	54.8	47.4	73.0	45.8

Total of the Means = 480.6

$$\text{Mean of the Means} \quad \frac{480.6}{10} = 48.06$$

Passage #8 is closest to the mean of the means, which is 48.06. Therefore, passage #8 is saved and the others are discarded.

Passage #8 is then given to new students with whom you may wish to use the text from which #8 was derived. If they can read passage #8 with an accuracy of between 44 and 56 percent, then this text would be appropriate for them at their Instructional reading level. If they scored at 43 percent or lower, the text would be at their Frustration reading level. If they scored at 57 percent or better, the text would be at their Independent reading level.

J

Scope and Sequence
of Reading Skills

Pages 301 to 303 present information on how the Scope and Sequence of Reading Skills was developed.

Pages 304 to 308 present the Scope and Sequence by grade level.

Pages 309 to 311 present the Scope and Sequence in alphabetical order.

SCOPE AND SEQUENCE OF READING SKILLS

Purpose

The purpose of the reading scope and sequence chart is to help developmental, corrective, and remedial reading teachers know the point at which most students should have mastered certain skills. While the author realizes that many students learn to read quite well with the mastery of only a few of these skills, they can be highly important to others.

Format

The chart appears in two forms. First, various reading skills are listed by the grade level at which they should have been mastered by most students. This should be especially helpful for developmental reading teachers to determine what skills should have generally been mastered by new students at each grade level, as well as what skills students should master during any particular year. Secondly, the chart appears with the skills listed alphabetically. This should be of value to teachers in corrective or remedial reading situations to quickly determine the point at which a certain skill, such as knowledge of a particular blend or digraph, should have been mastered. This will help these teachers know whether to test and teach certain skills or whether they would normally not be taught until later in a student's progress through the grades.

Designation of Levels

Levels are designated in the scope and sequence chart as follows: 1.3 = preprimer, 1.6 = primer, 1.9 = first reader (or end of first grade), 2.5 = mid-second grade, 2.9 = end of second grade, 3.5 = mid-third grade, 3.9 = end of third grade, 4.9 = end of fourth grade, etc. You will note that past the third year, grade levels are not split, but are listed only as 4.9, 5.9, etc. Most basal reader companies do not, of course, provide but one book per grade level past the third grade.

Important Notation Concerning Grade Levels

It should be noted that the levels following each skill *do not* represent the level at which the skill is, or should be, taught. Rather *the notation represents the first level at which most basal readers agree the skill should have been mastered or was, at least, taught.* For example, if a grade level of P appears, it would indicate that most of the basals examined would have taught that skill sometime during the first six months of school. Since a PP did not appear it would also mean that it had been taught, by most of the series examined, after the first three months (PP) or during the 4th, 5th, or 6th months.

Development

The scope and sequence chart was developed by determining the point at which six major publishers of basal readers teach each of the skills listed. The publishers were as follows: Macmillan-1983, Houghton Mifflin-1987, Economy-1986, Ginn-1984, Harcourt Brace Jovanovich-1982, and Scott Foresman-1981. For each skill, a matrix was developed as follows:

Skill	Econ.	Ginn	HBJ	H–M	Mac.	S–F	Consensus
"fl" blend	PP	P	P	PP	PP	PP	P = 1.6
soft "c"	PP	1	PP	PP	PP	PP	PP = 1.3

You will note that four out of the six series examined taught the fl blend at the preprimer level. However, since two did not teach it until the primer level, then the designation of "P" or 1.6 was used. On the other hand, with the soft c sound, five of the six series taught it by the end of the preprimer level. Since only one company was in disagreement, the "PP" or 1.3 designation was used.

In developing the scope and sequence chart the following rules and notations were generally observed:

1. Where only one company was in disagreement with the others, the designation of that company was ignored.
2. When two companies taught the skill after the others, the later designation of these two companies appears.

3. Following each skill listing throughout the chart is a range, e.g., following the *sc* sound is a range of "PP-2^1." This means that one or more series taught the skill as early as preprimer, while one or more did not teach it until the 2^1 level.

4. Following some ranges the word *varies* appears, such as with the "sn" blend. This means that the series were in considerable disagreement in the level at which the skill was taught.

5. On other ranges just as great as the *sn* blend, e.g., "PP-3^1," the word *varies* does not appear. In this case it would mean that, although the range varied a great deal, most of the series were in general agreement even though the overall range was great. In such cases, it was usually a case of one series varying considerably from the others.

6. A skill was *generally* not listed if it appeared in only one series.

7. If a skill was listed in only two series, then the words *2 only* appear following the range for that skill.

8. Where only one entry appears, such as "PP," it means that all six series, or all series in which that skill appeared, were in agreement as to when it was taught.

9. The designations K, R, and PP are all treated as prior to 1.3. (K = Kindergarten and R = Readiness)

10. Some graphemes such as "oo" stand for two phonemes; e.g., the /oo/ in *book* and the /oo/ in *moon*. Where this was the case, a word representing each phoneme appears beside that grapheme—note the word *book* beside one "oo" and the word *moon* beside the other.

11. Only a range is given for recognition of suffixes and prefixes. This is because each of the six series varied to such a large extent that no one meaningful point could be designated.

12. In the alphabetical list that follows the grade level listing, rules for *y*, vowel rules, syllable principles, accent generalizations, and dictionary skills are not repeated because most texts do not state them the same way, thus it would be difficult to use a standard alphabetical listing.

Initial Consonants

b	1.3 (K–PP)
c	1.3 (K–PP)
d	1.3 (K–PP)
f	1.3 (K–PP)
g	1.3 (K–PP)
h	1.3 (K–PP)
j	1.3 (K–PP)
k	1.3 (K–PP)
l	1.3 (K–PP)
m	1.3 (K–PP)
n	1.3 (K–PP)
p	1.3 (K–PP)
r	1.3 (K–PP)
s	1.3 (K–PP)
t	1.3 (K–PP)
v	1.3 (K–PP)
w	1.3 (K–PP)
y	1.3 (K–PP)
z	1.3 (K–PP)
soft c	1.3 (K–PP)
soft g	1.3 (K–PP)

Ending Consonant

x	1.3 (R-1)

Initial Consonant Clusters

pr	1.3 (PP–3^1)
qu	1.3 (R–2^1)
bl	1.6 (P–1)
br	1.6 (PP–P)
fl	1.6 (PP–P)
fr	1.6 (PP–2^1)
pl	1.6 (PP–P)
gr	1.6 (PP–3^1)
sl	1.6 (PP–1)
st	1.6 (PP–P)
ch	1.9 (PP–3^1)
cl	1.9 (PP–3^1)
cr	1.9 (PP–3^1)
dr	1.9 (PP–3^1)
gl	1.9 (PP–1)
sh	1.9 (PP–3^1)
sk	1.9 (PP–3^1)
sw	1.9 (PP–3^1) varies
th	1.9 (PP–1)
tr	1.9 (PP–1)
sc	2.5 (PP–2^1)
scr	2.5 (1–3^1)
sm	2.5 (PP–2^1)
sp	2.5 (P–2^1)
spl	2.5 (1 only)
spr	2.5 (1–2^1)
str	2.5 (PP–2^1)
thr	2.5 (1–2^2)
wh	2.5 (PP–2^1)
sn	2.9 (PP–3^1) varies
squ	2.9 (1–3^1)
tw	2.9 (1–3^2)
dw	3.5 (2^1–3^1) 2 only
ph	3.5 (2^2–3^1)
shr	3.5 (2^1–3^1) 2 only
sch	3.9 (2^1–3^2) 2 only

Ending Consonant Clusters

ck	1.3 (PP)
ng	1.6 (PP–1)
ld	1.9 (P–2^1)
lt	1.9 (P–2^1)
mp	1.9 (P–2^1)
nd	1.9 (P–1)
nk	1.9 (P–1)
nt	1.9 (P–2^1)
st	1.9 (PP–1)
ft	2.5 (1–2^1)

Silent Consonant Clusters

kn	2.5 (PP–2^1)
wr	2.9 (1–2^2)
gn	3.5 (2^2–3^1) 2 only
mb	3.5 (2^2–3^1) 2 only
ght	3.9 (1 only)

Short Vowels

a	1.6 (R–P)
e	1.6 (R–1)
i	1.6 (R–1)
o	1.6 (R–1)
u	1.6 (R–1)

Long Vowels

a	1.6 (R–1)
o	1.6 (R–1)
e	1.9 (R–2^1)
i	1.9 (R–1)
u	1.9 (R–1)

Vowel Teams and Special Letter Combinations

ai	1.9 (PP–2^1)
ea-each	1.9 (PP–2^1)
ee	1.9 (PP–2^1)
oa	1.9 (1–2^1)
ar	2.5 (P–2^2)
ay	2.5 (PP–2^1)
ea-lead	2.5 (1–3^1)
er	2.5 (P–3^1)
ir	2.5 (P–3^1)
oi	2.5 (PP–2^2)
ou	2.5 (P–3^2) varies
al	2.9 (PP–2^2)
ew	2.9 (2^1–3^1)
oe	2.9 (2^2) 2 only
oo-book	2.9 (1–3^1)
or	2.9 (P–3^1)

ow–cow	2.9 (P–3^1)
ow-snow	2.9 (P–3^1) varies
oy	2.9 (PP–2^2)
ur	2.9 (P–3^1)
au	3.5 (1–3^2)
aw	2.9 (1–3^1)
ie	3.5 (2^1–3^1)
oo-moon	3.5 (PP–3^2) varies

Word Endings

ed	1.3 (PP–P)
ing	1.3 (PP–P)
s	1.3 (PP)
es	1.6 (PP–1)
's	1.6 (PP–1)
er	2.5 (PP–2^1)
est	2.5 (PP–2^1)

Contractions

aren't	1.9 (PP–1)
can't	1.9 (PP–1)
couldn't	1.9 (PP–1) 2 only
didn't	1.9 (PP–1)
don't	1.9 (PP–1)
hadn't	1.9 (PP–1) 2 only
haven't	1.9 (PP–1)
isn't	1.9 (PP–1)
wasn't	1.9 (PP–2^2)
weren't	1.9 (PP–1) 2 only
won't	1.9 (PP–1)
wouldn't	1.9 (PP–1)
anybody'd	2.5 (2^1–4) 2 only
he'll	2.5 (PP–2^1)
here's	2.5 (PP–2^1)
I'll	2.5 (PP–2^1)
I'm	2.5 (1–2^1)
It's	2.5 (PP–2^1)
let's	2.5 (PP–2^1) 2 only
she'll	2.5 (PP–2^1)

that's	2.5 (PP–2^1)	in	(3^1–4)
there'll	2.5 (PP–2^1) 2 only	inter	(4–6) 2 only
there's	2.5 (PP–2^1)	mid	(4–5) 2 only
they'll	2.5 (PP–2^1)	mis	(3^1–5)
we'll	2.5 (PP–2^1)	non	(3^1–4) 2 only
what's	2.5 (PP–2^1)	over	(4) 2 only
where's	2.5 (PP–2^1)	pre	(3^1–6)
who'll	2.5 (PP–2^1) 2 only	pro	(4–6) 2 only
you'll	2.5 (PP–2^1)	re	(2^1–3^1)
doesn't	2.9 (PP–2^2)	sub	(5–6)
hasn't	2.9 (PP–2^2)	trans	(5) 2 only
he'd	2.9 (2^1–4)	un	(2^1–3^1)
he's	2.9 (PP–2^2)		
I'd	2.9 (2^1–4)		

Prefixes (Meaning)

I've	2.9 (2^1–2^1)	re (back/again)	2.9 (2^2–3^1)
she'd	2.9 (2^1–4)	un (not)	3.5 (2^1–4)
she's	2.9 (PP–2^2)	dis (part)	3.9 (3^1–3^2)
they'd	2.9 (2^1–4)	in (into)	3.9 (3^1–3^2) 2 only
they're	2.9 (1–2^2)	in (not)	3.9 (3^1–3^2) 2 only
they've	2.9 (2^1–2^2)	de (from/away)	4.9 (3^2–4) 2 only
we'd	2.9 (2^1–4)	ex (without)	4.9 (3^1–4) 2 only
we're	2.9 (1–2^2)	pre (before)	4.9 (3^1–4)
we've	2.9 (2^1–2^2)	en (into)	5.9 (3^2–5) 2 only
who'd	2.9 (2^1–4) 2 only	sub (under)	6.9 (5–6) 2 only
you'd	2.9 (2^1–4)		
you're	2.9 (1–2^2)		

Suffixes (Recognition only)

| you've | 2.9 (2^1–2^2) | able | (3^1–4) |
| | | al | (6) 2 only |

Prefixes (Recognition only)

		an	(4–5) 2 only
a	(P–2^1) 2 only	ance	(4–5) 2 only
ad	(5–6) 2 only	ant	(4–6) 2 only
anti	(5–6) 2 only	ation	(5–6) 2 only
be	(P–6) varies	en	(PP–5)
com	(4–5) 2 only	ence	(4–5) 2 only
con	(4–5) 2 only	ent	(4–6) 2 only
de	(3^2–4) 2 only	er	(PP–3^2)
dis	(2^2–4)	es	(PP–2^2)
ex	(2^1–4)	est	(PP–2^2)
fore	(5–7) 2 only		
im	(3^1–4)		

ful	(2^1-3^1)
hood	(5) 2 only
ian	(4-5)
	2 only
ible	(4-6)
ic	(4-6)
ion	(3-5)
ish	(3-5)
ist	(3-5)
ity	(6) 2 only
ive	(6-8)
less	(2^1-3^2)
ly	(P-3)
ment	(2^2-4)
ness	(2^2-4)
or	(2^2-5)
ous	(3^1-4)
ship	(5) 2 only
some	(6) 2 only
th	(2^2-3^2)
	2 only
tion	(2^1-5)
ty	(2^1-5)
	2 only
ure	(5-6)
	2 only
ward	(5—6)
	2 only
y	(2^2-3^1)

Rules for Y

Y at the end of a multisyllable word	2.5 $(1-3^1)$
Y at the end of a single syllable word	2.5 $(1-2^1)$

Vowel Rules

1. A single vowel in a closed syllable is usually short.	1.9 (1) 1 only
2. A single vowel at the end of a word is usually long.	1.9 (1) 1 only

Syllable Principles

1. When two like consonants stand between two vowels, the word is usually divided between the two consonants.	3.5 (2^1-4)
2. When two unlike consonants stand between two vowels, the word is usually divided between the consonants.	3.5 (2^1-4)
3. Prefixes and suffixes are usually separate syllables.	3.5 (3^1) 2 only
4. When a word ends in a consonant and "le," the consonant usually begins the last syllable.	3.9 (1 only)
5. Divide between compound words.	3.9 (3^1-4) 2 only
6. Do not divide between letters in a consonant digraph or consonant blend.	4.9 (3^1-4) 2 only

Accent Generalizations

1. In two syllable words the first syllable is usually accented.	3.9 (3^1-3^2) 2 only
2. In inflected or derived forms, the primary accent usually falls on the root word.	3.9 (3^1-3^2) 2 only

3. If two vowels are together in the last syllable of a word, it is a clue to an accented final syllable. $3.9 (3^1-6)$ 2 only

4. If there are two unlike consonants within a word, the syllable before the double consonant is usually accented. $3.9 (3^1-6)$ 2 only

Dictionary Skills

1. Learning the alphabet in order   1.6 (PP–1)

2. Alphabetizing letters   1.6 (PP–1)

3. Alphabetizing words $2.5 (R-2^1)$

4. Alphabetizing words to second letter $2.5 (P-2^1)$

5. Selecting word meaning from context $2.5 (2^1)$ 1 only

6. Alphabetizing words to third letter $2.9 (P-2^2)$ 2 only

7. Using guide words $2.9 (2^1-4)$

8. Interpreting syllables   2.9 (2^2-3^2)

9. Estimating location of a word in the dictionary $3.5 (3^1)$ 1 only

10. Interpreting accent or stress $3.9 (3^2)$ 1 only

11. Interpreting pronunciation key   3.9 (3^1-3^2) 2 only

12. Using first and second spellings $3.9 (3^2)$ 1 only

13. Learning about parts of speech   4.9 (4) 1 only

14. Using cross-reference   5.9 (5) 1 only

15. Learning about word origin   6.9 (6) 1 only

Initial Consonants

b	1.3 (K–PP)
c	1.3 (K–PP)
d	1.3 (K–PP)
f	1.3 (K–PP)
g	1.3 (K–PP)
h	1.3 (K–PP)
j	1.3 (K–PP)
k	1.3 (K–PP)
l	1.3 (K–PP)
m	1.3 (K–PP)
n	1.3 (K–PP)
p	1.3 (K–PP)
r	1.3 (K–PP)
s	1.3 (K–PP)
t	1.3 (K–PP)
v	1.3 (K–PP)
w	1.3 (K–PP)
y	1.3 (K–PP)
z	1.3 (R–1)
soft c	1.3 (PP–1)
soft g	1.3 (K–PP)

Ending Consonant

x	1.3 (R–1)

Initial Consonant Clusters

bl	1.6 (PP–1)
br	1.6 (PP–P)
ch	1.9 (PP–3^1)
cl	1.9 (PP–3^1)
cr	1.9 (PP–3^1)
dr	1.9 (PP–3^1)
dw	3.5 (2^1–3^1) 2 only
fl	1.6 (PP–P)
fr	1.6 (PP–2^1)
gl	1.9 (PP–1)
gr	1.6 (PP–3^1)
ph	3.5 (2^2–3^1)

pl	1.6 (PP–P)
pr	1.3 (PP–3^1)
qu	1.3 (R–2^1)
sc	2.5 (PP–2^1)
sch	3.9 (2^1–3^2) 2 only
scr	2.5 (1–3^1)
sh	1.9 (PP–3^1)
shr	3.5 (2^1–3^1) 2 only
sk	1.9 (PP–3^1)
sl	1.6 (PP–1)
sm	2.5 (PP–2^1)
sn	2.9 (PP–3^1) varies
sp	2.5 (P–2^1)
spl	2.5 (1 only)
spr	2.5 (1–2^1)
squ	2.9 (1–3^1)
st	1.6 (PP–P)
str	2.5 (PP–2^1)
sw	1.9 (PP–3^1) varies
th	1.9 (PP–1)
thr	2.5 (PP–2^2)
tr	1.9 (PP–1)
tw	2.9 (1–3^2)
wh	2.5 (PP–2^1)

Ending Consonant Clusters

ck	1.3 (PP)
ft	2.5 (1–2^1)
gh	2.9 (1–2^2)
ld	1.9 (P–2^1)
lt	1.9 (1–2^1)
mp	1.9 (P–2^1)
nd	1.9 (P–1)
ng	1.9 (P–1)
nk	1.9 (P–1)
nt	1.9 (P–2^1)
st	1.9 (PP–1)

Silent Consonant Clusters

ght	3.9 (3^2) 1 only
gn	3.5 (2^2–3^1) 2 only
kn	2.5 (PP–2^2)
mb	3.5 (2^2–3^1) 2 only
wr	2.9 (1–2^2)

Short Vowels

a	1.6 (R–P)
e	1.6 (R–1)
i	1.6 (R–1)
o	1.6 (R–1)
u	1.6 (R–1)

Long Vowels

a	1.6 (R–1)
e	1.9 (R–2^1)
i	1.9 (R–1)
o	1.6 (R–1)
u	1.9 (R–1)

Vowel Teams and Special Letter Combinations

ai	1.9 (PP–2^1)
al	2.9 (PP–2^2)
ar	2.5 (P–2^2)
au	3.5 (1–3^2)
aw	3.5 (1–3^1)
ay	2.5 (PP–2^1)
ea-bread	2.5 (1–3^1)
ea-each	1.9 (PP–2^1)
ee	1.9 (PP–2^1)
er	2.5 (P–3^1)
ew	2.9 (2^1–3^1)
ie	3.5 (2^1–3^1)
ir	2.5 (P–3^1)
oa	1.9 (1–2^1)
oe	2.9 (2^2) 2 only
oi	2.5 (PP–2^2)
oo-book	2.9 (1–3^1)
oo-moon	3.5 (PP–3^2) varies
or	2.9 (P–3^1)
ou	2.5 (P–3^2) varies
ow-cow	2.9 (P–3^1)
ow-snow	2.9 (P–3^1) varies
oy	2.9 (PP–2^2)
ur	2.9 (P–3^1)

Word Endings

ed	1.3 (PP–P)
er	2.5 (PP–2^1)
es	1.6 (PP–1)
est	2.5 (PP–2^1)
ing	1.3 (PP–P)
s	1.3 (PP)
's	1.6 (PP–1)

Contractions

anybody'd	2.5 (2^1–4) 2 only
aren't	1.9 (PP–1)
can't	1.9 (PP–1)
couldn't	1.9 (PP–1) 2 only
didn't	1.9 (PP–1)
doesn't	2.9 (PP–2^2)
don't	1.9 (PP–1)
hadn't	1.9 (PP–1) 2 only
hasn't	2.9 (PP–2^2)
haven't	1.9 (PP–1)
he'd	2.9 (2^1–4)
he'll	2.5 (PP–2^1)
he's	2.9 (PP–2^2)
here's	2.5 (PP–2^1)
I'd	2.9 (2^1–4)
I'll	2.5 (PP–2^1)
I'm	2.5 (1–2^1) 2 only
isn't	1.9 (PP–1)
It's	2.5 (PP–2^1)
I've	2.9 (2^1–2^2)

let's	2.5 (PP–2^1) 2 only
she'd	2.9 (2^1–4)
she'll	2.5 (PP–2^1)
she's	2.9 (PP–2^2)
that's	2.5 (PP–2^1)
there'll	2.5 (PP–2^1) 2 only
there's	2.5 (PP–2^1)
they'd	2.9 (2^1–4)
they'll	2.5 (PP–2^1)
they're	2.9 (1–2^2)
they've	2.9 (2^1–2^2)
wasn't	1.9 (PP–2^2)
we'd	2.9 (2^1–4)
we'll	2.5 (PP–2^1)
we're	2.9 (1–2^2)
we've	2.9 (2^1–2^2)
weren't	1.9 (PP–1) 2 only
what's	2.5 (PP–2^1)
where's	2.5 (PP–2^1)
who'd	2.9 (2^1–4) 2 only
who'll	2.5 (PP–2^1) 2 only
won't	1.9 (PP–1) 2 only
wouldn't	1.9 (PP–1)
you'd	2.9 (2^1–4)
you'll	2.5 (PP–2^1)
you're	2.9 (1–2^2)
you've	2.9 (2^1–2^2)

Prefixes (Recognition only)

a	(P–2^1) 2 only
ad	(5–6) 2 only
anti	(5–6) 2 only
be	(P–6) varies
com	(4–5) 2 only
con	(4–5) 2 only
de	(3^2–4) 2 only
dis	(2^2–4)
ex	(2^1–4)
fore	(5–7) 2 only
im	(3^1–4)

in	(3^1–4)
inter	(4–6) 2 only
mid	(4–5) 2 only
mis	(3^1–5)
non	(3^1–4) 2 only
over	(4) 2 only
pre	(3^1–6)
pro	(4–6) 2 only
re	(2^1–3^1)
sub	(5–6)
trans	(5) 2 only
un	(2^1–3^1)

Prefixes (Meaning)

de (from/away)	4.9 (3^2–4) 2 only
dis (part)	3.9 (3^1–3^2)
en (into)	5.9 (3^2–5) 2 only
ex (without)	4.9 (3^1–4) 2 only
in (into)	3.9 (3^1–3^2) 2 only
in (not)	3.9 (3^1–3^2) 2 only
pre (before)	4.9 (3^2–4)
re (back/again)	2.9 (2^2–3^1)
sub (under)	6.9 (5–6) 2 only
un (not)	3.5 (2^1–4)

Suffixes (Recognition only)

able	(3^1–4)
al	(6) 2 only
an	(4–5) 2 only
ance	(4–5) 2 only
ant	(4–6) 2 only
ation	(5–6) 2 only
en	(PP–5)
ence	(4–5) 2 only
ent	(4–6) 2 only
er	(PP–3^2)
est	(PP–2^2)
ful	(2^1–3^1)
hood	(5) 2 only
ian	(4–5) 2 only

A Phonics Primer

VOWEL SOUNDS

Short Sounds		Long Sounds	
a	bat	a	rake
e	bed	e	jeep
i	pig	i	kite
o	lock	o	rope
u	duck	u	mule

W is sometimes used as a vowel, as in the *ow* and *aw* teams. *W* is usually used as a vowel on word endings and used as a consonant at the beginning of words.

Y is usually a consonant when it appears at the beginning of a word and a vowel in any other position.

Three consonants usually affect or control the sounds of some, or all, of the vowels when they follow these vowels within a syllable. They are *r, w,* and *l*.

r (all vowels)	w (a, e, and o)	l (a)
car	*law*	*all*
her	*few*	
dirt	*now*	
for		
fur		

CONSONANT SOUNDS

b	bear	*k*	king	*s*	six
c	cat	*l*	lake	*t*	turtle
d	dog	*m*	money	*v*	vase
f	face	*n*	nose	*w*	wagon
g	goat	*p*	pear	*x*	xylophone
h	hen	*q*	queen	*y*	yellow
j	jug	*r*	rat	*z*	zebra

The following consonants have two or more sounds:

c	cat	*g*	goat	*s*	six	*x*	xylophone
c	ice	*g*	germ	*s*	is	*x*	exist
				s	sure	*x*	box

When *g* is followed by *e, i,* or *y,* it often takes the soft sound of *j,* as in *gentle* and *germ.* If it is not followed by these letters, it takes the hard sound illustrated in such words as *got* and *game.*

When *c* is followed by *e, i,* or *y,* it usually takes the soft sound heard in *cent.* If it is not followed by these letters, it usually takes the hard sound heard in *come.*

Qu usually has the sound of *kw*; however, in some words such as *bouquet* it has the sound of *k.*

CONSONANT BLENDS

Beginning

bl	blue	*pr*	pretty	*tw*	twelve
br	brown	*sc*	score	*wr*	wrench
cl	clown	*sk*	skill	*sch*	school
cr	crown	*sl*	slow	*scr*	screen
dr	dress	*sm*	small	*shr*	shrink
dw	dwell	*sn*	snail	*spl*	splash
fl	flower	*sp*	spin	*spr*	spring
fr	from	*st*	story	*squ*	squash
gl	glue	*sw*	swan	*str*	string
gr	grape	*tr*	tree	*thr*	throw
pl	plate				

Ending

ld	wild
mp	lamp
nd	wind
nt	went
rk	work
sk	risk

CONSONANT AND VOWEL DIAGRAPHS

Consonant

ch	*ch*ute	*sh*	*sh*ip
ch	*ch*oral	*th*	*th*ree
ch	*ch*ur*ch*	*th*	*th*at
gh	cou*gh*	*wh*	*wh*ich
ph	gra*ph*	*wh*	*wh*o

Vowel (Most common phonemes only)

ai	p*ai*n	*ie*	p*ie*ce	(A number of other phonemes are common for *ie*.)
ay	h*ay*			
ea	*ea*ch	*oa*	*oa*ts	
	or	*oo*	b*oo*k	
ea	w*ea*ther	*oo*	m*oo*n	
ei	w*ei*ght	*ou*	t*ou*gh	(*ou* may be either a digraph or diphthong.)
	or			
ei	*ei*ther			
		ow	l*ow*	(*ow* may be either a digraph or a diphthong.)
			or	
		ow	c*ow*	

DIPHTHONGS

au	h*au*l*	*oi*	s*oi*l
au	ha*w*k*	*ou*	tr*ou*t
ew	f*ew*	*ow*	c*ow*
ey	th*ey*	*oy*	b*oy*

---

*Some may hear *au* and *aw* as a digraph.

L

Phonograms and Words for Use in Teaching Phonics

In this appendix you will first find an explanation of how the phonogram list was developed. Following that on pp. 319–322 you will find an explanation of how to use the phonogram list (and word lists on pp. 323–355) to teach phonics. *Be sure to read both of these sections before using the list.*

HOW THE PHONOGRAM LIST WAS DEVELOPED

The phonogram list was developed by taking the phonograms from the words listed in the *Basic Reading Vocabularies*. This is a vocabulary list derived through an analysis of eight sets of basal readers. In the book *Basic Reading Vocabularies*, words are listed alphabetically, by frequency, and by grade level. The phonogram list was developed by using the list by grade level. The list is graded in the following order: Preprimer, primer, first reader, second reader, etc.

The phonogram lists are cumulative, that is to say, in the primer list all phonograms listed at preprimer are shown plus the additional ones at the primer level. Likewise, at first-reader level, you will find the preprimer, primer, and first-reader lists, etc. In developing the final list, the following rules were used:

1. Each word at preprimer, primer, first-reader level, etc., was examined, and the phonogram(s) in those words were listed. For example, in the list shown in *Basic Reading Vocabularies* the following ten words first appear at the preprimer level: *a, all, am, and, are, at, be, bear, big,* and *blue.* From this list one would then have the following phonograms: *all, am, and, are, at, ear, ig,* and *ue.*

2. Because certain of the phonograms listed above begin with vowel pairs or contain a vowel controlled by the consonant following it, e.g., *ea, ar, al,* that are not introduced at the preprimer level, they are not then listed in the phonogram list until that particular vowel pair or vowel-

controlled sound is introduced in the scope and sequence chart shown in appendix J. For example, the vowel pair *ea,* as in the word *each,* is not taught until the first-reader level; therefore, it does not appear in the phonogram list until first-reader level. Likewise the "1"-controlled *a* is not taught in most basal readers until the 2-2 level; therefore, it would not appear in the phonogram list until second-grade level.

3. In some cases words contain phonograms in which the phonogram is different from the sound it takes in most common words, e.g., *are.* When this was the case, it was not used at all. For example, it would be confusing to a student to first say *are* and then *bare, care,* and *dare,* etc.

4. Where a phonogram such as *is* appeared with only one common word such as *his,* it was not included in the list. The author's logic was that such phonograms would be akin to teaching an obscure rule in phonics that pertained to only a few words. The word and phonogram *is* is also somewhat confusing in that it appears in such words as *this* with a different *s* sound. In this case, of course, the student would also probably know *is* and *his* as sight words.

5. Certain phonograms such as *ull,* were omitted. This was done in some cases because the words in which they appear are of rather low utility, such as *dull, gull,* and *skull.* The *ull* sound heard in *gull* also takes on a slightly different pronunciation in words such as *bull.*

6. Only one-syllable words were used in making words from phonograms.

7. Vowel pairs are introduced in the phonogram list at the level at which they appear in the scope and sequence. For example, *oo* appears with the long /o/ sound as in moon at the third-reader level. The *oo* then appears with the short /o/ sound as in *book* at the second-reader level. Therefore, at the third-reader list of phonograms both appear. However, when both appear they are separated by a line so that students will tend to differentiate between the two different sounds. An example of this is shown below:

ook – book, brook, cook, crook, hook, look, shook, took

oof – goof, hoof, proof, spoof, woof

8. Vowel pairs do not appear by themselves (aa, ee, ii, oo, uu). Only vowels or vowel pairs with consonants appear in the phonogram list.

9. There are only about four vowel pairs that are consistent in following the rule that when two vowels appear the long sound of the first one is heard. Or as you may have been taught, "When two vowels go walking the first one does the talking." These vowels are *ai, ay, oa,* and *ee.* Vowel pairs of low utility or vowel pairs that stand for a number of different sounds have, for the most part, been omitted. However, there are several vowel pairs for which two sounds are rather common. Examples of these

are *ea* (each-head), *ow* (crow-owl), *oo* (moon-book). When these appear they are handled as described in number 7 above.

USING THE PHONOGRAM LIST TO TEACH PHONICS

Research in the field of reading shows that the practice of looking for little words in big or longer words is a poor practice since the shorter word often changes in longer words. For example, in the word *government* we would find the words *go, over,* and *men,* yet of these three words only *men* retains the normal sound of the shorter or smaller word. You may wish to experiment with other words.

There is, however, another similar approach that works well for students who need help with word attack skills. In using this approach one looks for phonograms in words. A phonogram, as defined here, is a common word family beginning with a vowel or vowel pair followed by a consonant or consonants, and sometimes ending in *e*. A high percentage of phonograms retain the same sounds in longer words that they stand for in the simple phonograms themselves (See *How the Phonogram List was Developed)*. Helping students learn many phonograms will, in turn, help them immediately identify these same sounds in longer words. In learning phonograms, students also learn many consonant and consonant cluster sounds, as well as the sounds for long and short vowels, vowel pairs, and *r,- l,-* and *w*-controlled vowels.

Many students who have problems in learning to read also seem to have problems learning various rules for vowel and consonant sounds. These same students also have difficulty learning sounds in isolation. In using the phonogram approach the student learns automatically and is not required to learn rules. The author has found that many students can greatly expand their knowledge of phonics in a very short time using the phonogram list. Below is an example that illustrates how you can use the phonogram list to teach students vowel sounds as well as the sounds represented by various consonants and consonant clusters.

Recording and Learning Phonograms by Row

You will note that the phonogram list that follows has each of the rows numbered by grade level. The first three rows of phonograms, at the preprimer level, appear as follows:

1. ake – bake, cake, fake, lake, make, take, rake, wake
2. am – ham, dam, jam, ram, Sam, yam
3. ame – came, dame, game, fame, lame, name, same, tame

Using a tape recorder, record the following script:

"I am going to say a number and then some words. As I say the words you are to point to each word and say it right after you hear it on the tape recorder. Be sure to point to the word as you say it. Number one: *ake, bake, cake, fake, lake, make, take, rake, wake.* Number two: *am, ham, dam, jam, ram, Sam, yam.* Number three: *ame, came, dame, game, fame, lame, name, same, tame.*"

In recording the words, pause slightly after each word so that the student will have time to look at the word and say it before you say the next word on the recording. *However, it is very important to keep a rather brisk pace so the student does not become bored. It is also very important that the student be required to point to each word as she says it. The importance of this cannot be overemphasized.*

When teachers first begin to use this method the question is often asked, "How many rows should I expect the student to learn at one time?" The answer to this is not a simple one, but will depend on how fast the student learns. To make this determination, begin with about ten rows on the first recording. Have the student listen to the tape enough times so that she can do the exercise without listening to the tape recording. That is, have her point to the words and say them just as she did when listening to the tape recorder. If you find the student does not know nearly all of the phonograms already studied, or that it takes an inordinate amount of time for her to learn ten rows, then next time do only five rows. Adjust the number of rows so that the student can learn all the words without a great deal of difficulty. However, this is not to say that the student should not have to listen to the tape and go over the words many times.

Another question that you may have is, "How many times should the student have to listen to the tape recording and say the words before she learns them? Again, the answer to this question is not a simple one. The best approach to this is probably to simply tell the student that you want her to listen to the words enough times to learn all of them on the recording. The student will then probably be the best judge of just how many times she needs to listen to the tape to learn all of the words.

If you find that approximately ten rows is best for the student, then continue to give her about ten rows at a time until all of the phonograms and words up to her grade level are known. When she has mastered this task, she will not only know the phonograms found in most words, but also will have learned nearly all of the initial consonants and consonant clusters. The student will probably also have internalized several of the most common vowel rules.

Using the Phonogram List and Word List to Teach the Most Common Vowel Rules

Following the phonogram list you will find a word list for teaching the most common vowel rules. The two vowel rules that beginning readers should learn are as follows:

1. *When a single vowel appears in a closed syllable, it usually stands for the short sound of the vowel.* (This is often referred to as the CVC rule.)

A closed syllable is one that has a consonant at the end; for example, the words *in, did, on,* and *Fred* are all closed syllables. On the other hand, the words *go, he,* and *me* are open syllables. Remember that a closed syllable is one that has a consonant at the end and an open syllable is one that has a vowel at the end.

2. *When a word has a vowel, consonant, and final* e, *the first vowel will be more likely to be long and the final* e *will be silent.* (This is often referred to as the VCE rule.) More accurately, the student should probably be taught that when she encounters a word with a VCE ending, she should try the long sound first.

In order to use the phonogram and word list to teach the two rules listed above, do exercises as follows:

a. Write the following words and ask the student to say each word (or help her, if necessary):

> can   cap   dam   pan

After doing this, explain to the student that the *a* sound heard in these words stands for the short *a* sound. Have the student give you more words in which the short *a* sound is heard.

b. Write the following words and then ask the student to say each word (again help her, if necessary):

> cane   cape   dame   pane

Following this, explain to the student that the *a* sound heard in these words stands for the long *a* sound. Have her give you some more words in which the long *a* sound is heard.

Now write the word *cane*. Then cross off the *e* at the end. Ask the student what word you now have. Do the same with the words *cape, dame,* and *pane*. Following this, ask the student what happens to the vowel sounds in the words when you remove the *e* from the end. She should, of course, tell you that removing the *e* changes the vowel sound of the first vowel from long to short.

Following this, do words the other way around. That is, take words such as *gag, rag,* and *stag* and have the student pronounce them. (Help her again, if necessary.) Then put an *e* at the end of each word and ask her to pronounce the words as they now appear. Ask her what happens when you add an *e* to the end of words such as these. The student should, of course, tell you that the first vowel sound changes from short to long when an *e* is added.

In doing this it is not necessary to use real words all of the time; therefore, you may wish to use the phonogram list to supplement the word list. Students enjoy doing the same exercises with nonsense words; for example, changing *slam* to *slame,* or *gam* to *game.*

After teaching the two rules stated above, dictate various words and nonsense words to students and have them write them from your dictation. *This is a very important part of the learning of these rules.*

PREPRIMER

1. ake   – bake, cake, fake, lake, make, quake, rake, sake, take, wake
2. am   – cam, dam, ham, jam, lam, ram, Sam, tam, yam
3. ame   – came, dame, game, fame, lame, name, same, tame
4. an   – ban, can, Dan, fan, Jan, man, pan, ran, tan, van
5. and   – band, hand, land, sand
6. at   – bat, cat, fat, hat, mat, pat, rat, sat, tat, vat
7. ed   – bed, fed, Jed, led, Ned, red, Ted, wed, Zed
8. elp   – help, kelp, yelp
9. et   – bet, get, jet, let, met, net, pet, set, wet, yet
10. id   – bid, did, hid, kid, lid, mid, rid
11. ide   – bide, hide, pride, ride, side, tide, wide
12. ig   – big, dig, fig, gig, jig, pig, prig, rig, wig
13. ike   – bike, dike, hike, like, Mike, pike
14. ill   – bill, dill, fill, gill, hill, Jill, kill, mill, pill, sill, till, will
15. ime   – dime, lime, mime, prime, rime, time
16. in   – bin, din, fin, gin, kin, pin, sin, tin, win
17. ing   – ding, king, ling, ring, sing, wing, zing
18. ish   – dish, fish, wish
19. it   – bit, fit, hit, kit, lit, pit, quit, sit, wit
20. og   – bog, cog, dog, fog, hog, log, tog
21. old   – bold, cold, fold, gold, hold, mold, sold, told
22. op   – cop, fop, hop, lop, mop, pop, prop, sop, stop, top
23. ot   – cot, dot, got, hot, jot, lot, mot, not, pot, rot, sot, tot
24. ump   – bump, dump, hump, jump, lump, pump, rump, sump
25. un   – bun, dun, fun, gun, nun, pun, run, sun, tun
26. up   – cup, pup, sup
27. ut   – but, cut, gut, hut, jut, nut, rut

PRIMER

1. ace   – brace, face, grace, lace, mace, pace, place, race
2. ack   – back, black, hack, jack, lack, pack, quack, rack, sack, slack, stack, tack
3. ad   – bad, brad, cad, dad, fad, gad, had, lad, mad, pad, sad
4. ade   – blade, fade, grade, jade, lade, made, wade
5. ag   – bag, brag, flag, gag, hag, lag, nag, rag, sag, slag, stag, tag, wag, zag
6. ake   – bake, brake, cake, fake, flake, lake, make, quake, rake, sake, slake, stake, take, wake
7. alk   – balk, calk, stalk, talk, walk
8. am   – cam, dam, gram, ham, jam, lam, ram, Sam, slam, tam, yam
9. ame   – blame, came, dame, fame, flame, frame, game, lame, name, same, tame
10. an   – ban, bran, can, Dan, fan, Jan, man, pan, plan, ran, tan, van
11. and   – band, bland, brand, grand, hand, land, sand, stand
12. ank   – bank, blank, dank, flank, frank, Hank, plank, rank, sank, stank, tank, yank
13. ask   – bask, cask, flask, mask, task
14. ast   – blast, cast, fast, last, mast, past, vast
15. at   – bat, brat, cat, fat, flat, hat, mat, pat, plat, rat, sat, slat, vat
16. ate   – bate, date, fate, gate, grate, hate, late, mate, Nate, plate, rate, slate, state
17. aw   – caw, flaw, haw, jaw, law, maw, paw, raw, saw, slaw, taw, yaw
18. each   – beach, bleach, breach, leach, peach, preach, reach, teach

Primer page 1

19. ed   – bed, bled, bred, fed, fled, Jed, led, Ned, pled, red, sled, Ted, wed, Zed
20. ell – bell, cell, dell, fell, hell, jell, Nell, quell, sell, tell, well, yell
21. elp – help, kelp, yelp
22. em   – gem, hem, stem
23. en   – Ben, den, fen, hen, Ken, men, pen, ten, yen, wen, zen
24. end – bend, blend, fend, lend, mend, rend, send, tend, vend, wend
25. ent – bent, Brent, cent, dent, lent, pent, rent, sent, tent, vent, went
26. et   – bet, fret, get, jet, let, met, net, pet, set, wet, yet
27. ext – next, text
28. ick – brick, Dick, flick, kick, lick, nick, pick, prick, quick, sick, slick, stick, wick
29. id   – bid, did, grid, hid, kid, lid, mid, rid, slid
30. ide – bide, hide, pride, ride, side, slide, tide, wide
31. ig   – big, brig, dig, fig, gig, jig, pig, prig, rig, wig
32. ike – bike, dike, hike, like, Mike, pike
33. ill – bill, dill, fill, gill, grill, hill, Jill, kill, mill, pill, sill, still, till, will
34. im   – brim, dim, grim, him, Jim, Kim, rim, slim, Tim
35. ime – dime, grime, lime, slime, time
36. in   – bin, chin, din, fin, gin, grin, kin, pin, sin, tin, win
37. ing – bring, ding, fling, king, ling, ping, ring, sing, sling, sting, wing, zing
38. ish – dish, fish, wish
39. it   – bit, fit, flit, grit, hit, kit, lit, pit, quit, sit, skit, slit, wit
40. ive – dive, five, hive, live, rive, wive

Primer page 2

325

41. ix   – fix, mix, nix, six
42. ob   – blob, bob, cob, fob, gob, job, lob, mob, rob, slob, sob
43. og   – bog, cog, dog, fog, flog, frog, grog, jog, hog, log, slog, tog
44. old   – bold, cold, fold, gold, hold, mold, sold, told
45. op   – cop, flop, fop, hop, lop, mop, pop, plop, sop, slop, stop, top
46. ost   – host, most, post
47. ot   – blot, cot, dot, got, hot, jot, lot, mot, not, pot, plot, rot, sot, slot, tot
48. ox   – box, fox, lox, pox, sox
49. uch   – much, such
50. uck   – buck, duck, luck, muck, puck, pluck, stuck, suck, tuck
51. ump – jump, bump, dump, frump, grump, hump, lump, pump, plump, rump, sump, slump, stump
52. un   – bun, dun, fun, gun, nun, pun, stun, sun, tun
53. up   – cup, pup, sup
54. us   – bus, flus, nus, plus, pus
55. ust   – bust, dust, gust, just, must, rust
56. ut   – but, cut, gut, hut, jut, nut, rut

Primer page 3

FIRST READER

1. able — cable, table, stable
2. ace — brace, face, grace, lace, mace, pace, place, race, trace
3. ack — back, black, hack, jack, lack, pack, quack, rack, sack, slack, shack, stack, tack, track
4. ad — bad, cad, dad, brad, fad, gad, had, lad, mad, pad, sad
5. ade — blade, fade, grade, jade, lade, made, wade
6. ag — bag, brag, drag, flag, gag, hag, lag, nag, rag, sag, slag, stag, tag, wag, zag
7. aid — braid, laid, maid, paid, raid
8. ail — bail, brail, fail, frail, hail, jail, mail, nail, pail, quail, rail, sail, tail, trail, wail
9. ain — brain, chain, drain, gain, grain, lain, main, pain, plain, rain, slain, stain, vain
10. aint — faint, paint, quaint, saint, taint
11. air — chair, fair, flair, hair, lair, pair, stair
12. alk — balk, calk, chalk, talk, stalk, walk
13. ake — bake, brake, cake, drake, fake, flake, lake, make, quake, rake, sake, shake, slake, stake, take, wake
14. am — cam, clam, cram, dam, dram, gram, ham, jam, lam, ram, Sam, sham, slam, swam, tam, tram, yam
15. ame — blame, came, dame, fame, flame, frame, game, lame, name, same, shame, tame
16. an — ban, bran, can, clan, Dan, fan, Jan, man, pan, plan, ran, tan, than, van
17. and — band, bland, brand, gland, grand, hand, land, sand, stand
18. ang — bang, fang, gang, hang, rang, sang, slang

19. ank — bank, dank, blank, flank, frank, Hank, plank, rank, sank, stank, tank, thank, yank
20. ant — pant, plant, slant
21. ask — bask, cask, flask, mask, task
22. ass — bass, brass, class, glass, grass, lass, mass, pass
23. ast — blast, cast, fast, last, mast, past, vast
24. aste — baste, haste, paste, taste, waste
25. at — bat, brat, cat, chat, fat, flat, hat, mat, pat, plat, rat, sat, slat, that, vat
26. ate — bate, crate, date, fate, gate, grate, hate, late, mate, Nate, plate, rate, skate, slate, state
27. ave — brave, cave, crave, Dave, gave, grave, nave, pave, rave, save, shave, slave, stave, wave
28. aw — caw, claw, draw, flaw, haw, jaw, law, maw, paw, raw, saw, taw, thaw, yaw
29. each — beach, bleach, breach, leach, peach, preach, reach, teach
30. eal — deal, heal, meal, peal, real, seal, steal, teal, veal
31. ean — bean, clean, dean, glean, Jean, lean, mean, skean, wean
32. ear — clear, dear, fear, gear, hear, near, rear, sear, shear
33. ease — please, tease
34. eat — beat, bleat, cheat, cleat, feat, heat, meat, neat, peat, pleat, seat, treat
35. ed — bed, bled, bred, fed, fled, Jed, led, Ned, pled, shed, sled, Ted, red, wed, Zed
36. eed — bleed, breed, creed, deed, feed, freed, greed, heed, need, reed, seed, steed, teed, treed, weed
37. eel — creel, feel, keel, peel, reel, steel
38. een — green, keen, peen, queen, seen, sheen, teen
39. eep — beep, cheep, creep, deep, jeep, keep, peep, sheep, sleep, steep, sweep, weep

40. eet — beet, feet, fleet, greet, meet, sheet, sleet, sweet
41. elf — pelf, self, shelf
42. ell — bell, cell, dell, fell, hell, jell, Nell, quell, sell, shell, swell, tell, well, yell
43. elp — help, yelp, kelp
44. em — gem, hem, stem, them
45. en — Ben, den, fen, Glen, hen, Ken, men, pen, ten, then, wen, yen, zen
46. end — bend, blend, fend, lend, mend, rend, send, tend, trend, vend, wend
47. ent — bent, Brent, fent, dent, lent, rent, pent, sent, tent, vent, went
48. ere — here, mere, sere
49. ess — bless, chess, cress, dress, guess, less, mess, press, tress
50. est — best, blest, chest, crest, jest, lest, nest, quest, pest, rest, test, vest, west, zest
51. et — bet, fret, get, jet, let, met, net, pet, set, wet, yet
52. ext — next, text
53. ice — dice, lice, mice, nice, price, rice, slice, trice, vice
54. ick — brick, chick, click, crick, Dick, flick, kick, lick, nick, Rick, pick, prick, quick, sick, slick, stick, thick, trick, wick
55. id — bid, did, grid, hid, kid, lid, mid, rid, skid, slid
56. ide — bide, chide, glide, hide, pride, ride, side, slide, tide, wide
57. ig — big, brig, dig, fig, gig, jig, pig, prig, rig, swig, trig, twig, whig, wig
58. ike — bike, dike, hike, like, Mike, pike
59. ill — bill, chill, dill, drill, fill, gill, grill, hill, Jill, kill, mill, pill, sill, skill, still, thrill, till, will

First Reader page 3

60. im   – brim, dim, grim, him, Jim, Kim, prim, rim, shim, skim, slim, swim, Tim, trim

61. ime   – chime, clime, crime, dime, grime, lime, mime, prime, rime, slime, time

62. in   – bin, chin, din, fin, gin, grin, kin, pin, shin, sin, skin, tin, thin, win

63. ine   – brine, dine, fine, line, mine, nine, pine, shine, swine, tine, thine, wine

64. ing   – bring, cling, ding, fling, king, ling, ping, ring, sing, sting, string, swing, thing, wing, zing

65. ink   – blink, brink, chink, drink, fink, kink, link, mink, pink, rink, shrink, sink, slink, stink, think, wink

66. int   – flint, glint, hint, lint, mint, print, quint, stint, tint

67. ip   – blip, chip, clip, dip, drip, flip, grip, hip, jip, kip, lip, nip, pip, quip, rip, ship, sip, skip, slip, tip, trip, zip

68. irl   – girl, swirl

69. ish   – dish, fish, swish, wish

70. iss   – bliss, kiss, hiss, miss, Swiss

71. it   – bit, fit, grit, hit, kit, lit, pit, quit, sit, skit, slit, wit

72. ive   – chive, dive, drive, five, hive, live, rive, wive

73. ix   – fix, mix, nix, six

74. oad   – goad, load, road, toad

75. oat   – boat, bloat, coat, float, gloat, groat, moat, shoat, stoat, throat

76. ob   – bob, blob, cob, fob, glob, gob, job, lob, mob, rob, slob, sob

77. og   – bog, clog, cog, dog, fog, flog, frog, grog, jog, hog, log, slog, tog

78. ole   – bole, dole, hole, mole, role, pole, sole, stole, tole

79. ood   – brood, food, mood, rood

80. oom   – bloom, broom, boom, doom, gloom, groom, loom, room, zoom

81.	ong	– gong, long, prong, song, thong, tong
82.	oon	– boon, coon, croon, loon, moon, noon, soon, swoon
83.	op	– cop, chop, crop, drop, fop, flop, glop, hop, lop, mop, pop, plop, sop, shop, slop, stop, top
84.	ope	– cope, dope, grope, hope, lope, mope, pope, rope, slope, trope
85.	ose	– chose, close, hose, nose, pose, rose, those
86.	ost	– host, most, post
87.	ot	– blot, clot, cot, dot, got, hot, jot, lot, mot, not, pot, plot, rot, shot, slot, sot, tot, trot
88.	ote	– cote, dote, mote, note, quote, rote, tote, vote
89.	ove	– clove, cove, drove, grove, stove
90.	ox	– box, fox, lox, pox, sox
91.	uch	– much, such
92.	uck	– buck, chuck, cluck, duck, luck, muck, puck, pluck, shuck, stuck, suck, truck, tuck
93.	ump	– bump, chump, clump, dump, frump, grump, hump, jump, lump, plump, pump, rump, slump, stump, sump, thump, trump
94.	un	– bun, dun, fun, gun, nun, pun, stun, sun, tun
95.	unch	– brunch, bunch, crunch, hunch, lunch, munch, punch
96.	ung	– bung, clung, dung, flung, hung, lung, rung, slung, stung, sung, swung
97.	up	– cup, pup, sup
98.	us	– bus, flus, nus, plus, pus, thus
99.	ust	– bust, crust, dust, gust, just, must, rust, trust
100.	ut	– but, cut, glut, gut, hut, jut, nut, rut, shut

First Reader page 5

SECOND READER

1. ab — blab, cab, crab, dab, drab, flab, grab, jab, nab, scab, slab, stab, tab

2. ace — brace, face, grace, lace, mace, pace, place, race, space, trace

3. ack — back, black, clack, crack, hack, jack, lack, pack, quack, rack, sack, shack, slack, smack, snack, stack, tack, track, wack

4. ad — bad, brad, cad, clad, dad, fad, gad, glad, had, lad, mad, pad, sad, shad

5. ade — blade, fade, grade, jade, lade, made, shade, spade, trade, wade

6. afe — chafe, safe, strafe

7. ag — bag, brag, crag, drag, flag, gag, hag, lag, nag, rag, sag, shag, slag, snag, stag, swag, tag, wag, zag

8. age — cage, gage, page, rage, sage, stage, wage

9. aid — braid, laid, maid, paid, raid

10. ail — bail, fail, flail, frail, hail, jail, mail, nail, pail, quail, rail, sail, snail, tail, trail, wail

11. ain — brain, chain, drain, gain, grain, lain, main, pain, plain, rain, slain, Spain, sprain, stain, strain, swain, train, twain, vain

12. aint — faint, paint, plaint, quaint, saint, taint

13. air — chair, fair, flair, hair, lair, pair, stair

14. ake — bake, brake, cake, drake, fake, flake, lake, make, quake, rake, sake, shake, slake, snake, stake, take, wake

15. ale — bale, Dale, gale, hale, Kale, male, pale, sale, scale, shale, stale, tale, wale, whale

16. alk — balk, calk, chalk, stalk, talk, walk

17. all   – ball, call, fall, gall, hall, mall, pall, small, squall, stall, tall, wall
18. am   – cam, clam, cram, dam, dram, gram, ham, jam, lam, ram, Sam, scam, scram, sham, slam, swam, tam, tram, yam
19. amb   – jamb, lamb
20. ame   – blame, came, dame, fame, flame, frame, game, lame, name, same, shame, tame
21. amp   – camp, champ, clamp, cramp, damp, lamp, ramp, scamp, stamp, tamp, tramp, vamp
22. an   – ban, bran, Dan, can, clan, fan, Jan, man, pan, plan, ran, scan, span, tan, than, van
23. and   – band, bland, brand, grand, hand, land, sand, stand, strand
24. ane   – bane, cane, crane, Dane, lane, mane, pane, plane, sane, Shane, vane, wane
25. ang   – bang, clang, fang, gang, hang, pang, rang, sang, slang, sprang, twang
26. ange   – change, grange, mange, range, strange
27. ank   – bank, blank, clank, crank, dank, drank, flank, frank, Hank, lank, plank, prank, rank, sank, shank, spank, stank, swank, tank, thank, yank
28. ant   – pant, plant, slant
29. ap   – cap, chap clap, crap, flap, gap, hap, lap, map, nap, pap, rap, sap, scrap, slap, snap, strap, tap, trap, wrap, yap, zap
30. ape   – cape, drape, grape, nape, scrape, shape, tape
31. ar   – bar, car, char, far, gar, jar, mar, par, scar, spar, star, tar
32. arch   – larch, march, parch, starch
33. ard   – bard, card, guard, hard, lard, sward, yard
34. arge   – barge, charge, large

Second Reader page 2

35. ark   – bark, Clark, dark, hark, lark, mark, quark, park, shark, spark, stark

36. arm   – charm, farm, harm

37. arn   – barn, darn, tarn, yarn

38. arp   – carp, harp, sharp

39. art   – cart, chart, dart, hart, mart, part, smart, start, tart

40. ase   – base, case, chase, vase

41. ash   – bash, brash, cash, clash, crash, dash, flash, gash, gnash, hash, lash, mash, rash, sash, slash, smash, stash, splash, thrash, trash

42. ask   – bask, cask, flask, mask, task

43. ass   – bass, brass, class, crass, glass, grass, lass, mass, pass

44. ast   – blast, cast, fast, last, mast, past, vast

45. aste   – baste, haste, paste, taste, waste

46. at   – bat, brat, cat, chat, fat, flat, knat, hat, mat, pat, plat, rat, sat, scat, slat, spat, sprat, that, vat

47. ate   – bate, crate, date, fate, gate, grate, hate, late, mate, Nate, pate, plate, rate, sate, skate, slate, spate, state

48. ath   – bath, lath, math, path

49. ause   – cause, clause, pause

50. ave   – brave, cave, crave, Dave, gave, grave, lave, nave, pave, rave, save, shave, slave, stave, wave

51. aw   – caw, claw, draw, flaw, gnaw, haw, jaw, law, maw, paw, raw, saw, slaw, squaw, straw, taw, thaw, yaw

52. awl   – bawl, brawl, crawl, drawl, pawl, shawl, scrawl, sprawl, trawl, yawl

53. awn   – brawn, dawn, drawn, fawn, lawn, pawn, prawn, spawn, yawn

Second Reader page 3

54. ay   — bay, bray, cray, day, Fay, flay, fray, gay, gray, hay, jay, lay, may, nay, pay, play, pray, quay, ray, say, slay, spay, splay, spray, stay, stray, sway, tray, way

55. ayed — bayed, brayed, flayed, frayed, grayed, payed, played, prayed, rayed, spayed, sprayed, stayed, swayed

---

56. ead — bread, dead, dread, head, lead, read, spread, thread, tread

---

57. each — beach, bleach, breach, leach, peach, preach, reach, teach

58. ead — bead, lead, plead, read, stead

59. eal — deal, heal, meal, peal, real, seal, squeal, steal, teal, veal

60. eam — beam, cream, dream, gleam, ream, scream, seam, steam, stream, team

61. ean — bean, clean, dean, glean, Jean, lean, mean, skean, wean

62. eap — cheap, heap, leap, reap

63. ease — please, tease

64. east — beast, feast, least, yeast

65. eat — beat, bleat, cheat, cleat, feat, heat, meat, neat, peat, pleat, seat, teat, treat, wheat

66. ear — clear, dear, fear, hear, near, rear, smear, shear, spear, rear, sear

67. earn — learn, yearn

68. eck — check, deck, neck, peck, speck, wreck

69. ed   — bed, bled, bred, fed, fled, Jed, led, pled, Ned, shed, sled, sped, red, wed, Zed

70. edge — hedge, ledge, sedge, wedge

Second Reader page 4

71. eed — bleed, breed, creed, deed, feed, freed, greed, heed, need, reed, seed, speed, steed, teed, treed, tweed, weed

72. eek — cheek, creek, Greek, leek, meek, reek, peek, seek, sleek, week

73. eel — creel, feel, heel, keel, kneel, peel, reel, steel, wheel

74. eem — deem, seem, teem

75. een — green, keen, peen, preen, queen, screen, seen, sheen, spleen, teen

76. eep — beep, cheep, creep, deep, jeep, keep, peep, seep, sheep, sleep, steep, sweep, veep, weep

77. eer — beer, cheer, deer, freer, jeer, leer, peer, queer, seer, sheer, sneer, steer, veer

78. eet — beet, feet, fleet, greet, meet, sheet, skeet, sleet, street, sweet, tweet

79. eeze — breeze, freeze, sneeze, squeeze, tweeze, wheeze

80. eft — cleft, deft, left, theft, weft

81. eg — beg, dreg, Greg, keg, leg, peg

82. eld — held, geld, meld, weld

83. elf — pelf, self, shelf

84. ell — bell, cell, dell, fell, hell, jell, Nell, quell, sell, shell, smell, spell, swell, tell, well, yell

85. elp — help, kelp, whelp, yelp

86. elt — belt, felt, melt, pelt, smelt, welt

87. em — gem, hem, stem, them

88. en — Ben, den, fen, hen, Glen, Ken, men, pen, ten, then, when, wen, wren, yen, zen

89. ence — fence, hence, pence, thence, whence

90. ench — bench, blench, clench, drench, French, quench, stench, trench, wrench

91. end — bend, blend, fend, lend, mend, rend, send, spend, tend, trend, vend, wend

92. ent   – bent, Brent, cent, dent, lent, pent, rent, scent, sent, spent, tent, vent, went
93. ept   – crept, kept, slept, swept, wept
94. er   – her, per
95. esh   – flesh, fresh, mesh, thresh
96. ess   – bless, chess, cress, dress, guess, less, mess, press, stress, tress
97. est   – best, blest, chest, crest, guest, jest, nest, pest, quest, rest, test, vest, west, zest
98. et   – bet, fret, get, jet, let, met, net, pet, set, wet, whet, yet
99. ew   – blew, brew, chew, clew, crew, dew, drew, few, flew, grew, hew, Jew, knew, mew, new, pew, screw, skew, slew, spew, stew, strew, threw, yew
100. ext   – next, text
101. ice   – dice, lice, mice, nice, price, rice, slice, spice, splice, thrice, trice, twice, vice
102. ick   – brick, chick, click, crick, Dick, flick, kick, lick, nick, pick, prick, quick, sick, slick, stick, thick, tick, trick, wick
103. id   – bid, did, grid, hid, kid, lid, mid, rid, skid, slid, squid
104. ide   – bide, bride, chide, glide, hide, pride, ride, side, slide, snide, stride, tide, wide
105. idge   – bridge, midge, ridge
106. ife   – fife, knife, life, rife, strife, wife
107. ift   – drift, gift, lift, rift, sift, shift, swift, thrift
108. ig   – big, brig, dig, fig, gig, jig, pig, prig, rig, sprig, swig, trig, twig, whig, wig
109. ike   – bike, dike, hike, like, Mike, pike, spike, strike

Second Reader page 6

337

110. ile — bile, file, mile, Nile, pile, rile, smile, stile, tile, vile, while, wile
111. ilk — bilk, milk, silk
112. ill — bill, chill, dill, drill, fill, gill, grill, hill, Jill, kill, mill, pill, sill, skill, spill, still, thrill, till, will
113. im — brim, dim, grim, Jim, Kim, him, prim, rim, shim, skim, slim, swim, Tim, trim, whim, vim
114. ime — chime, clime, crime, dime, grime, lime, mime, prime, rime, slime, time
115. in — bin, chin, din, fin, gin, grin, kin, pin, sin, shin, skin, spin, thin, tin, twin, win
116. ince — mince, prince, quince, since, wince
117. ine — brine, dine, fine, line, mine, nine, pine, sine, shine, spine, spline, swine, tine, thine, twine, vine, whine, wine
118. ing — bring, cling, ding, fling, king, ling, ping, ring, sing, sling, spring, sting, string, swing, thing, wing, wring, zing
119. ink — blink, brink, chink, clink, drink, fink, kink, link, mink, pink, rink, sink, stink, think, wink
120. int — dint, flint, glint, hint, lint, mint, print, quint, splint, sprint, squint, stint, tint
121. ip — blip, chip, clip, dip, drip, flip, grip, hip, Kip, lip, nip, pip, quip, rip, scrip, ship, sip, skip, slip, snip, strip, tip, trip, whip, zip
122. ipe — gripe, pipe, ripe, snipe, stripe, swipe, tripe, wipe
123. ird — bird, gird, third
124. ire — dire, fire, hire, lire, mire, quire, shire, spire, squire, sire, tire, wire
125. irl — girl, twirl, swirl, whirl
126. irt — dirt, flirt, girt, shirt, skirt, squirt
127. ish — dish, fish, swish, wish

Second Reader page 7

128.	iss	— bliss, kiss, hiss, miss, Swiss
129.	ist	— fist, jist, grist, list, mist, twist, wist, wrist
130.	it	— bit, fit, flit, grit, hit, kit, knit, lit, pit, quit, sit, skit, slit, spit, split, twit, whit, wit, writ
131.	ite	— bite, cite, kite, mite, rite, quite, site, smite, spite, sprite, trite, white, write
132.	ive	— chive, dive, drive, five, hive, live, rive, strive, thrive, wive
133.	ix	— fix, mix, nix, six
134.	ize	— prize, size
135.	oach	— broach, coach, poach, roach
136.	oad	— goad, load, road, toad
137.	oak	— cloak, croak, soak
138.	oal	— coal, foal, goal, shoal
139.	oar	— boar, roar, soar
140.	oast	— boast, coast, roast, toast
141.	oat	— bloat, boat, coat, float, gloat, goat, groat, moat, shoat, stoat, throat
142.	ob	— blob, bob, cob, fob, glob, gob, job, lob, knob, mob, rob, slob, snob, sob, throb
143.	ock	— block, bock, chock, clock, cock, crock, dock, flock, frock, hock, knock, lock, mock, pock, rock, shock, smock, sock, stock
144.	od	— clod, cod, hod, God, mod, nod, plod, pod, prod, rod, scrod, shod, sod, trod
145.	ode	— bode, code, lode, mode, node, rode, strode
146.	oft	— loft, soft
147.	og	— bog, clog, cog, dog, flog, fog, frog, grog, hog, jog, log, slog, smog, tog
148.	oice	— choice, voice
149.	oil	— boil, broil, coil, foil, moil, roil, soil, spoil, toil

Second Reader page 8

339

150.	oin	– coin, groin, join, loin, quoin
151.	oke	– broke, choke, coke, joke, poke, smoke, spoke, stoke, stroke, woke, yoke
152.	old	– bold, cold, fold, gold, hold, mold, scold, sold, told
153.	ole	– bole, dole, hole, mole, pole, role, sole, stole, tole, whole
154.	ond	– blond, bond, fond, frond, pond
155.	ong	– gong, long, prong, song, strong, thong, throng, tong

156.	ood	– good, hood, stood, wood

157.	ood	– brood, food, mood, rood

158.	ook	– book, brook, cook, crook, hook, look, nook, rook, shook, took

159.	oof	– goof, poof, proof, spoof
160.	ool	– cool, drool, fool, pool, spool, stool, tool
161.	oom	– bloom, boom, broom, doom, gloom, groom, loom, room, zoom
162.	oon	– boon, coon, croon, moon, noon, soon, spoon, swoon
163.	oot	– boot, coot, hoot, loot, moot, root, scoot, shoot, toot
164.	op	– cop, chop, crop, drop, fop, flop, glop, hop, lop, mop, plop, pop, prop, sop, shop, slop, stop, top, whop
165.	ope	– cope, dope, grope, hope, lope, mope, pope, rope, scope, slope, trope
166.	ore	– bore, chore, core, fore, gore, lore, more, pore, score, shore, snore, sore, spore, store, swore, tore, wore, yore
167.	ork	– cork, fork, pork, stork, York
168.	orn	– born, corn, horn, morn, scorn, shorn, sworn, thorn, torn, worn
169.	ort	– fort, port, short, snort, sort, sport, tort, wort

170. ose   — chose, close, hose, nose, pose, prose, rose, those
171. oss   — boss, cross, floss, gloss, loss, moss, toss
172. ost   — host, most, post
173. ot   — blot, clot, cot, dot, got, hot, jot, knot, lot, mot, not, pot, plot, rot, Scot, shot, slot, spot, sot, tot, trot
174. ote   — cote, dote, mote, note, quote, rote, smote, tote, vote, wrote
175. oud   — cloud, loud, proud
176. ought — bought, brought, fought, sought, thought, wrought
177. ould   — could, should, would
178. ound   — bound, found, ground, hound, mound, pound, round, sound, wound
179. ount   — count, fount, mount
180. our   — dour, flour, hour, scour, sour
181. ouse   — blouse, douse, grouse, house, louse, mouse, souse, spouse
182. out   — bout, clout, flout, gout, grout, lout, pout, rout, scout, shout, snout, spout, stout, trout
183. ow   — brow, chow, cow, how, now, plow, pow, prow, scow, vow, wow

184. ow   — blow, crow, flow, glow, grow, low, mow, row, show, slow, snow, throw, tow
185. ox   — box, fox, lox, pox, sox
186. oy   — boy, cloy, coy, joy, ploy, Roy, soy, toy, troy
187. ube   — cube, rube, tube
188. uch   — much, such
189. uck   — buck, chuck, cluck, duck, luck, muck, pluck, puck, shuck, snuck, struck, stuck, suck, truck, tuck
190. udge   — budge, drudge, fudge, grudge, judge, nudge, sludge, smudge, trudge
191. uff   — bluff, cuff, fluff, huff, gruff, muff, puff, ruff, scuff, scruff, sluff, snuff, stuff

Second Reader page 10

192.	ug	– bug, chug, drug, dug, hug, jug, lug, mug, plug, pug, rug, slug, smug, snug, thug, tug
193.	um	– bum, chum, drum, glum, gum, hum, plum, rum, scum, slum, strum, sum, swum, thrum
194.	umb	– crumb, dumb, numb, plumb, thumb
195.	ump	– bump, chump, clump, dump, frump, grump, hump, jump, lump, plump, pump, rump, slump, stump, sump, thump, trump
196.	un	– bun, dun, fun, gun, nun, pun, spun, stun, sun, tun
197.	unch	– brunch, bunch, crunch, hunch, lunch, munch, punch, scrunch
198.	une	– dune, June, prune, rune, tune
199.	ung	– bung, clung, dung, flung, hung, lung, rung, slung, sprung, strung, stung, sung, swung
200.	up	– cup, pup, sup
201.	ur	– blur, bur, cur, slur, spur, fur
202.	ure	– cure, lure, pure, sure
203.	urn	– burn, churn, spurn, turn
204.	urse	– curse, nurse, purse
205.	us	– bus, flus, nus, plus, pus, thus
206.	usk	– dusk, husk, musk, rusk, tusk
207.	uss	– buss, cuss, fuss, muss, truss
208.	ust	– bust, crust, dust, gust, just, must, rust, thrust, trust
209.	ut	– but, cut, glut, gut, hut, jut, nut, rut, shut, smut
210.	uzz	– buzz, fuzz

THIRD READER

1. ab   — blab, cab, crab, dab, drab, flab, grab, jab, nab, scab, slab, stab, tab
2. ace   — brace, face, grace, lace, mace, pace, place, race, space, trace
3. ack   — back, black, clack, crack, hack, jack, lack, pack, quack, rack, sack, shack, slack, smack, snack, stack, tack, track, wack
4. ad   — bad, brad, cad, clad, dad, fad, gad, glad, had, lad, mad, pad, sad, shad
5. ade   — blade, fade, grade, jade, lade, made, shade, spade, trade, wade
6. afe   — chafe, safe, strafe
7. ag   — bag, brag, crag, drag, flag, gag, hag, lag, nag, rag, sag, shag, slag, snag, stag, swag, tag, wag, zag
8. age   — cage, gage, page, rage, sage, stage, wage
9. aid   — braid, laid, maid, paid, raid
10. ail   — bail, fail, flail, frail, hail, jail, mail, nail, pail, quail, rail, sail, snail, tail, trail, wail
11. ain   — brain, chain, drain, gain, grain, lain, main, pain, plain, rain, slain, Spain, sprain, stain, strain, swain, train, twain, vain
12. aint   — faint, paint, plaint, quaint, saint, taint
13. air   — chair, fair, flair, hair, lair, pair, stair
14. ake   — bake, brake, cake, drake, fake, flake, lake, make, quake, rake, sake, shake, slake, snake, stake, take, wake
15. ale   — bale, Dale, gale, hale, Kale, male, pale, sale, scale, shale, stale, tale, wale, whale
16. alk   — balk, calk, chalk, stalk, talk, walk

17. all   – ball, call, fall, gall, hall, mall, pall, small, squall, stall, tall, wall

18. am   – cam, clam, cram, dam, dram, gram, ham, jam, lam, ram, Sam, scam, scram, sham, slam, swam, tam, tram, yam

19. amb   – jamb, lamb

20. ame   – blame, came, dame, fame, flame, frame, game, lame, name, same, shame, tame

21. amp   – camp, champ, clamp, cramp, damp, lamp, ramp, scamp, stamp, tamp, tramp, vamp

22. an   – ban, bran, Dan, can, clan, fan, Jan, man, pan, plan, ran, scan, span, tan, than, van

23. and   – band, bland, brand, grand, hand, land, sand, stand, strand

24. ane   – bane, cane, crane, Dane, lane, mane, pane, plane, sane, Shane, vane, wane

25. ang   – bang, clang, fang, gang, hang, pang, rang, sang, slang, sprang, twang

26. ange   – change, grange, mange, range, strange

27. ank   – bank, blank, clank, crank, dank, drank, flank, frank, Hank, lank, plank, prank, rank, sank, shank, shrank, spank, stank, swank, tank, thank, yank

28. ant   – pant, plant, slant

29. ap   – cap, chap, clap, crap, flap, gap, hap, lap, map, nap, pap, rap, sap, scrap, slap, snap, strap, tap, trap, wrap, yap, zap

30. ape   – cape, drape, grape, nape, scrape, shape, tape

31. ar   – bar, car, char, far, gar, jar, mar, par, scar, spar, star, tar

32. arch   – larch, march, parch, starch

33. ard   – bard, card, guard, hard, lard, sward, yard

Third Reader page 2

34. arge   – barge, charge, large
35. ark   – bark, Clark, dark, hark, lark, mark, quark, park, shark, spark, stark
36. arm   – charm, farm, harm
37. arn   – barn, darn, tarn, yarn
38. arp   – carp, harp, sharp
39. art   – cart, chart, dart, hart, mart, part, smart, start, tart
40. ase   – base, case, chase, vase
41. ash   – bash, brash, cash, clash, crash, dash, flash, gash, gnash, hash, lash, mash, rash, sash, slash, smash, stash, splash, thrash, trash
42. ask   – bask, cask, flask, mask, task
43. ass   – bass, brass, class, crass, glass, grass, lass, mass, pass
44. ast   – blast, cast, fast, last, mast, past, vast
45. aste   – baste, haste, paste, taste, waste
46. at   – bat, brat, cat, chat, fat, flat, gnat, hat, mat, pat, plat, rat, sat, scat, slat, spat, sprat, that, vat
47. ate   – bate, crate, date, fate, gate, grate, hate, late, mate, Nate, pate, plate, rate, sate, skate, slate, spate, state
48. ath   – bath, lath, math, path
49. ause   – cause, clause, pause
50. ave   – brave, cave, crave, Dave, gave, grave, lave, nave, pave, rave, save, shave, slave, stave, wave
51. aw   – caw, claw, draw, flaw, gnaw, haw, jaw, law, maw, paw, raw, saw, slaw, squaw, straw, taw, thaw, yaw
52. awk   – hawk, squawk
53. awl   – bawl, brawl, crawl, drawl, pawl, shawl, scrawl, sprawl, trawl, yawl

Third Reader page 3

54. awn   — brawn, dawn, drawn, fawn, lawn, pawn, prawn, swawn, spawn, yawn

55. ay   — bay, bray, cray, day, Fay, flay, fray, gay, gray, hay, jay, lay, may, nay, pay, play, pray, quay, ray, say, slay, spay, splay, spray, stay, stray, sway, tray, way

56. ayed   — bayed, brayed, flayed, frayed, grayed, payed, played, prayed, rayed, spayed, sprayed, stayed, swayed

---

57. ead   — bread, dead, dread, head, lead, read, spread, thread, tread

---

58. each   — beach, bleach, breach, leach, peach, preach, reach, teach

59. ead   — bead, lead, plead, read, stead

60. eal   — deal, heal, meal, peal, real, seal, squeal, steal, teal, veal

61. eam   — beam, cream, dream, gleam, ream, scream, seam, steam, stream, team

62. ean   — bean, clean, dean, glean, Jean, lean, mean, skean, wean

63. eap   — cheap, heap, leap, reap

64. ease   — please, tease

65. east   — beast, feast, least, yeast

66. eat   — beat, bleat, cheat, cleat, feat, heat, meat, neat, peat, pleat, seat, teat, treat, wheat

67. ear   — clear, dear, fear, hear, near, rear, smear, shear, spear, rear, sear

68. earn   — learn, yearn

69. eck   — check, deck, neck, peck, speck, wreck

70. ed   — bed, bled, bred, fed, fled, Jed, led, pled, Ned, shed, sled, sped, red, shred, wed, Zed

71. edge   — hedge, ledge, sedge, wedge

72. eed — bleed, breed, creed, deed, feed, freed, greed, heed, need, reed, seed, speed, steed, teed, treed, tweed, weed

73. eek — cheek, creek, Greek, leek, meek, reek, peek, seek, sleek, week

74. eel — creel, feel, heel, keel, kneel, peel, reel, steel, wheel

75. eem — deem, seem, teem

76. een — green, keen, peen, preen, queen, screen, seen, sheen, spleen, teen

77. eep — beep, cheep, creep, deep, jeep, keep, peep, seep, sheep, sleep, steep, sweep, veep, weep

78. eer — beer, cheer, deer, freer, jeer, leer, peer, queer, seer, sheer, sneer, steer, veer

79. eet — beet, feet, fleet, greet, meet, sheet, skeet, sleet, street, sweet, tweet

80. eeze — breeze, freeze, sneeze, squeeze, tweeze, wheeze

81. eft — cleft, deft, left, theft, weft

82. eg — beg, dreg, Greg, keg, leg, peg

83. eld — held, geld, meld, weld

84. elf — pelf, self, shelf

85. ell — bell, cell, dell, dwell, fell, hell, jell, Nell, quell, sell, shell, smell, spell, swell, tell, well, yell

86. elp — help, kelp, whelp, yelp

87. elt — belt, dwelt, felt, melt, pelt, smelt, welt

88. em — gem, hem, stem, them

89. en — Ben, den, fen, hen, Glen, Ken, men, pen, ten, then, when, wen, wren, yen, zen

90. ence — fence, hence, pence, thence, whence

91. ench — bench, blench, clench, drench, French, quench, stench, trench, wrench

92. end — bend, blend, fend, lend, mend, rend, send, spend, tend, trend, vend, wend

Third Reader page 5

93.	ent	— bent, Brent, cent, dent, lent, pent, rent, scent, sent, spent, tent, vent, went
94.	ept	— crept, kept, slept, swept, wept
95.	er	— her, per
96.	ere	— here, mere, sere
97.	esh	— flesh, fresh, mesh, thresh
98.	ess	— bless, chess, cress, dress, guess, less, mess, press, stress, tress
99.	est	— best, blest, chest, crest, guest, jest, nest, pest, quest, rest, test, vest, west, zest
100.	et	— bet, fret, get, jet, let, met, net, pet, set, wet, whet, yet
101.	ew	— blew, brew, chew, clew, crew, dew, drew, few, flew, grew, hew, Jew, knew, mew, new, pew, shrew, screw, skew, slew, spew, stew, strew, threw, yew
102.	ext	— next, text
103.	ice	— dice, lice, mice, nice, price, rice, slice, spice, splice, thrice, trice, twice, vice
104.	ick	— brick, chick, click, crick, Dick, flick, kick, lick, nick, pick, prick, quick, sick, slick, stick, thick, tick, trick, wick
105.	id	— bid, did, grid, hid, kid, lid, mid, rid, skid, slid, squid
106.	ide	— bide, bride, chide, glide, hide, pride, ride, side, slide, snide, stride, tide, wide
107.	idge	— bridge, midge, ridge
108.	ife	— fife, knife, life, rife, strife, wife
109.	ift	— drift, gift, lift, rift, sift, shift, swift, thrift
110.	ig	— big, brig, dig, fig, gig, jig, pig, prig, rig, sprig, swig, trig, twig, whig, wig
111.	ike	— bike, dike, hike, like, Mike, pike, spike, strike

Third Reader page 6

112.	ile	– bile, file, mile, Nile, pile, rile, smile, stile, tile, vile, while, wile
113.	ilk	– bilk, milk, silk
114.	ill	– bill, chill, dill, drill, fill, gill, grill, hill, Jill, kill, mill, pill, sill, shrill, skill, spill, still, thrill, till, will
115.	im	– brim, dim, grim, Jim, Kim, him, prim, rim, shim, skim, slim, swim, Tim, trim, whim, vim
116.	ime	– chime, clime, crime, dime, grime, lime, mime, prime, rime, slime, time
117.	in	– bin, chin, din, fin, gin, grin, kin, pin, sin, shin, skin, spin, thin, tin, twin, win
118.	ince	– mince, prince, quince, since, wince
119.	inch	– cinch, clinch, finch, flinch, pinch, winch
120.	ine	– brine, dine, fine, line, mine, nine, pine, sine, shine, shrine, spine, spline, swine, tine, thine, twine, vine, whine, wine
121.	ing	– bring, cling, ding, fling, king, ling, ping, ring, sing, sling, spring, sting, string, swing, thing, wing, wring, zing
122.	ink	– blink, brink, chink, clink, drink, fink, kink, link, mink, pink, rink, shrink, slink, sink, stink, think, wink
123.	int	– dint, flint, glint, hint, lint, mint, print, quint, splint, sprint, squint, stint, tint
124.	ip	– blip, chip, clip, dip, drip, flip, grip, hip, Kip, lip, nip, pip, quip, rip, scrip, ship, sip, skip, slip, snip, strip, tip, trip, whip, zip
125.	ipe	– gripe, pipe, ripe, snipe, stripe, swipe, tripe, wipe
126.	ird	– bird, gird, third
127.	ire	– dire, fire, hire, lire, mire, quire, shire, spire, squire, sire, tire, wire

Third Reader page 7

128.	irl	— girl, twirl, swirl, whirl
129.	irt	— dirt, flirt, girt, shirt, skirt, squirt
130.	ish	— dish, fish, swish, wish
131.	iss	— bliss, kiss, hiss, miss, Swiss
132.	ist	— fist, jist, grist, list, mist, twist, wist, wrist
133.	it	— bit, fit, flit, grit, hit, kit, knit, lit, pit, quit, sit, skit, slit, spit, split, twit, whit, wit, writ
134.	ite	— bite, cite, kite, mite, rite, quite, site, smite, spite, sprite, trite, white, write
135.	ive	— chive, dive, drive, five, hive, live, rive, shrive, strive, thrive, wive
136.	ix	— fix, mix, nix, six
137.	ize	— prize, size
138.	oach	— broach, coach, poach, roach
139.	oad	— goad, load, road, toad
140.	oak	— cloak, croak, soak
141.	oal	— coal, foal, goal, shoal
142.	oar	— boar, roar, soar
143.	oast	— boast, coast, roast, toast
144.	oat	— bloat, boat, coat, float, gloat, goat, groat, moat, shoat, stoat, throat
145.	ob	— blob, bob, cob, fob, glob, gob, job, lob, knob, mob, rob, slob, snob, sob, throb
146.	ock	— block, bock, chock, clock, cock, crock, dock, flock, frock, hock, knock, lock, mock, pock, rock, shock, smock, sock, stock
147.	od	— clod, cod, hod, God, mod, nod, plod, pod, prod, rod, scrod, shod, sod, trod
148.	ode	— bode, code, lode, mode, node, rode, strode
149.	oft	— loft, soft
150.	og	— bog, clog, cog, dog, flog, fog, frog, grog, hog, jog, log, slog, smog, tog

Third Reader page 8

151.	oice	– choice, voice
152.	oil	– boil, broil, coil, foil, moil, roil, soil, spoil, toil
153.	oin	– coin, groin, join, loin, quoin
154.	oke	– broke, choke, coke, joke, poke, smoke, spoke, stoke, stroke, woke, yoke
155.	old	– bold, cold, fold, gold, hold, mold, scold, sold, told
156.	ole	– bole, dole, hole, mole, pole, role, sole, stole, tole, whole
157.	olt	– bolt, colt, dolt, jolt, molt, volt
158.	ond	– blond, bond, fond, frond, pond
159.	ong	– gong, long, prong, song, strong, thong, throng, tong
160.	ood	– good, hood, stood, wood
161.	ood	– brood, food, mood, rood
162.	ook	– book, brook, cook, crook, hook, look, nook, rook, shook, took
163.	oof	– goof, poof, proof, spoof
164.	ool	– cool, drool, fool, pool, school, spool, stool, tool
165.	oom	– bloom, boom, broom, doom, gloom, groom, loom, room, zoom
166.	oon	– boon, coon, croon, moon, noon, soon, spoon, swoon
167.	oop	– coop, droop, goop, hoop, loop, scoop, sloop, snoop, stoop, swoop, troop, whoop
168.	oose	– goose, moose, loose, noose
169.	oot	– boot, coot, hoot, loot, moot, root, scoot, shoot, toot
170.	op	– cop, chop, crop, drop, fop, flop, glop, hop, lop, mop, plop, pop, prop, sop, shop, slop, stop, top, whop
171.	ope	– cope, dope, grope, hope, lope, mope, pope, rope, scope, slope, trope

Third Reader page 9

172.	ore	— bore, chore, core, fore, gore, lore, more, pore, score, shore, snore, sore, spore, store, swore, tore, wore, yore
173.	ork	— cork, fork, pork, stork, York
174.	orn	— born, corn, horn, morn, scorn, shorn, sworn, thorn, torn, worn
175.	ort	— fort, port, short, snort, sort, sport, tort, wort
176.	ose	— chose, close, hose, nose, pose, prose, rose, those
177.	oss	— boss, cross, floss, gloss, loss, moss, toss
178.	ost	— host, most, post
179.	ot	— blot, clot, cot, dot, got, hot, jot, knot, lot, mot, not, pot, plot, rot, Scot, shot, slot, spot, sot, tot, trot
180.	ote	— cote, dote, mote, note, quote, rote, smote, tote, vote, wrote
181.	oud	— cloud, loud, proud, shroud
182.	ought	— bought, brought, fought, sought, thought, wrought
183.	ould	— could, should, would
184.	ound	— bound, found, ground, hound, mound, pound, round, sound, wound
185.	ount	— count, fount, mount
186.	our	— dour, flour, hour, scour, sour
187.	ouse	— blouse, douse, grouse, house, louse, mouse, souse, spouse
188.	out	— bout, clout, flout, gout, grout, lout, pout, rout, scout, shout, snout, spout, stout, trout
189.	ove	— clove, cove, drove, grove, stove
190.	ow	— brow, chow, cow, how, now, plow, pow, prow, scow, sow, vow, wow

---

191.	ow	— blow, crow, flow, glow, grow, low, mow, row, show, slow, snow, sow, throw, tow

Third Reader page 10

192.	ox	— box, fox, lox, pox, sox
193.	oy	— boy, cloy, coy, joy, ploy, Roy, soy, toy, troy
194.	ube	— cube, rube, tube
195.	uch	— much, such
196.	uck	— buck, chuck, cluck, duck, luck, muck, pluck, puck, shuck, snuck, struck, stuck, suck, truck, tuck
197.	udge	— budge, drudge, fudge, grudge, judge, nudge, sludge, smudge, trudge
198.	uff	— bluff, cuff, fluff, huff, gruff, muff, puff, ruff, scuff, scruff, sluff, snuff, stuff
199.	ug	— bug, chug, drug, dug, hug, jug, lug, mug, plug, pug, rug, shrug, slug, smug, snug, thug, tug
200.	um	— bum, chum, drum, glum, gum, hum, plum, rum, scum, slum, strum, sum, swum, thrum
201.	umb	— crumb, dumb, numb, plumb, thumb
202.	ump	— bump, chump, clump, dump, frump, grump, hump, jump, lump, plump, pump, rump, slump, stump, sump, thump, trump
203.	un	— bun, dun, fun, gun, nun, pun, spun, stun, sun, tun
204.	unch	— brunch, bunch, crunch, hunch, lunch, munch, punch, scrunch
205.	une	— dune, June, prune, rune, tune
206.	ung	— bung, clung, dung, flung, hung, lung, rung, slung, sprung, strung, stung, sung, swung
207.	up	— cup, pup, sup
208.	ur	— blur, bur, cur, slur, spur, fur
209.	ure	— cure, lure, pure, sure
210.	urn	— burn, churn, spurn, turn
211.	urse	— curse, nurse, purse
212.	us	— bus, flus, nus, plus, pus, thus
213.	usk	— dusk, husk, musk, rusk, tusk

Third Reader page 11

214. uss   — buss, cuss, fuss, muss, truss
215. ust   — bust, crust, dust, gust, just, must, rust, thrust, trust
216. ut   — but, cut, glut, gut, hut, jut, nut, rut, shut, smut
217. uzz   — buzz, fuzz

WORDS FOR TEACHING THE CVC & CVCE RULE

A Vowels

can	cane
cap	cape
dam	dame
fad	fade
fat	fate
gap	gape
hat	hate
mad	made
mat	mate
nap	nape
pal	pale
pan	pane
Sam	same
tam	tame
tap	tape
plan	plane
scrap	scrape
shad	shade
sham	shame

E Vowels

bed	bede
pet	Pete
met	mete

I Vowels

bid	bide
bit	bite
dim	dime
din	dine
fin	fine
hid	hide
kit	kite
mil	mile
mit	mite
pin	pine
rid	ride
rip	ripe
Sid	side
sit	site
Tim	time

I Vowels (continued)

tin	tine
quit	quite
grim	grime
grip	gripe
prim	prime
shin	shine
slid	slide
slim	slime
snip	snipe
spin	spine
spit	spite
strip	stripe
trip	tripe
twin	twine

O Vowels

rob	robe
cod	code
dot	dote
hop	hope
lop	lope
mop	mope
not	note
pop	pope
rod	rode
rot	rote
ton	tone
tot	tote
glob	globe
slop	slope

U Vowels

Long *u* sound:

cub	cube
cut	cute

Long *oo* sound:

dun	dune
jut	jute
tub	tube
crud	crude
plum	plume

M

Prepositional Phrases

Appendix M is a list of prepositional phrases that may be used in teaching some of the most common words in the English language as well as the most common prepositions and noun words. Some teachers object, perhaps rightly so, to the teaching of basic sight words or any high utility word in isolation. For students who are having difficulty with any of the most commonly used prepositions, you may wish to use these phrases as you would with individual word flash cards. The author has found it helpful to make an audio tape of the phrases to be sent home with students who are having difficulties with these words. The tape may be made as follows:

1. Copy the first page, so that you will have it for further reference.
2. Number the first 10 to 15 phrases of the copy you have made. Once you have worked with a student for a short while, you will know how many he or she is capable of learning. If you find that you send 15 phrases on an audio tape home and the student has easily mastered all of them, then send home 20 more the next week. Increase these to the maximum that the student can successfully master in the time between meetings. Place a *1* by the first phrase, a *2* by the second phrase, etc. Then make an audio tape with a script much the same as the one that follows:

"You will hear some phrases on this tape recording. First you will hear a number and then you will hear the phrase. Look at each word as it is pronounced on this tape recording. There will then be a short pause for you to say the phrase. Be sure to point to each of the words as you say them. Number one, about his dog (pause); be sure to point to each word as you say it. Number two about my cat (pause); Number three about dinner, . ."

The author believes that it is extremely important to point to each word as it is pronounced. This way the student makes the connection between the spoken word and the written word. This seems to be the key to the successfulness of

357

the neurological-impress method and the successful use of the language-experience approach with students who are lacking in their sight vocabularies.

The following are commonly used phrases. Most of the words are also in the Fry list of the 600 most frequently used words in reading and writing the English language.*

about
about his dog
about my cat
about dinner
about my sister
about the room

after
after we've gone
after three years
after work
after his mother
after the bell

along
along the ground
along the water
along the wall
along the road
along the way

around
around the garden
around the school
around here
around eight o'clock
around the trees

as
as a house
as a girl
as a boy
as a man
as a woman

at
at the house
at the door
at the party
at the water
at the half

before
before winter
before bed
before the fire
before eight
before we go

but
but the outside
but the poor
but the yard
but his head
but her eyes

by
by the hair
by the horse
by the week
by the government
by her eyes

down
down the hill
down the side
down the front
down the street
down the stairs

---

*Edward Fry, *Reading Instruction for Classroom and Clinic* (New York: McGraw-Hill, 1972), pp. 58-63.

for
for the law
for the doctor
for the money
for a guess
for tomorrow

in
in the hour
in the music
in the spring
in the picture
in his voice

like
like the wind
like snow
like you
like her hat
like a bird

next
next turn
next president
next to me
next to him
next in line

off
off the wall
off the water
off the horse
off the table
off of it

out
out of paper
out to study
out of school
out of line
out in public

over
over his clothes
over the ice
over the city
over the thing
over his name

from
from the cows
from her need
from my cousin
from the cold
from the story

into
into the box
into the floor
into the train
into the bank
into the office

near
near the fish
near the war
near the bridge
near the farm
near the airplane

of
of the sun
of my life
of the farm
of the paper
of the church

on
on one afternoon
on Friday morning
on her smile
on the house
on her face

outside
outside the country
outside the woods
outside the town
outside the third grade
outside the grocery store

to
to the summer
to the fair
to the state
to the world
to the house

through
through them
through his heart
through twenty
through the day
through the water

up
up the window
up the river
up the table
up in the air
up to speak

until
until the night
until they come
until tomorrow
until this minute
until he knew

with
with his suit
with my uncle
with her aunt
with a present
with the baby

N

Prefixes and Suffixes

PREFIXES

Prefix	Meaning	Examples
a	on, in, at	alive asleep abed
a (an)	not, without	anhydrous anhydride anarchy
*ab, abs	*from*	abduct abrogate abstain
*ad (ac, af, ag, al, an, ap, ar, as, at)	*to*, at, toward	adapt accuse aggrade acclaim affirm
ambi (amb)	both	ambicoloration ambivalent ambidextrous
amphi (amph)	both, around	amphibian amphitheatre amphibolite

---

*Prefixes that appeared most frequently and accounted for 82 percent of the 61 different basic forms of prefixes studied by Stauffer. The italicized word represents the meaning of the prefix in the study referred to here. From Russell G. Stauffer, *Teaching Reading as a Thinking Process* (New York: Harper & Row, 1969), p. 348.

Prefix	Meaning	Examples
ana	back, again, up, similar to	analysis analogy anabaptist
ante	before, earlier date	antechamber antedate antetype
anti (ant, anth)	against, counteracts, prevents	antilabor antiaircraft antitoxin
apo (ap)	off, away from, used before	apology aphelion apocrine
archi (arch)	chief, extreme	architect archenemy archfiend
auto	self-propelling, self	automobile autotruck autobiography
*be	to make, about, by	belittle beguile befriend
bene	well	benefit benefactor benevolent
bi	having two, double	bicycle bilingual biweekly
by	near, extra	bystander by-pass by-product
cata (cat, cath)	down, against	catastrophic catacomb catheter
centi	one hundred	centigrade centimeter centipede

Prefix	Meaning	Examples
circum	around, about	circumnavigate circumpolar circumspect
*com (co, col, con, cor)	*with,* together, intensification	combine copilot collect confided corrupt
contra	against	contradict contraband contrarious
counter	opposite, in retaliation, opposed to but like	counterclockwise counterattack counterpart
*de	*from,* away	deport detract devitalize
deca (dec, deka, dek)	ten	decimal decade decagon
di (dis)	twice, double	dissect dichroism dichloride
dia	through, across	diagonal diagram diagnose
*dis	opposite, refuse to, *apart*	disagree disintegrate disable disengage
ec (ex)	out of, from	eccentric exodus exaggerate
*en	*in,* into make	encircle enact encourage

Prefix	Meaning	Examples
enter	to go into, among	enterprise entered entertain
epi (ep)	upon, after, over	epitaph epilogue epicene
equi	equal	equilibrium equilateral equiangular
*ex	*out*	exile exhale exhaust
eu	well	euphony euphonism eugenic
extra	beyond	extraordinary extrajudicial extracurricular
for	very, neglect, away	forlorn forbid forget
fore	before, in front	forepaws forehand foreleg
geo	earth, ground, soil	geography geographic geology
hemi	half	hemisphere hemicycle hemistich
hexa (hex)	six	hexagon hexapod hexachord
hyper	over, above	hypersensitive hyperactive hyperacid

Prefix	Meaning	Examples
hypo	under, beneath	hypocrite hypocycloid hypodermic
*in (il, im, ir)	in, within, *into*	inbreed instigate infect
*in (il, im, ir)	no, *not*, without	illiterate immaterial insignificant irresponsible
inter	between, with	interurban interlock interact
intra	within, inside of	intrastate intravenous intramural
intro	into, within	introvert introspective introduce
kilo	one thousand	kilowatt kilogram kilocycle
mal (male)	bad, wrong, ill	maladjust malediction maladroit
meta (met)	after, change in place or form	metacarpal metabolism metaprotein
milli	one thousand	milligram millimeter milliard
mis (miso)	wrong	misplace misadventure misanthrope
mono (mon)	one	monosyllable monologue monolayer

Prefix	Meaning	Examples
multi	many	multitude multiply multiphase
non	not	nonunion nondemocratic nonzero
ob (oc, of, op)	to, upon, totally	object occur offer oppose
oct (octa, octo)	eight	octopus octagon octopod
off	from	offspring offset offstage
out	beyond, excels	outtalk outweigh outmaneuver
over	too much	overactive overheated overage
par (para)	by, past, accessory	parrallel paragraph parasympathetic
penta (pent)	five	pentagon Pentateuch pentane
per	through, completely	perceive persuade perchloride
peri	around, about	perimeter periphery periscope
phono (phon, phone)	voice, sound	phonograph phonate phoneme

Prefix	Meaning	Examples
poly	many	polygon polygamy polysulfide
post	later, behind	postgraduate postaxial postlude
*pre	*before,* in front (of), superior	prewar preaxial pre-eminent
*pro	moving forward, acting for, defending, favoring, *in* *front of*	progress pronoun prosecutor prolabor prologue
quadr	four	quadrant quadrangle quadrennial
quint	five	quintuplets quintet quintillion
*re (red)	*back,* again	review regain recall
retro	backwards	retroactive retrospect retroflex
semi	half, partly, twice in (period)	semicircle semicivilized semiannually
sex (sexi)	six	sextant sexpartite sexivalent
*sub (suc, suf, sug, sup, sur, sus)	*under*	submarine succeed suffix
super	above, exceeding	superior superstructure superscribe

Prefix	Meaning	Examples
sur	over, above, beyond	surcoat surface surbase
syn (sym)	with, together	sympathy synthesis symptom
tele (tel)	afar, of, in, or by	television telescope telephoto
trans	across	transcontinental transport transatlantic
tri	three	triangle tricycle triweekly
ultra	beyond, excessively	ultraviolet ultramodern ultramarine
*un	*not,* opposite	unannounced unburden uncrowned
uni	consisting of only one	unicellular uniform unicorn
under	below	underpaid underworked underpass
vice	in place of	viceroy vice-president vice-consul
with	against, away	withstand withdraw withhold

SUFFIXES

Suffix	Meaning	Examples	Used to Form
able (ible, ble)	able to, worthy of	obtainable divisible breakable	adjectives
ac (ic, al, an)	characteristic of, having to do with, caused by	cardiac alcoholic comical American	adjectives
aceous (acious)	characterized by, like	carbonaceous crustaceous tenacious	adjectives
ade	action, product	blockade limeade lemonade	nouns
age	act of, cost of	tillage passage postage	nouns
al	relating to, of, pertaining to	directional fictional dismissal	adjectives
al	action process	rehearsal arrival acquittal	nouns
an (ian, ean)	pertaining to, of, born in	diocesan Christian European	adjectives
an	one who, belonging to	artisan African American	nouns
ance (ence)	act of, state of being	continuance reference performance	nouns
ancy (ency)	state of being, act	efficiency piquancy emergency	nouns

Suffix	Meaning	Examples	Used to Form
ant (ent)	one who	accountant suppliant superintendent	nouns
ant	performing, promoting	litigant expectorant expectant	adjectives
ar	relating to, like, of the nature of	regular polar singular	adjectives
ard (art)	one who (excessively)	braggart dullard pollard	nouns
arium	place relating to	planetarium sanitarium aquarium	nouns
ary (ar)	relating to	military dictionary scholar	nouns
ate	office, function	directorate vicarate magistrate	nouns
ate	acted on	temperate determinate animate	adjectives
ate	to become, combine, arrange for	evaporate chlorinate orchestrate	verbs
ation (ition)	state of	translation realization nutrition	nouns
cle	little, small	article particle corpuscle	nouns
dom	state of being	wisdom martyrdom freedom	nouns

Suffix	Meaning	Examples	Used to Form
ed	tending to, having	cultured versed bigoted	adjectives
en	cause to have, made of	strengthen woolen wooden	nouns
en	to make, made of	deepen strengthen fasten	verbs
ent (ence)	quality, act, degree	solvent emergence despondence	nouns
er (ar ior, yer)	a thing or action, connected with, or associated	batter beggar interior lawyer	nouns
ery (erie)	place to or for collection of	nunnery jewelry tanneries	nouns
esce	to begin	effervesce fluoresce coalesce	verbs
escent	starting to be	obsolescent fluorescent alkalescent	adjectives
esque	like, having quality or style of	picturesque Romanesque statuesque	adjectives
ess	female	patroness giantess princess	nouns
et (ette)	little, female	dinette suffragette pullet	nouns
ful	full of	hopeful playful joyful	adjectives

Suffix	Meaning	Examples	Used to Form
fy	to make, become	liquefy purify glorify	verbs
hood	state of, condition	womanhood childhood priesthood	nouns
eer	one who, calling or profession	auctioneer buccaneer profiteer	nouns
ic (ics)	relating to, affected with	alcoholic allergic volcanic	adjectives
ic (ical)	one that produces	magic cosmetic radical	nouns
ice	condition or quality of	malice justice practice	nouns
ie	small, little	doggie lassie	nouns
ile (il)	appropriate to, suited for, capable of	docile missile civil	adjectives
ing	related to, made of	farthing banking cooking	nouns
ion (sion)	result of act, state	regulation hydration correction	nouns
ise (ize)	to make, treat with	sterilize summarize finalize	verbs
ish	having	boyish purplish fortyish	adjectives

Suffix	Meaning	Examples	Used to Form
ism	act of, state of	baptism invalidism animalism	nouns
ist	practicer or believer in one who, the doer	evangelist pianist violinist	nouns
ive	related to, tending to	creative massive amusive	adjectives
ize	to become, become like	Americanize crystallize socialize	verbs
kin	little	catkin manikin napkin	nouns
le (el)	small, a thing used for for doing	icicle handle mantle	nouns
less	without, lacking	careless hopeless painless	adjectives
ling	young, small	duckling hireling suckling	nouns
ly	in a way, manner	softly quietly hoarsely	adverbs
ment	concrete result, state, process	embankment development amazement	nouns
ness	state of being	happiness cheerfulness hopefulness	nouns
ock	small one	hillock bullock paddock	nouns

Suffix	Meaning	Examples	Used to Form
or	state of, does certain thing	pallor grantor elevator	nouns
orium	place for, giving	sanatorium auditorium haustorium	nouns
ory	tending to, producing	auditory gustatory justificatory	adjectives
ose	full of, containing, like	verbose cymose morose	adjectives
ous	having, full of	religious generous poisonous	adjectives
ship	state of, office, art	friendship clerkship horsemanship	nouns
ster	one that does or is	spinster teamster youngster	nouns
th	act of, state of	growth length spilth	nouns
tude	condition	certitude gratitude finitude	nouns
ty (ity)	state of, degree, quality	masculinity priority timidity	nouns
ulent	tending to, abounds in	fraudulent flocculent opulent	adjectives
ure	act, office	exposure legislature procedure	nouns

Suffix	Meaning	Examples	Used to Form
ward	in specified direction	southward seaward backward	adverbs
wise	manner, way	likewise clockwise lengthwise	adverbs
y	like a, full of	rosy fishy glassy	adjectives
y (acy)	state of, action, condition, position	jealousy inquiry celibacy	nouns

Samples of the Author, Title, and Subject Cards

Call number

Author

Title

Publisher & date
of publication

Total number of
pages in book

Indicates subject
heading in library
card catalog
Indicates there is
a title card in
card catalog

395 G	
	Parker, Pamela
	Table Manners around the World. Illus. by Lilia Lavender Merrill, 1989.
	260p. illus.
	1. Etiquette I. Title

TITLE CARD

Call number	395 G
Title	Table Manners around the World

Parker, Pamela
Table Manners around the World.
Illus. by Lilia Lavender
Merrill, 1989.

260p. illus.

1. Etiquette   I. Title

Call number — 395 G

Title — Table Manners around the World

Author

Publisher & date
of publication

Total number of
pages in book

Indicates subject
heading in library
card catalog
Indicates there is
a title card in
card catalog

SUBJECT CARD

Call number	395 G
Subject	Etiquette

Parker, Pamela
Table Manners around the World.
Illus. by Lilia Lavender
Merrill, 1989.

1. Etiquette   I. Title
64

Call number

Subject

Author
Title

Publisher & date
of publication

Indicates subject
heading in library
card catalog
Indicates there is
a title card in
card catalog

P

Charts for Graphing Words per Minute and Comprehension

Appendix P is for students to use in graphing their reading rate in words per minute, as well as graphing their percentage of comprehension. A number of available study skills or reading rate books present passages to be read by the student. These are usually followed by comprehension questions for the student to answer. In most cases there are ten questions. You may wish to use the system of graphing each factor separately that appears on page 382 or the one on the preceding page which takes both percentage of comprehension and reading rate in words per minute into account. It will, of course, do the student little good to improve reading rate if comprehension suffers considerably in the process. In using the combination chart on page 382, multiply the number of words per minute by the percentage of comprehension and then graph the combination of these two factors. On page 381 you will find a sample of Fred's reading scores graphed for six trials. Note that there are blank lines on the left side of the graph to be filled in by the student. The lines have been left blank because every student will tend to read at a different rate. As the student gains in competence, he or she will probably improve in overall comprehension. Although percentage of comprehension may *decrease* as the child increases reading speed, it will usually increase after practice. Start the number representing the combination of the words per minute and percentage of comprehension on the third line from the bottom (as shown in the example with Fred), since it is quite possible that the student may decrease in overall score slightly before beginning to increase that score. The method of computing Fred's scores is shown below the graph of Fred's reading performance. This is the system that you should, of course, use if you wish to graph your own scores.

Name

Progress Chart

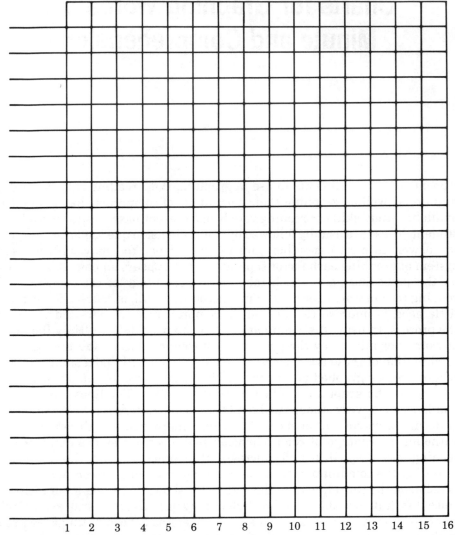

Name **Fred**

Progress Chart

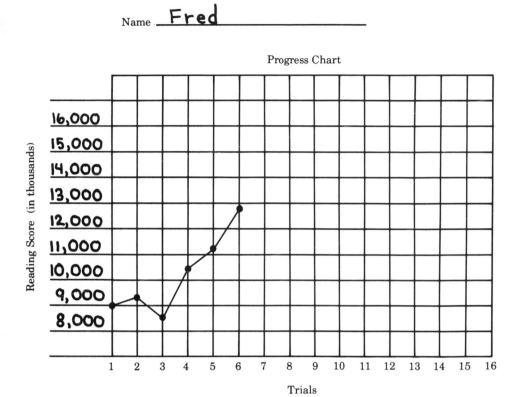

Reading Score (in thousands)

16,000
15,000
14,000
13,000
12,000
11,000
10,000
9,000
8,000

1   2   3   4   5   6   7   8   9   10   11   12   13   14   15   16

Trials

On Fred's first trial he read at 150 words per minute and had a comprehension score of 60 percent. There his score was $150 \times 60 = 9000$. This score was then put as the first trial using the third line from the bottom, in case in any future trials his score might decrease instead of increase.

On the following five trials, Fred's scores are shown below and graphed above.

Trial 2: 155 words per minute with a comprehension score of 60 percent = 9,300

Trial 3: 170 words per minute with a comprehension score of 50 percent = 8,500

Trial 4: 175 words per minute with a comprehension score of 60 percent = 10,500

Trial 5: 185 words per minute with a comprehension score of 60 percent = 11,100

Trial 6: 185 words per minute with a comprehension score of 70 percent = 12,950

ILLUSTRATING WORDS PER MINUTE AND
PERCENT OF COMPREHENSION

Name _____

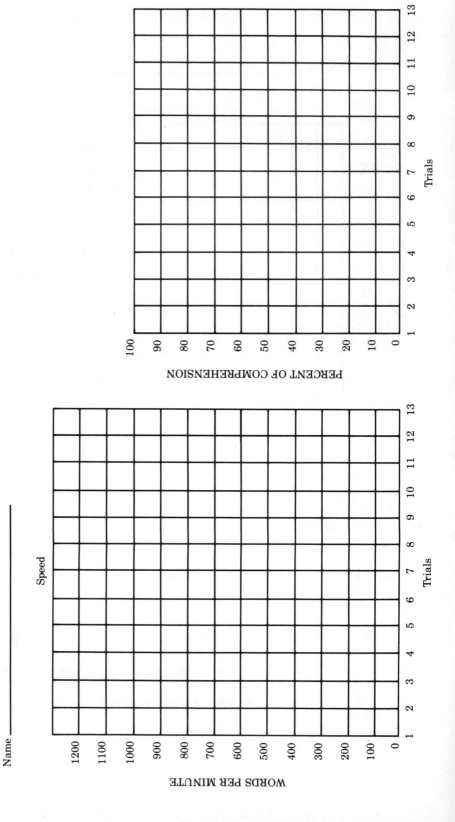

Repeated Readings Chart

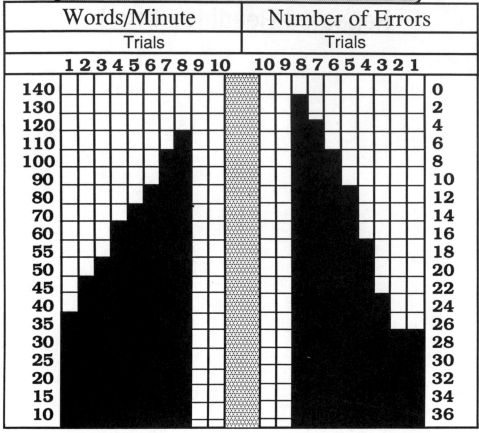

Repeated Readings Chart

This is an example of a repeated readings chart in which the student began reading at 35 words/minute and, after eight trials, was reading at 120 words/minute. The student also began this passage with 26 errors and, after eight trials, made no errors. To compute words/minute count the number of words the student will be reading and then determine the time it takes the student to read that passage in seconds. The words/minute equals the number of words read divided by the number of seconds it took to read the passage, multiplied by 60. A student who reads 220 words in 110 seconds would then be reading at: $220/110 = 2.0$ X $60 = 120$ words/minute. In doing repeated readings, it is recommended that you use 100 words/grade level X .75. Thus a student in the fourth grade should read 400 X .75 or 300 words. A student in the fifth grade should read 500 X .75 or a 375-word passage, etc.

Repeated Readings Chart

Words/Minute		Number of Errors	
Trials		Trials	
1 2 3 4 5 6 7 8 9 10		10 9 8 7 6 5 4 3 2 1	
140			0
130			2
120			4
110			6
100			8
90			10
80			12
70			14
60			16
55			18
50			20
45			22
40			24
35			26
30			28
25			30
20			32
15			34
10			36

Name of Student: _____

Number of Words in Passage: _____

R

Sources of Reading Materials

Programs	Reading Skills	Specific Titles	Reading Grade Level	Interest Grade Level
Benefic Press **10300 W. Roosevelt Rd.** **Westchester, IL 60153**				
Alley Alligator Series. A series of five books written at the pre-primer to third-grade level; develops an understanding and respect for the natural environment.	Reading skills	Alley Alligator	PP	1–2
		Alley Alligator and the Fire	PP	1–3
		Alley Alligator and the Hurricane	1.0	1–4
		Alley Alligator and the Big Race	2.0	2–5
		Alley Alligator and the Hunters	3.0	3–6
Animal Adventure Series. A series of 12 books provides high-interest readers with use of humor and provides low-difficulty readers in areas of children's natural interest. Includes an activity section with questions and "Things to Do."	Reading skills Comprehension	Becky the Rabbit	PP	1–3
		Squeaky, the Squirrel	PP	1–3
		Doc, the Dog	PP	1–3
		Pat, the Parakeet	PP	1–3
		Kate, the Cat	PP	1–3
		Gomer, the Gosling	PP	1–3
		Skippy, the Skunk	P	1–3
		Sandy, the Swallow	P	1–3
		Sally, the Screech Owl	P	1–3
		Pudgy, the Beaver	1.0	1–4
		Hamilton, the Hamster	1.0	1–4
		Horace, the Horse	1.0	1–4

Description	Skill area	Title	Level	Grade
Butternut Bill Series. A series of eight books written at the pre-primer to first-grade reading level. Features high-interest, low-difficulty readers. Story situations are humorous and taken from everyday life. Provides carefully controlled vocabulary. Available with correlated cassettes. Program may be used as remediation as well as supplemental grade level.	Reading skills Word perception	Butternut Bill	PP	PP–2
		Butternut Bill and the Bee Tree	PP	PP–2
		Butternut Bill and the Big Catfish	PP	PP–2
		Butternut Bill and the Bear	P	P–3
		Butternut Bill and Little River	P	P–3
		Butternut Bill and the Big Pumpkin	P	P–3
		Butternut Bill and His Friends	1.0	1–3
		Butternut Bill and the Train	1.0	1–4
Comprehension-Critical Reading Kits. A program designed to develop reading-comprehension skills. Includes content in Language Arts, Social Studies, and Science. Features 10 sequentially developed major strands of reading comprehension. Placement test, post-test, and record keeping.	Comprehension	Kit #46		4–6
		Kit #57		5–7
		Kit #68		6–8
Comprehension and Critical Reading Workbooks. A program designed to develop a student's comprehension skills. Provides instruction and practice in four areas of reading comprehension: identifying main ideas, understanding details, seeing relationships, thinking critically.	Comprehension Reading skills	Book #35	3.0	3-5
		Book #46	4.0	4-6
		Book #57	5.0	5-7
		Book #68	6.0	6-8

389

Programs	Reading Skills	Specific Titles	Reading Grade Level	Interest Grade Level
Vocabulary Mastery. This series consists of easy-to-use duplicating master books designed to improve and expand vocabulary. Activities include: matching word and meaning, word categories, dictionary use, meaning from context, games and puzzles.	Vocabulary	Mastery A		3
		Mastery B		4
		Mastery C		5
		Mastery D		6
		Mastery E		7
		Mastery F		8
Cowboy Sam Series. A series of 15 books with reading levels ranging from preprimer to third grade. These books are exciting and humorous. Easy vocabulary permits even slow readers to share adventure. Program includes readers and cassettes. The interest levels run two to three grades above the books' reading levels.	Vocabulary skills Reading skills	Cowboy Sam and Big Bill	PP	PP–2
		Cowboy Sam and Freckles	PP	PP–2
		Cowboy Sam and Dandy	PP	PP–2
		Cowboy Sam and Miss Lily	P	P–3
		Cowboy Sam and Porky	P	P–3
		Cowboy Sam	P	P–3
		Cowboy Sam and Flop	1.0	1–4
		Cowboy Sam and Shorty	1.0	1–4
		Cowboy Sam and Freddy	1.0	1–4
		Cowboy Sam and Sally	2.0	2–5
		Cowboy Sam and the Fair	2.0	2–5
		Cowboy Sam and the Rodeo	2.0	2–5
		Cowboy Sam and the Airplane	3.0	3–6
		Cowboy Sam and the Indians	3.0	3–6
		Cowboy Sam and the Rustlers	3.0	3–6

Tom Logan Series. A series of 10 books with reading levels ranging from preprimer to third grade. Tom Logan books spark readers' enthusiasm at the primary level. Slower readers find success with carefully controlled vocabulary. Children easily identify with the young characters. Available with correlated cassettes.

	Reading skills Word perception		
Pony Rider		PP	PP–2
Talking Wire		PP	PP–2
Track Boss		P	P–3
Cattle Drive		P	P–3
Secret Tunnel		1.0	1–4
Gold Train		1.0	1–4
Gold Nugget		2.0	1–5
Cattle Cars		2.0	2–5
Stagecoach Driver		3.0	3–6
Circus Train		3.0	3–6

Dan Frontier Series. A series of 11 books with reading levels ranging from preprimer to fourth grade. Their interest runs two to three grades above their reading level. Content is high interest, while the readability is controlled. Social and personal values are emphasized.

	Reading skills Word perception		
Dan Frontier and the New House		PP	P–2
Dan Frontier		PP	P–2
Dan Frontier and the Big Cat		P	P–3
Dan Frontier Goes Hunting		P	P–3
Dan Frontier, Trapper		1	1–4
Dan Frontier with the Indians		1	1–4
Dan Frontier and the Wagon Train		2	2–5
Dan Frontier Scouts with the Army		2	2–5
Dan Frontier the Sheriff		3	3–6
Dan Frontier Goes Exploring		3	3–6

Helicopter Adventure Series. A series of six books written at the primer to third-grade level with interest levels that range from primer to fourth grade. Progressive difficulty for easy measurement of reading progress.

	Reading skills Word attack		
Chopper Malone and the New Pilot		P	P–1
Chopper Malone and Susie		P	P–1
Chopper Malone and the Big Snow		1	1–2
Chopper Malone and Trouble at Sea		1	1–2
Chopper Malone and the Mountain Rescue		2	2–3
Chopper Malone and the Skylarks		3	3–4

Programs	Reading Skills	Specific Titles	Reading Grade Level	Interest Grade Level
Treat Truck Series. A series of eight books developed to provide enjoyable and interesting stories for young readers. Skill development is provided in a controlled and increasingly more difficult progression.	Reading skills	Mike and the Treat Truck	PP	PP–2
		Treat Truck and the Fire	PP	PP–2
		Treat Truck and the Dog Show	P	P–2
		Treat Truck and the Big Rain	P	P–2
		Treat Truck and the Parade	1	1–2
		Treat Truck and the Lucky Lion	1	1–2
		Treat Truck and the Storm	2	2–4
		Treat Truck and the Bank Robbery	3	3–5
The Moonbeam Series. A series of 10 books written at the primer to third-grade level. High-interest, low-difficulty stimulates interest in reading about real-life experiences. Controlled vocabulary provides reading practice for increased skills. Questions help develop critical thinking skills.	Reading skills Vocabulary	Moonbeam	PP	P–3
		Moonbeam is Caught	PP	P–3
		Moonbeam and the Captain	PP	P–3
		Moonbeam is Lost	P	P–3
		Moonbeam and the Big Jump	P	P–3
		Moonbeam and the Rocket Ride	1	1–4
		Moonbeam and Dan Starr	1	1–4
		Moonbeam Finds a Moon Stone	2	2–5
		Moonbeam and Sunny	3	3–6
Space Science Fiction Series. A series of six books, grades fourth to twelfth. This series provides interesting reading with controlled readability. High-interest controlled vocabulary allows reluctant readers to succeed.	Reading skills Vocabulary	Space Pirate	2	4–12
		Milky Way	2	4–12
		Bone People	3	4–12
		Planet of the Whistlers	4	4–12
		Inviso Man	5	4–12
		Ice-Men of Rime	6	4–12

Inner City Series. A series of five books written at the second- to fourth-grade reading level with interest levels that run from two to three grades above their reading grade levels.

Reading skills

Beat the Gang	2	2–5
Tough Guy	3	3–6
Runaway	3	3–6
New Boy in School	4	4–7
No Drop Out	4	4–7

Mystery Adventure Series. A series of six books written at the second- to sixth-grade level. These mystery stories about teenage boys and girls, have high interest levels two to ten grades above their reading grade levels.

Reading skills

Mystery Adventure of the Talking Statues	2	4–12
Mystery Adventure of the Jeweled Bell	2	4–12
Mystery Adventure at Cave Four	3	4–12
Mystery Adventure of the Indian Burial Ground	4	4–12
Mystery Adventure at Longcliff Inn	5	4–12
Mystery Adventure of Smuggled Treasure	6	4–12

World Adventure Series. A series of eight books written at the second- to sixth-grade levels. Helps to build and review the vocabulary of basal reading series.

Reading skills

Lost Uranium Mine	2	4–9
Flight to South Pole		4–9
Hunting Grizzly Bears	3	4–9
Fire on The Mountain		4–9
City Beneath the Sea	4	4–9
The Search for Piranha	4	4–9
Sacred Well of Sacrifice	5	4–9
Viking Treasure	6	4–9

Programs	Reading Skills	Specific Titles	Reading Grade Level	Interest Grade Level
Sports Mystery Series. A series of 12 books written at the second- to fourth-grade levels. These stories are about teenagers, their problems, and sports activities. This series is valuable in remedial programs.	Reading skills	Luck of The Runner	2	4–12
		Ten Feet Tall	2	4–12
		No Turning Back	2	4–12
		Gymnast Girl	3	4–12
		Ski-Mountain Mystery		4–12
		Fairway Danger	3	4–12
		Tip Off	3	4–12
		Pitcher's Choice	3	4–12
		Scuba Diving	4	4–12
		Face Off	4	4–12
		Swimmer's Mark	4	4–12
		Tennis Champ	4	4–12
Racing Wheels Series. A series of 12 books written at the second- to fourth-grade levels.	Reading skills Vocabulary	Hot Rod	2	4–12
		Motorcycle Scramble		4–12
		Destruction Derby	2	4–12
		Motorcycle Racer	2	4–12
		Drag Race	3	4–12
		Baja 500	3	4–12
		Stock Car Race	3	4–12
		Safari Rally	3	4–12
		Road Race	4	4–12
		Grand Prix Races	4	4–12
		Indy 500	4	4–12
		Le Mans Race	4	4–12
Target Today Series. A series of 10 books written at the preprimer to third-grade levels. Easy-to-read life of the Old West.	Reading skills	Here It Is	1.9–2.5	4–12
		Action Now	2.5–3.5	4–12
		Move Ahead	3.5–4.5	4–12
		Lead On	4.5–4.9	4–12

Bowmar Noble Publishers, Inc.
4563 Colorado Boulevard
Los Angeles, CA 90039

Bowmar Noble Skills Series. This is a workbook program designed to teach the skills shown.

Skills	Title	Reading Level	Grade
Vocabulary			3–6
Dictionary skills			
Map-reading skills			
Spelling skills			
Library and reference skills			

Double Play Reading Series: Triple Play Series. These kits capitalize on students' interest in sports. Provides skill-building tools to improve reading comprehension. Teacher's guide included.

Skills	Title	Reading Level	Grade
Comprehension development	Big League Baseball	2.0–4.3	4–8
	NFL Reading	2.0–4.3	4–8
	Pro Basketball	2.0–4.3	4–8

Primary Reading Series. This kit consists of high-interest story cards written at the interest level of young readers. Teacher's guide included.

Skills	Title	Reading Level	Grade
Word recognition	Laugh & Secrets	1.3–2.5	1–3
Vocabulary development	Toys	1.3–2.5	1–3
Comprehension development	Mikie	1.3–2.5	1–3
	Sydney	1.3–2.5	1–3
	Pets	1.3–2.5	1–3
	Morton	1.3–2.5	1–3

Reading Comprehension Series. This series consists of high-interest story cards. Questions are provided to teach and evaluate comprehension skills. Teacher's guide included.

Skills	Title	Reading Level	Grade
Comprehension development	Aviation	3.0–4.4	4–8
	Dogs	3.0–4.4	4–8
	Marguerite	3.0–4.4	4–8
	Henry's Horse	3.0–4.4	4–8
	Crime Fighters	3.0–4.4	4–8
	Cars and Cycles	3.0–4.4	4–8
	Fads	3.0–4.4	4–8
	Special People	3.0–4.4	4–8
	Escape	3.0–4.4	4–8

395

Programs	Reading Skills	Specific Titles	Reading Grade Level	Interest Grade Level
Quicksilver Books. This series includes high-interest selections and quizzes to review basic comprehension skills and a set of questions that lead students through the process of writing a book report.	Comprehension review Book-report writing skills	Horses Dogs Aviation Cars & Cycles Fads Crime Fighters	3.0–4.5 3.0–4.5 3.0–4.5 3.0–4.5 3.0–4.5 3.0–4.5	4–8 4–8 4–8 4–8 4–8 4–8
Letter Sounds All Around. This is a program to teach the alphabet. Included are filmstrips, cassettes, workbooks, and a teacher's guide.	Consonant and vowel recognition	Alphabet Soup Tick Tock Time Jelly Jars Blues	PP PP PP	P P P
Gold Dust Books. This series encourages students' independent reading habits.	Reading skills	Includes 36 volumes written at 2.0–2.9 reading levels		4–6
Reading Zingo. Children listen to letters or words from a record, then mark the right place on their cards, much like Bingo.	Vocabulary development Word recognition Consonant blends and contractions	Beginning Consonants Consonant Blends Contractions Word Building		3–6 3–6 3–6 3–6

Drier Educational Systems
P.O. Box 1291
Highland Park, NJ 08904

Storybooks for Beginners. A series of four books with phonetically controlled vocabulary written at the first-grade level.

Skills	Products	Grade
Phonic skills	Dragon Don (total of 15 vocabulary)	1–4
Vocabulary skills	Dragon Don and Tim (total of 27 vocabulary)	1–4
	Sailboat (total of 39 vocabulary)	1–4
	Sailboat in the Wind (total of 53 vocabulary)	1–4

Scholastic Magazine & Book Service
50 West 44th Street
New York, NY 10036

Scope Visuals. For individual skills reinforcement or classwide instruction. Helps you pinpoint specific reading problems.

Skills	Products	Grade
Comprehension skills	Reading Anthology for each grade level.	7–12
Spelling skills	Spelling Skills for each grade level.	7–12
Writing skills	Writing Skills for each grade level.	7–12
Language skills	Language Skills for each grade level.	7–12
	Grammar & Composition for each grade level.	7–12

Programs	Reading Skills	Specific Titles	Reading Grade Level	Interest Grade Level
Action Program. Teaches below-level students reading comprehension skills that bring them closer to on-level performance. It is the only complete core-instructional and remedial reading system for secondary students that teaches essential reading material.	Comprehension skills	Duration of instruction: 1/2 yr.		
	Reading skills	Unit I	2.0–2.2	
		Unit II	2.2–2.5	
		Unit III	2.6–2.9	
		Library 1A	2.0–2.4	7–12
		Library 1B	2.0–2.4	7–12
		Library 1	2.0–2.4	7–12
		Library 2A	2.5–2.9	7–12
		Library 2B	2.5–2.9	7–12
		Library 2	2.5–2.9	7–12
		Library 3A	3.0–3.4	7–12
		Library 3B	3.0–3.4	7–12
		Library 3	3.0–3.4	7–12
		Library 4A	3.5–3.9	7–12
		Library 4B	3.5–3.9	7–12
		Library 4	3.5–3.9	7–12
Double Action. Skills are reinforced and extended through a variety of practice exercises that relate to stories being read.	Comprehension skills	Duration of instruction: 1/2 yr. Action Library 15,000 to 20,000 words		
		Library 1A	3.0–3.4	7–12
		Library 1	3.0–3.4	7–12
		Library 2	3.5–3.9	7–12
		Library 3	4.0–4.4	7–12
		Library 4	4.5–4.9	7–12
Triple Action. Three unit books teach skills via prereading exercises. Stories, post-reading exercise, and skill-building lessons.	Comprehension skills	Unit I	4.0–6.0	7–12
	Reading skills	Unit II	4.0–6.0	7–12
		Unit III	4.0–6.0	7–12
		Duration of instruction: 1 yr.		

Individualized Reading from Scholastic. This develops the student's own reading program by choosing what he or she wants to read from a wide range of children's literature. Good to use as text extenders; many companies to choose from.

Basic sight words
Vocabulary
Comprehension development
Word analysis
Dictionary
Study skills
Oral reading skills

Ginn Reading Program		
Little Dog Laughed/Fish & Not Fish	PP	P–Jr
Inside My Hat/Birds Fly, Bears Don't	PP	P–Jr
Glad to Meet You/Give Me a Clue		2.1–2.2
Mystery Sweater/Ten Times Around		3.1–3.2
Barefoot Island	4.0	P–Jr
Ride the Sunrise	5.0	P–Jr
Flights of Color	6.0	P–Jr

Scholastic Literature Units. This program focuses on themes of vital interest, provides for individual differences, emphasizes major literary forms, and develops good reading habits.

Vocabulary development
Comprehension skills
Study skills

Communication	Jr.H.
The Individual	Sr.H.
Society	Sr.H.

Bell & Howell Co.
7100 McCormick Rd.
Chicago, IL 60645

The Reading Game. A five-box instructional program designed to teach as sight words the 440 core words common to the basal reading programs.

Vocabulary development
Reading skills

Student Levels:
Primary Students
Elementary Students
Elementary & Secondary Remedial Students
ESL Students
Special Ed. Students

PP–Elementary

399

Programs	Reading Skills	Specific Titles	Reading Grade Level	Interest Grade Level
Vocabulary Master Program. A set of six instructional programs that teach the understanding and use of 300 commonly misused or misunderstood words.	Vocabulary skills	Student Levels: Grades 5–7 supplementary Grades 8–9 remedial		
Word Picture Program. A highly visual sequential program created to expand the student's sight-recognition vocabulary to include 376 graphic nouns, verbs, and auxiliary words essential to reading proficiency.	Vocabulary skills	Student Levels: Primary-Sixth Elementary & Secondary Remedial ESL Students Special Ed. Students		
Language Master. An electronic card reader that employs sight, touch, and hearing.	Vocabulary skills Phonetic analysis Structural analysis	Card Reader Readiness Word Attack Vocabulary Language Development Comprehension Special Ed. & ESL		K.–Adults
	Word attack:	TGR Sound System		K–8
		Phonics Program		1–6
		Linguistic Word Pattern		1–3
	Vocabulary:	Vocabulary Mastery		1–6
		TGR Sight Vocabulary		2–6
		Word Picture Program		5–12
	Language:	ALAP		K–1
		Reading Through Pictures		2–6
		Articulation Therapy		2–12
		English Development		1–6
		ESL		3–8
	Comprehension:	STAR		5–9

400

Source	Title / Description	Skills	Components / Notes		
Phonovisual Products 12216 Parklawn Drive Rockville, MD 20853	*Phonics Charts.*	Phonics	Beginning Level		
Prentice-Hall, Inc **Englewood Cliffs, NJ 07632**	*Reading For Every Day: Survival Skills.* Students develop reading competency by applying reading skills to everyday experiences.	Survival reading skills	50 Activity Cards 10 Books	4.0 4.0	4–7 4–7
Webster Division **McGraw-Hill Book Co.** **28th Floor** **1121 Avenue of the Americas** **New York, NY 10020**	*Webster Word Wheels.* This program contains 63 wheels, of which 17 are beginning blends, 20 prefix wheels, 18 suffix wheels, 8 two-letter consonant wheels, and a file box. The purpose of this is to teach students basic phonetic and structural-analysis skills.	Phonics Word analysis	Use for Elementary & Junior-High Students.		

Programs	Reading Skills	Specific Titles	Reading Grade Level	Interest Grade Level
Sunburst Communication **RM U23** **39 Washington Avenue** **Pleasantville, NY 10570**				
Hi-Lo Reading Activity Card Program. This is a remedial-reading program for improving reading comprehension.	Comprehension development	18 Paperback Books	5.0–7.0	4–12
		20 Activity Cards	5.0–7.0	4–12
		12 Paperback Books	3.0–5.0	3–7
		20 Activity Cards	3.0–5.0	3–7
Science Research Associates, Inc. **259 East Erie Street** **Chicago, IL 60611**				
Getting It Together. A reading series about people. This program consists of a text, a student resource book, and a teacher's guide. The text contains stories about concerns of adolescents. The student resource has three sections.	Comprehension development	Level I	3.0	3–12
		Level II	4.0	3–12
		Level III	5.0	3–12
Schoolhouse: Comprehension Patterns. This comprehension-skill program provides a variety of increasingly sophisticated sentences for interpretation.	Comprehension skills	195 Activity Cards arranged in 10 units. Teacher's Guide and 10 plastic overlays. Includes remedial teaching lessons and provides for flexibility.		3–8

402

Description	Skills	Material	Reading Levels	Grade Levels
Individualized Reading Skills Program. This program consists of four pupil books and a teacher's guide. Each book emphasizes a different vowel-skill program.	Phonics Vocabulary Structural analysis	Gilligan Milligan (short vowel) Risky Ride (long vowel) Strawberry Emergency (variant vowel) Sky Diver (variant vowel)		2–6 2–6 2–6 2–6
Mark II Reading Laboratory Series. Each kit contains 150 power-builder cards, 150 rate-builder cards, and 150 skill-development cards.	Word study Comprehension Study skills Vocabulary skills Dictionary skills	Kit 2A reading levels: Kit 2B reading levels: Kit 2C reading levels:	2.0, 2.5, 3.0, 3.5, 4.0, 4.5, 5.0, 5.5, 6.0, 7.0, 2.5, 3.0, 3.5, 4.0, 4.5, 5.0, 5.5, 6.0, 7.0, 8.0, 3.0, 3.5, 4.0, 4.5, 5.0, 5.5, 6.0, 7.0, 8.0, 9.0	2–7 2–8 3–9
Readers' Workshop. Each readers' workshop gives students a five-grade span of sequential material, covering 25 comprehension skills.	Comprehension skills Study skills Literary skills	Readers' Workshop I Readers' Workshop II	3–7 5.9	3–12 3–12
SRA Lunchbox Libraries. This is a recreational reading series of short books to motivate young readers. Each kit contains two copies each of 32 selections. There are two levels in each kit, written a level below the level at which students are working in their basal readers.	Word recognition Vocabulary comprehension	Preprimer Kit Preprimer Pink Kit IA Kit IA Yellow Kit IA Red Kit IB Kit IB Blue Kit IB Orange	PP-2.0 PP-2.0 PP-2.0 PP-2.0 PP-2.0 PP-2.0 PP-2.0 PP-2.0	1–3 1–3 1–3 1–3 1–3 1–3 1–3 1–3
SRA Skills Series. There are three skill sets to this series. Each kit contains 48 independent teaching units with instruction and practice for specific skills.	Phonics Structural analysis Comprehension	Phonics Skills Structural Analysis Comprehension Skills	1.0–3.0 3.0–7.0 4.0–8.0	1–8 1–8 1–8

Programs	Reading Skills	Specific Titles	Reading Grade Level	Interest Grade Level
Super Kits. This is a high-interest, controlled-vocabulary comic book series designed for reluctant readers with limited word-attack and comprehension skills.	Vocabulary Comprehension skills Oral reading Phonics	Super A Super AA Super B Super BB	2.0 3.0 4.0 5.0	4–8 4–8 4–8 4–8
Vocabulary 3 Program. This kit contains 20 explora-wheels that show the elements of word structures such as prefixes, suffixes, and roots. Also included are 150 vocabulary builders that contain stories, articles, exercises, and activities in 10 areas.	Vocabulary development	3 Kits	5.0–14.0	5–jr.
SRA Pilot Libraries. This program is designed to bridge the gap between reading training and independent reading by using short excerpts, complete in themselves, from full-length books.	Comprehension	Pilot Library Kit IC 2.0, 3.0, 4.0, 5.0, 6.0 Pilot Library Kit 2A 2.0, 3.0, 4.0, 5.0, 6.0, 7.0 Pilot Library Kit 2B 3.0, 4.0, 5.0, 6.0, 7.0 Pilot Library Kit 2C 4.0, 5.0, 6.0, 7.0, 8.0, 9.0 Pilot Library Kit 3B 5.0, 6.0, 7.0, 8.0, 9.0, 10.0, 11.0, 12.0		3–9 3–9 3–9 3–9 3–9
SRA Reading for Understanding. This program is a set of 400 reading comprehension exercises designed to aid each student in improving ability to get mean-	Comprehension skills	Reading for Understanding I Reading for Understanding II Reading for Understanding III	3–7 7–12	1–3 3–Adult 3–Adult

Program	Skills	Content	Grade Level
SRA Reading Laboratories. This program contains reading labs from IA to IC, 2A to 2C, 3A to 3B and 4A, pupil booklets for labs, and is an individualized reading system.	Basic sight words Vocabulary skills Word-attack skills Dictionary skills Study skills Comprehension	Reading Laboratory Kit IA: 1.2, 1.4, 1.6, 1.8, 2.0, 2.2, 2.4, 2.6, 2.8, 3.0, 3.2, 3.5	3–9
		Kit IB: 1.4, 1.6, 1.8, 2.0, 2.2, 2.4, 2.6, 2.8, 3.0, 3.5, 4.0, 4.5	3–9
		Kit IC: 1.6, 1.8, 2.0, 2.2, 2.4, 2.6, 3.0, 3.5, 4.0, 4.5, 5.0, 5.5	3–9
		Kit 2A: 2.0, 2.5, 3.0, 3.5, 4.0, 4.5, 5.0, 5.5, 6.0, 7.0	3–9
		Kit 2B: 2.5, 3.0, 3.5, 4.0, 4.5, 5.0, 5.5, 6.0, 7.0, 8.0	3–9
		Kit 2C: 3.0, 3.5, 4.0, 4.5, 5.0, 5.5, 6.0, 7.0, 8.0, 9.0	3–9
		Kit 3A: 3.5, 4.0, 4.5, 5.0, 6.0, 7.0, 8.0, 9.0	3–9
		Kit 3B: 5.0, 5.5, 6.0, 7.0, 8.0, 9.0, 10.0, 11.0, 12.0	3–9
		Kit 4A: 8.0, 9.0, 10.0, 11.0, 12.0, 13.0, 14.0	3–9
The Phonograms Series. This kit contains vowel and vowel digraphs emphasis. There are 36 games with sounds, vocabulary, and reading. Includes 72 stories.	Word analysis Phonics	Readiness skills	K–3 / K–1
		The Phonics Explorer	K–3 / K–3
		The Phonics Express	1–3 / K–3

Programs	Reading Skills	Specific Titles	Reading Grade Level	Interest Grade Level
Reading Laboratory I: Word Game. This kit includes phonics and structural-analysis exercise for 1-3 and games that help students match their listening vocabulary.	Phonics Structural analysis	Kit IA Kit IB Kit IC		1-3 1-3 1-3
Schoolhouse Reading Kits. All three of these kits contain activity cards with duplicates, plastic response overlays, markers, pupil progress sheets, and teacher's guide.	Phonics Structural analysis Word meaning Word attack Dictionary skills	Schoolhouse Word Attack Schoolhouse Word Attack IC Schoolhouse Comprehension Patterns	1.0–3.0 3.0–4.0 3.0–8.0	1-8 1-8 1-8
SRA Basic Reading Series. This contains an alphabet book for the readiness-level readers from A-F, workbooks from A-F, and teacher's guide.	Basic sight words Vocabulary skills Word analysis Comprehension	Readiness Level Level A Level B Levels C-F	PP–K K–1.0 1.0–2.0 1.0–2.0	PP–Jr PP–Jr PP–Jr PP–Jr
Reader's Digest Service, Inc. Educational Division Pleasantville, NY 10570				
Reader's Digest Advanced Skill Builders. Each kit contains readers, matching cassette tapes, workbooks, and teacher's manual.	Vocabulary Comprehension development Study skills	4 Books, 16 Audio Lessons Level 7 Level 8 Level 9		7-9 7-9 7-9
Reader's Digest Reading Skill Practice Pads. These are high-utility workbooks that extend basic reading, writing, vocabulary, and word-study skills.	Vocabulary development Word analysis Comprehension development	Level 3 Main Ideas Level 4 Main Ideas Inference Level 5 Main Ideas Inference Level 6 Main Ideas Inference Level 7 Main Ideas Inference		1-6

Program / Description	Skills	Title	Grades	Reading Level
Reading Skills Library. This is a reading and listening resource unit that will help in building critical reading skills.	Comprehension development, Study skills	About America	P–12	
		Nature Books	P–12	
		True Stories for Mystery Buffs	P–12	
		Reference Books	P–12	
		Song Books	P–12	
		How to Books	P–12	
Reading Tutors. This program is a compact reading and listening unit that will offer "private reading lessons" for pupils in the classroom.	Comprehension development, Study skills	Skill Builder Tutor		
		Grades	1–6	
Vocabulary Audio Skills. This program extends the audio program with dramatizations from 30 additional skill-builder stories. Six vocabulary lessons on three cassettes at each level.	Vocabulary skills, Word-analysis skills	Vocabulary Audio Level	P–JrH	2–6
New Series Reading Skill Builders. Helps to develop a specific reading skill, such as recognizing the main ideas and noting the sequence of events.	Vocabulary skills, Comprehension skills, Study skills	Skills Builder A	1–8	1–2
		Skills Builder B	1–8	4–4.8
		Skills Builder C	1–8	4.2–5.0
Comprehension Audio Lessons. Each audio lesson helps to develop a specific skill.	Oral-reading skills, Comprehension skills	Primary Audio Center	1–8	1–3
		Intermediate Audio Center	1–8	4–6
New Top-Picks Series B. Because students never get enough of the subjects they enjoy, this new series adds science fiction, sports, mystery, adventure, comedy, and people. Covers 26 important comprehension, literary, and study skills.	Comprehension skills, Study skills	People	5–9	5.0–6.9
		Sports	5–9	5.0–6.9
		Science Fiction	5–9	5.0–6.9
		Adventure	5–9	5.0–6.9
		Comedy	5–9	5.0–6.9
		Mystery	5–9	5.0–6.9

Programs	Reading Skills	Specific Titles	Reading Grade Level	Interest Grade Level
Original Series Reading Skill Builders. This series improves aural comprehension and oral reading, helps diagnose a pupil's ability to comprehend ideas and demonstrate correct pronunciation and intonation, and serves as a model for class dramatization.	Vocabulary development Comprehension skills Study skills Oral-reading skills	Piper Skills Builder Skills Builder for the Advanced	PP–1 1–6 7–9	PP–Jr PP–Jr PP–Jr
RD2000 Labs or Reading Centers. This is a comprehensive reading program in colorfully illustrated, high-interest magazine form.	Comprehension and vocabulary development Word recognition Oral-reading skills	Decoding (2 books, 12 audio) Level I (2 books, 12 audio) Level II Level III Level IV Level V	PP–1.9 2.5–3.9 3.5–4.9 4.5–5.9 5.5–6.9	P–JrH P–JrH P–JrH P–JrH P–JrH
Lit Kits: Cricket Magazine. This program saves you time as a teacher, money and energy you would have spent sorting through thousands of paperback books in print to find quality classroom library editions. This program has already selected the best stories and packaged them by grade level. Special interest kits built around "how to books," mysteries, myths, science fiction, and adventure will appeal to all young readers.	Language skills Reading skills Vocabulary skills	Each kit contains 8 to 20 selections and includes from grades K-6.		

McGraw-Hill Book Co.
1221 Avenue of the Americas
New York, NY 10020

Bilingual/Bicultural/ESL. A new basal reading series that helps Spanish-speaking students make a natural transition to English reading.

Skills	Material	Level	Grade
Comprehension	Textos del Alumno	P–2.2	K–5
Reading skills	Libros de Actividades	P–5	K–5
Writing skills	Tarjetas (cards)	PP–1	K–5
Vocabulary skills	Tarjetas	2.1–2.2	K–5
	Tarjetas	3.1–3.2	K–5

Phonetic Key to Reading Early; decoding and comprehension skills emphasis. Good as a supplement to any basal reading program.

Skills	Material	Level	Grade
Reading skills, Comprehension skills	Charts, Cards, and Pictures	2.0–4.0	1–3

T–10 Vocabulary Booster

Skills	Material
Vocabulary skills	Level 4 and up

Stanford–McGraw Hill Vocabulary

Skills	Material
Vocabulary	Level 7–8

Open Court Publishing Co.
Box 559
LaSalle, Il 61301

Catching on Comprehension. This is a cognitive skill-building program. It has five sequenced books designed A–E, with over-printed teacher's edition.

Skills	Material	Level	Grade
Comprehension development, Critical-reading skills	Level A	2.0–3.0	2–6
	Level B	3.1–3.9	2–6
	Level C	4.0–4.9	2–6
	Level D	5.0–5.9	2–6
	Level E	6.0–6.9	2–6

Programs	Reading Skills	Specific Titles	Reading Grade Level	Interest Grade Level
Headway Program. The goals of this program are to teach children to read, write, and communicate independently and to acquaint them with outstanding literary selections and to give students the cognitive benefits that result when reading and language arts are correlated in a single learning system.	Communication skills Vocabulary skills Language skills	Level A Letters and Sounds	K	K–6
		Level B	K–1.0	K–6
		Level C–J		K–6
		On a Blue Hill		1.0–1.2
		A Flint Holds Fire		1.2–2.2
		From Sea to Sea		2.2–3.1
		The Place Called Morning		3.2–4.0
		Cities All About		4.1–4.2
		Burning Bright		4.2–4.9
		The Spirit of the Wind		5.0–6.0
		Close to the Sun		5.1–6.0
The Rise Program. An alternative program based on colorful readers that contain classic literature and informational selections from a wide range of subject areas and material that will be interesting and motivational.	Reading Comprehension Spelling	Reading and language-arts program for advanced intermediate-level and average middle-grade students.		
		What Joy Awaits You		4–up
		But Life is Calling You		4–up
		Awake to Worlds Unfolding		4–up
Merrill Phonics Skilltext. A series designed to teach accuracy and independence in word recognition and comprehension. Level A is alphabet order, level B vowels, diphthongs, antonyms, synonyms, and homophones, and level C reviews, looks at plural, prefixes, suffixes, and possessives. Level D is a review of A and C.	Reading skills Dictionary skills Phonics skills	Level A (Alphabet Order)		1–4
		Level B (Review of Antonyms and Synonyms)		1–4
		Level C (Review of A&B plus vowels)		1–4
		Level D (Review of A&C)		1–4

Harcourt Brace Jovanovich
6277 Sea Harbor Drive
Orlando, FL 32887

Plays for Echo Reading. 60 pupil's plays, 32 accompanied by cassettes or records; helps improve word and phrase perception and oral-reading confidence.

Vocabulary
Comprehension

Elementary and Secondary Education Books. Includes reading, math, science, computer science, and engineering.

Vocabulary and comprehension skills

Levels 4–8

To use with all elementary students, even those students with special needs, because it includes hearing, visual, and physical needs.

Holt, Rinehart, and Winston Co.
1627 Woodland Ave.
Austin, TX 78741

Sounds of Language Readers. This series has 15 books and cassettes. Children experience the joy of reading by first listening.

Comprehension skills
Writing skills

Title	Level	Grade
Sounds I Remember	PP–1.0	K–8
Sounds of Number	PP–1.9	K–8
Sounds of a Hound Dog	2.9	K–8
Sounds Around the Clock	1.0–2.9	K–8
Sounds in the Wind	1.0–2.9	K–8
Sounds of a Pow-Wow	2.0	K–8
Sounds of Laughter	2.0–2.9	K–8
Sounds After Dark	3.0–3.9	K–8
Sounds of the Storyteller	3.2–3.9	K–8
Sounds of Mystery	4.0	K–8
Sounds of a Young Hunter	4.0–5.9	K–8
Sounds of Jubilee	7.0–8.9	K–8
Sounds Freedom Rings	8.0–8.9	K–8

Programs	Reading Skills	Specific Titles	Reading Grade Level	Interest Grade Level
Time Readings. Helps the students increase their reading speed while they maintain comprehension. Questions accompany each selection. A mixture of questions from recall to thought questions.	Build speed	Book 1	4.0	4–12
		Book 2	5.0	4–12
		Book 3	6.0	4–12
		Book 4	7.0	4–12
		Book 5	8.0	4–12
		Book 6	9.0	4–12
		Book 7	10.0	4–12
		Book 8	11.0	4–12
		Book 9	12.0	4–12
Skimming and Scanning. Helps students develop two valuable reading skills: skimming, for covering large amounts of material quickly, and scanning, for locating specific information.	Develop faster readers	Middle Level	4–6	4–8
		Advance Level	7–10	9–up
Vocabulary Drills. Helps students learn to build their vocabularies. Concentrates on two of the best-known approaches: the use of context clues and the analysis of the roots of unfamiliar words.	Vocabulary	Middle Level	6–8	6–8
		Advance Level	9–12	9–up
Comprehension Skills Drill. A series of skill drills in a high-interest, low-readability comprehension program designed to teach the process of comprehension. Reading levels 4–6 and interest levels 6–12.	Comprehension development	Volume I	4.5	4–12
		Volume II	5.5	4–12
		Volume III	6.5	4–12

Description	Skill	Titles	Level
Graphical Comprehension. A text workbook designed to teach students how to read graphs, as well as how to make graphs based on what they read. Reading level 7-10, interest level 9–college.	How to read and make graphs	Graphical Comprehension	7–10
Reading Drills. These text workbooks contain 30 timed passages, each followed by comprehension questions, cloze test and a vocabulary exercise. There are two levels, middle and advanced. The middle level has a reading level of 4-8 and an interest level of 4-8; advanced level, reading 7-10 and an interest level 9-college.	Vocabulary development Comprehension development	Middle Level: Harriet the Spy The Story of Doctor Doolittle Charlie and the Chocolate Factory Little House in the Woods The World of Robots	4–6
		Advance Level: Animal Education High Up in the Tropics The History of Books Education Out of School Walking in Space	7–10
3000 Instant Words. This contains the most common words in the English language. All words constitute a basic reading and spelling vocabulary for students in the elementary grades, or remedial vocabulary at the secondary level.	Vocabulary development	Primary/Junior High	

Programs	Reading Skills	Specific Titles	Reading Grade Level	Interest Grade Level
Borg-Warner **600 West University Drive** **Arlington Heights, IL 60004**				
Learning Essential Vocabulary. Reading words in context and improving reading skills.	Vocabulary skills	Levels K-6 Levels 4-12 Levels 6-12 Level 6		
Merrill Publishing Co. **1300 Alum Creek Drive** **Columbus, Ohio 43216**				
The Basic Vocabulary Series. A series of eight books with true-life and folklore stories from all over the world. Written at the second-grade level.	Reading skills Vocabulary	First Reading Books	1.0	1-4
		Animal Folklore		1-6
		Basic Vocabulary	2.0	2-8
		Folklore of the World		
		Pleasure Reading	4.0	3-up
		Reading Builder	1.0	1-3
		Puzzle Books	K-2.0	K-6
Grossett & Dunlap, Inc. **51 Madison Avenue** **New York, NY 10010**				
Easy Readers. A series of easy readers with short sentences, familiar words, and a high percentage of repeat words.	Reading skills Vocabulary	Mother Goose		PP-1.0
		Come Out And Play		PP-1.0
		Make-Believe		PP-1.0
		My Animal Friend		PP-1.0
		Fairyland		PP-1.0
		Faraway Friends		PP-1.0

Jamestown Publishers
P.O. Box 6743
Providence, RI 02940

Jamestown Classics. These are classics adapted from the world's greatest writers. Each 48-page booklet contains an illustrated story written at fifth grade level. There are four in the series from Jack London, four from Bret Harte, and four from Arthur Conan Doyle.

Reading skills	Law of Life	4.5–5.5	6–12
	Nan-Bok, the Liar	4.5–5.5	6–12
	The Marriage of Lit-Lit	4.5–5.5	6–12
	Diable, A Dog	4.5–5.5	6–12
	Mliss	4.5–5.5	6–12
	The Girl from Pike County	4.5–5.5	6–12
	The Outcasts of Poker Flat	4.5–5.5	6–12
	The Luck of Roaring Camp	4.5–5.5	6–12
	The Musgrave Ritual	4.5–5.5	6–12
	The Case of the Six Napoleons	4.5–5.5	6–12
	The Red-Headed League	4.5–5.5	6–12
	The Case of the Five Orange Pips	4.5–5.5	6–12

Comprehension Crossroads. Crossword puzzles designed to stimulate interest at the student's specific level. Duplicating masters are included.

Vocabulary development	Comprehension Crosswords:		
Comprehension development	Book 1	3.0	3–12
	Book 2	4.0	3–12
	Book 3	5.0	3–12
	Book 4	6.0	3–12
	Book 5	7.0	3–12
	Book 6	8.0	3–12
	Using Context and Word Elements	B	1–4
	Possessive Words, Contractions, and Comparison	C	1–4
	Prefixes & Suffixes, syllabication & word root	D	1–4

415

Programs	Reading Skills	Specific Titles	Reading Grade Level	Interest Grade Level
Garrard Publishing **607 North Market Street** **Champaign, IL 61820**				
First Reading Book. A series of 18 books written at the first-grade level. Books that stimulate the imagination.	Reading skills	Dog House for Sale	1.5	K–3
		Henrietta Goes to the Fair	1.9	K–4
		If I Could, I Would	2.3	1–5
		The Pirate's Adventure On Spooky Island	2.0	1–4
		Henrietta Circus Star	1.8	K–4
		Wish Upon A Birthday	2.2	1–4
		Henrietta Lays Eggs	2.1	K–4
		Henrietta, The Early Bird	1.9	K–4
		A Holiday for August	2.5	1–5
		If We Could Make Wishes		2–6
		Jack Frost and the Magic Paint Brush	2.0	K–5
		Riddles & Rhyme	P	1–5
		Spiders, Crabs and Creepy Crawlers	2.3	1–5
		What Makes a Grumble Smile?	2.2	1–5
		Where Did My Little Fox Go?	1.5	K–3
		Where is My Little Joey?	1.8	K–4
		Who is Root Beer?	1.5	K–3
		Why Won't the Dragon Roar?	2.2	1–5
Pleasure Reading Books. Level of books about fourth grade. This series of books has been re-written using a simpler vocabulary than the original editions.	Reading skills Vocabulary	Once Upon an ABC	K–1.0	2–4
		American Folktales	1–2.0	4–5
		Around the World Holidays	1–2.0	6–8
		Famous Animal Stories	1.2	4–6
		Johnny and Joe	K–1.0	2–3
		Old Witch Book	1–2.0	3
		Poetry	3.0	4–6
		Small Bear Adventures	1–3.0	2–5
		Target Books	3–4.0	5–up

Series	Skill area	Component	Grade level
Specific Skills Series. This level of booklets reinforces the pupil's basic sight vocabulary while providing skill instruction.	Vocabulary	Picture Level 8 skills	PP
	Comprehension	Preparatory 8 skills	K–1
	Word attack	Elementary 6 books	1–6
		Secondary 6 books	7–12
Identifying Inference, 1988. A complete comprehension program at each grade level.	Comprehension	Picture Level	PP
		Preparatory	K
		Level A	1.0
		Level B	2.0
		Level C	3.0
		Level D	4.0
		Level E	5.0
		Level F	6.0
		Level G	7.0
		Level H	8.0
Supportive Reading Series. A diagnostic and prescriptive reading program that complements and supplements the specific skills series.	Vocabulary	Phonic Analogies 2 books	1–3
	Comprehension	Rhyme Time 2 books	1–3
		Phonic Analogies Level 3	1–3
		Mastering Multiple 8 books	1–4
		Mastering Multiple 8 books levels 2-4	1–4
		Understanding Word Groups & Questions Levels 1–9	1–9
		Syllabication Levels 2–9	2–9
		Interpreting Idioms Levels 2–9	1–9
Word Theatre. This series uses all three modes of learning: language, observation, and performance. Promotes pupil participation, language interaction, and creative writing.	Vocabulary	Word Theatre Level 3	3–6
		Word Theatre Level 4	3–6
		Word Theatre Level 5	3–6
		Word Theatre Level 6	3–6

417

			Reading Grade Level	Level
Programs	**Reading Skills**	**Specific Titles**		
Picto-Cabulary Series. This series is also available in Spanish editions. Basic word sets for beginning readers.	Vocabulary	Words Around the Neighborhood		4–6
		Words Around the House		4–6
		Words to Eat		4–6
		Words to Wear		4–6
		Words to Meet		4–6
Word Recognition Program. Phonics, word elements, using context, structural analysis, and syllabication.	Word recognition	Initial & Final Consonant	A1	1–4
	Readiness comprehension	Consonant Blends	A2	1–4
		Digraphs, Long & Short Vowels		
Beginner Books. A series of 27 books written at levels 2.1 to 2.5 grade levels.	Reading skill	Dr. Seuss Collection		K–3
	Word recognition	Real Life Animal Books		K–3
	Comprehension	Alfred Hitchcock's Mystery Collection		4–6
	Vocabulary	Walter Farley's Horse Collection		4–6
		Star Wars Galaxy Packs		4–8
		Mission Read		5–7
Achievement Program in Comprehension. Each lesson features a reading selection—fiction, nonfiction, drama, or poetry—to capture the reader's interest. Questions about the selection encourage students' use of high-level thinking skills including literal, interpretive, and critical comprehension.	Comprehension	Level 1		1–8
		Level 2		1–8
		Level 3		1–8
		Level 4		1–8
		Level 5		1–8
		Level 6		1–8
		Level 7		1–8
		Level 8		1–8
Competency in Reading. Emphasis is on key word study, comprehension, and study skills. Emphasis is also given to reading literature, short stories, plays, poems, and to writing	Comprehension	Program 1	2.0–2.6	4–6
	Word study	Program 2	4.0–9.0	6–9
	Study skills			

Eight Essential Skills. Program includes eight skills books on seven separate levels. Carefully controlled instructional passages with margin clue guides. Exercises for students to complete and correct themselves allow learners to progress at their own pace.

Comprehension

Skills Set
Main Idea
Sequence
Story Elements
Critical Reading
Details
Vocabulary
Charts, Graphs & Maps

1 each level

2–8

Barnell Loft, LTD
958 Church Street
Baldwin, NY 11510

Multiple Skills Series. This series contains true stories that guarantee high-interest levels. Applies multilevel approach to make the series effective with all students. Spanish edition available.

Vocabulary
Reading
Comprehension

Picture Level 4 books — PP–K
Introductory 4 books — K–1
Preparatory 4 books — K–1
Levels 1 & 2 8 books — K–2
Levels 3–6 16 books — 2–6
Levels 7–9 12 books — 7–9

Learning with Laughter.

Vocabulary
Word attack
Language
Mechanics
Study skills

Beginning level

Coping with Computers in the Elementary & Secondary Schools. Features special chapters on exceptional students, easy and early learning, use of utility programs, word processing, database management systems, and electronic spread sheet.

Managing
Instruction
Subject area
Facilitating
Problem-solving

Used in Elementary, Middle and Secondary Schools

Programs	Reading Skills	Specific Titles	Reading Grade Level	Grade Level
Macmillan Publishing Co. **866 Third Avenue** **New York, NY 10022**				
Spectrum of Skills. A program of sequential instruction in word analysis, vocabulary, and reading comprehension.	Vocabulary & Comprehension Skills Word Attack	Intermediate and Upper Grades		
Hip Reader Program. A reading program for teenagers and adults who are nonreaders.	Word analysis	Written on grade levels	1–4	
Random House School Division **201 East 50th Street** **New York, NY 10022**				
Microcomputer Courseware. A series of eight programs each designed for different skills and grade levels from K–9. Special features of each program are customized drills and practice, variable levels of difficulty, and immediate correction and feedback.	Reading skills Study skills Readiness Phonics/word attack Structural analysis Vocabulary comprehension	Alphabet/Keyboard Alphabet/Sequence alphabetizing Customized Alphabet Drill Fundamental Phonics and Word Attack Fundamental Word Focus Homonyms in Context New Landmark Series: Comprehension Vocabulary Vocabulary B Tutorial Comprehension: Word Blaster Word Count		K–2 K–6 K–12 1–4 1–9 4–6 4–6 4–6 4–6 6–9 2–6 2–6

Index